REINVENTING
PROJECT
MANAGEMENT

REINVENTING
PROJECT
MANAGEMENT

The

DIAMOND APPROACH
TO SUCCESSFUL GROWTH
AND INNOVATION

Aaron J. Shenhar ◆ Dov Dvir

Harvard Business School Press

Boston, Massachusetts

Library of Congress Cataloging-in-Publication Data

Shenhar, Aaron
    Reinventing project management: the diamond approach to successful growth and innovation / Aaron J. Shenhar and Dov Dvir.
        p. cm.
    Includes bibliographical references.
    ISBN-13: 978-1-59139-800-4 (hardcover: alk. paper)
    ISBN-10: 1-59139-800-2
    1. Project management. I. Dvir, Dov. II. Title.
    HD69.P75S52 2007
    658.4'092—dc22

                                                                    2007009137

The paper used in this publication meets the requirements of the American National Standard for Permanence of Paper for Publications and Documents in Libraries and Archives Z39.48-1992.

To our children
Ayelet, Galit, and Ben
and
Ori, Hilla, and Omer

CONTENTS

Acknowledgments   *ix*

PART ONE

A NEW MODEL FOR MANAGING PROJECTS

1. Why Your Business Success Depends on Projects   3
2. What Makes a Project Successful   21
3. The Diamond Framework   37

PART TWO

THE FOUR BASES OF SUCCESSFUL PROJECTS

4. Novelty   63
5. Technology   79
6. Complexity   101
7. Pace   123

PART THREE

PUTTING THE DIAMOND APPROACH TO WORK

8. Managing Projects for Business Innovation   139
9. Managing Projects Within the Existing Organization   161
10. How Markets and Industries Affect Project Management   189
11. Reinventing Project Management for Your Organization   205

RESEARCH APPENDIXES

1. Our Research Steps 215
2. Project Success Assessment Questionnaire 219
3A. Building the Contingency Approach to Project Management 221
3B. Project Classification Questionnaire 224
3C. Principles and Design of Classification Systems 226
4. Project Novelty and Traditional Project Management 231
5A. Empirical Results for Project Technology 233
5B. Project Technology and Traditional Project Management 236
6A. Empirical Results for Project Complexity 239
6B. Project Complexity and Traditional Project Management 242
7. Project Pace and Traditional Project Management 245

Notes 249
Index 267
About the Authors 275

ACKNOWLEDGMENTS

There are never too many people to thank, particularly for a work that extended beyond a decade and a half, with its seeds planted even earlier. My early inspiration came from Ze'ev Bonen, Rafael's CEO, who has always promoted the idea that projects differ and who developed a four-type categorization of projects, which later inspired this research. I will ever be grateful to him and to some exceptional managers such as Yorm Valfish, Reuven Regev, Aharale Shapira, and Giora Shalgi, who taught me the art of project management and demonstrated what excellence really means.

As a practitioner turned academician, I was lost at first, and I needed guidance in uncharted territory. My new colleagues at Tel-Aviv University, Dov Eden, Shimcha Ronen, Asya Pazy, Zeev Neumann, Niv Ahituv, Yair Aharoni, Zvi Adar, Shlomo Globerson, Boaz Ronen, Israel Shpigler, Gadi Ariav, Igal Ayal, Yechiel Zif, Shoshi Anily, Yehuda Kahane, Yair Tauman, Avraham Beza, Elie Segev, and Dalia Etzion, helped to keep my thinking straight and my standards high within a unique culture of strong scholarship. Their support and energy never failed; I will forever cherish what they taught me.

A great deal of the research that Dov and I did for this book was performed in collaboration with others. The friendship and interaction with these outstanding colleagues made this endeavor particularly rewarding. They are Asher Tishler, Avi Grossfeld-Nir, Tzvi Raz, Hans Thamhain, Dragan Milosevic, Andy Sage, Stanislav Lipovetsky, Paul Adler, Yechiel Shulman, Joca Stefanovic, Rias van Wyk, Ofer Levy, Alan Maltz, Michael Poli, Richard Reilly, Brian Sauser, Jerry Mulenberg, Zvi Ahronson, Peerasit Patanakul, Thomas Lechler, William Guth, Gus Gaynor, Alex Laufer, Shlomo Alkaher, Arik Sadeh, Amnon Shefi, Daniel Kuhn, Michael Cooper, Larry French, Gary Lynn, Lynn Crawford, Max Wideman, Scott Fricke, Sabin Srivannaboon, Moshe Ayal, Tim Phelan, Nancy Tighe, Ayala Malach-Pines, Arie Ben-David, and Michael Ryan.

Other colleagues and scholars were no less supportive. Often reading drafts of the work or engaging in discussions about it, they offered advice and encouragement that put me back on track more than once. Such people as Clayton Christensen, Jim Collins, David Cleland, Ed Roberts, Ralph Katz, Karlos Arrto, Alan Pearson, Rodney Turner, Jeff Butler, Dundar Kocaolgu, Peter Morris, Rajan Anand, Pritesh Shah, Bob Mason, Ari Plonski, Dick Cardozo, George Farris, Harold Linstone, Isak Kruglianskas, Janice Thomas, Louis Lefebvre, Mel Silverman, Miriam Erez, Yehouda Shenhav, Josh Weston, Elie Geisler, Roberto Sbragia, Jacob Levy, and Roland Gareis were an inseparable part of this journey. I was often inspired by the works of great scholars, including Kathleen Eisenhardt, Michael Tushman, Robert Burgleman, Rebecca Henderson, Christoph Loch, Kim Klark, Steve Wheelwright, Richard Rosenbloom, Dorothy Leonard, James Utterback, Tom Allen, Gary Pisano, Marco Iansiti, Harold Kerzner, Gideon Kunda, Jeff Pinto, Terry Williams, Tim Kloppenborg, Alan McCormack, Stephen Thomke, Eric von Hippel, Geoffrey Moore, and Andy van de Ven.

Administrators and colleagues at Stevens Institute of Technology provided a highly supportive environment. This group includes Harold Raveche, James Tietjen, Jerry Hultin, Arthur Shapiro, Lex McCuster, George Korfiatis, Edward Friedman, Erich Kunhardt, Peter Koen, Murrae Bowden, Audrey Curtis, Ted Stohr, Ann Mooney, Hosen Fallah, Steve Savitz, Donald Merino, Tim Koeller, Bernard Gallois, Bernard Skwon, Dinesh Verma, Bob Ubell, Charles Suffel, Christos Christodoulatos, Dinesh Verma, Elliot Fishman, Frank Fernandez, Helena Wisniewski, Jerry Luftman, Joe Moeller, Jeff Nickerson, Larry Gastwirt, Patrick Berzinski, Lem Tarshis, Lu Terminello, Pete Dominick, Peter Jurkat, Mary Gaspar, Melissa Vinch, and Susan Pavelchack.

We are extremely indebted to many executives and employees in industry and government who supported this work in so many ways within their organizations. To each of the following people, we express our hope that this work may reward their efforts in some way: Sefi Katzenelson and Iris Elia-Shaul at Mafat, the Israeli Minsitry of Defense; Ed Hoffman, Lewis Peach, David Holdridge, Tony Maturo, Jon Boyle, Jerry Mulenburg, and Bruce Sauser at NASA; Harry Stefanou, Ed Andrews, Eva Godlman, Shellie Gaddy, Mary Devon, and Ed Miller at PMI; Karen Sorenson, Tony Rodriguez, Pamela Au, and Mike Bakaletz at Johnson & Johnson; Carole Hedden, Greg Hamilton, and Tony Velocci at Aviation Week; David Gutman, Joe Incremona, Barry Dayton, Ron Kubinski, and Mark Hynnek at 3M; Dennis Dorman and Paul Glamn at Trane; Jim Schneidmuller at AT&T; Mike Devine, Joe Lehman, and Vic Lindner at U.S. Army ARDEC; Paul Malinowski and Brendan McDonald at Becton Dickenson; Cheryl Badger and Mike Salvatore at Dow Jones & Co.; Tom Rabaut at United

Defense; Joe Hennessey and Don Senich at NSF; Roy Nicolosi at ISO; and Miles Braffett at BMG.

But the finest gratitude goes to the many students whose endless intelligence and inquisitive minds kept reminding me how much I don't know. They were the real drivers of this research by offering invaluable ideas and helping produce some of its case studies. This group includes Atish Babu, Donald Olson, Tim Phelan, William Sverapa, Doris Schultz, Michael Peled, Shlomo Klein, Zadok Hougui, Arie Lagerwaard, Paula Richards, Brian Cohn, Brian Nofzinger, David Walden, Kevin Lay, Zvi Yami, Derek Jensen, Givi Peradze, Balazs Vandor, Nancy Conrad, Maureen Lanucci, Arnold Lo, Stefan Merino, David Morgan, Seham Salazar, Daniel Marionni, Marc Martinez, Steve Szalanczi, Randall Vendetti, Xiang Yu, Anthony Mueller, Jody Berk, Kevin Pettersen, Mani Guruswamy, Mohesh Punjabi, Chris Switzer, Paul Tupaczewski, Nilesh Shringarpure, John Tracy, Ned Rogers, David Walter, Matthew Gilvey, Durga Bhogal, Fernando de la Vega, Deborah Ehrlich, Stan Jadwinski, Chris Long, Raj Sundar, Brian Coughlin, Mark Eppedio, Sumen Gupta, Joyce Jordan, Darren Birmingham, Alan Bader, Biren Desai, Jinsoo Kim, William Judge, Milton Maisonet, Darryl Clark, Michele Macleod, Wesley Patterson, Shashi Sinha, Anand Chouthai, Shawn Hopkins, Kalyan Narayanan, Nick Stampone, Eda Kilic, Jorymel Shada Jaquinet, and Todd Dennison.

Several agencies supported this research at different phases. We are indebted to them for their generous help and for their trust in this direction. They are Israeli Ministry of Defense, Mafat, the National Science Foundation, the Project Management Institute, and the Center for Project and Program Management Research at NASA's USRA.

Dov and I owe special thanks to Kirsten Sandberg, our editor at Harvard Business School Press. She was a wonderful mentor, teacher, and colleague and an outstanding friend who never failed to get the best from us. And to the rest of the Harvard Business School Publishing team, Dino Malvone, Michelle Morgan, Mark Bloomfield, Zeenat Potia, Allison Monro, Todd Berman, Sarah Mann, Liz Baldwin, Daisy Blackwell Hutton, Seana McInerney, and Leslie Zheutlin, for their commitment and enthusiastic support. To George Calhoun for his investment in editing part of the work; to Lucy McCauley, for a superior job of developmental editing; to Betsy Hardinger, for copyediting the manuscript; and especially to Sarah Weaver, our production manager, for never missing a bit and finding all the loose ends we left behind.

This work represents an outstanding collaboration with my coauthor Dov Dvir, who joined me on this journey in the early 1990s and has since been an exceptional colleague. His intelligence and brightness have challenged me to rectify the endless gaps in my logic and filter everything through his disciplined and sharp academic lenses. I deeply appreciate his continuous dedication, humbleness, selflessness, and persistence.

Finally, I am indebted to Hava for her unconditional love, unusual intelligence, and endless support.

—Aaron J. Shenhar
Hoboken, NJ

My journey in project management started in the defense industry and defense forces in Israel. I owe special gratitude to Arie Ben-Tov who gave me the "once-in-a-lifetime" chance to manage large and complex projects. I am also grateful to other exceptional managers such as Reuven Yeredor, Moti Dor-On, Oded Zach, and Shmulik Rothman, who always pursued managerial excellence and remarkable teamwork.

The experience that shaped my career as a researcher occurred during my doctoral studies under the supervision of Aaron (Aharale) Shenhar and Eli Segev. Both provided support and guidance from two different perspectives, which helped me integrate the often impossible connection between the practical and academic worlds.

Aharale Shenhar has since become one of my closest personal friends and colleagues. Our joint work represents an outstanding and productive collaboration. Aharale was and still is the engine behind our joint work. His endless enthusiasm, entrepreneurial spirit, and scholarly ability generated the ideas and resources for most of our studies in project management and related areas, which are represented by this book.

Finally, I am grateful to my wife and dearest friend, Yael, for over thirty-five years of continuous support. Without her encouragement I could not have survived the unending hours of work and later research that led to this book.

—Dov Dvir
Hertzlia, Israel

A NEW MODEL FOR MANAGING PROJECTS

WHY YOUR BUSINESS SUCCESS DEPENDS ON PROJECTS

G ENERALLY SPEAKING, you can divide your organization's activity into two categories: operations and projects. *Operations* involve repetitive, ongoing activities, such as manufacturing, service, and production, whereas *projects* involve unique, one-time initiatives, such as launching new products, new organizations, or new ventures, improving existing products, and investing in the company's infrastructure. Projects drive business innovation and change; in fact, the only way organizations can change, implement a strategy, innovate, or gain competitive advantage is through projects. Furthermore, if you think about it, every operational process began as a project that put things in motion.

With high demand for growth and innovation, the share of operations in most organizations is declining and the share of projects is on the rise (see figure 1-1). This trend began in the early 1900s, and it is accelerating in almost every organization and industry: not only do product life cycles become shorter, but also customers today demand greater variety and more choices, forcing companies to offer more products in almost every market. For example, in 2003 GM offered eighty-nine models, selling an average of fifty thousand cars per model; in the 1950s, in contrast, a single model would sell in the millions.[1]

In addition, market globalization is forcing businesses to respond to local demands and to low-cost competition around the world. Moreover, the information technology (IT) and Internet revolution is not slowing

FIGURE 1-1

The increasing share of projects

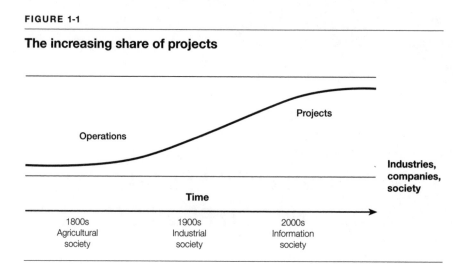

down. Even in stable industries such as banking and insurance, organizations must continuously invest in new IT infrastructure to keep up with growing demand and competition. Each of these trends intensifies the project activity in almost every organization and industry.

Ironically, during most of the twentieth century many organizations focused on improving their operations but not their projects. This trend began with the scientific management principles of Frederick Taylor, which greatly influenced the evolution of efficient mass production systems.[2] The efforts to improve operational efficiency continued for decades with more recent concepts such as just in time, lean manufacturing, reengineering, supply-chain management, and six sigma.

Although operational efficiency remains important, there is a limit to how much you can improve. With time, at least in theory, all companies can reach a similar level of efficiency. For example, think about quality. In the 1980s, high quality was considered an important source of competitive advantage. Not any more. Customers now take quality for granted, rather than view it as a unique advantage. High quality has become a must, and essentially a license to do business. A similar case can be made for organizational efficiency.[3]

No business enterprise can survive if it is focused only on improving its operations. The next untapped candidate for significant improvements in a company's pursuit of competitiveness is the project activity of the organization. Projects are the engines that drive innovations from idea to commercialization. But projects are also the drivers that make organizations better, stronger, and more efficient. And because most organizations accelerate toward a project-based world, shouldn't you ask yourself how your organization is doing with its projects? Are you doing a better job than your competitors?

This situation presents a tremendous opportunity. It is time to unleash the underutilized potential that exists in projects. The premise of this book is that organizational success depends more and more on projects. The good news is that because all organizations—commercial companies, government agencies, educational institutions, and charitable funds—have projects, managers at all levels can play a critical role in turning project management into an organizational competitive asset. The time has come to recognize that *project management is everyone's business.*

For the purpose of this book we define a project as *a temporary organization and process set up to achieve a specified goal under the constraints of time, budget, and other resources.* Project management is the *set of managerial activities needed to lead a project to a successful end.*[4]

The Bad News: Most Projects Still Fail

As the data proves, most projects fail to meet their goals. They do not meet time and budget goals, do not meet their business objectives, or both. Consider the following:

- The Standish Group found that in 2000 only about 28 percent of IT projects were successful. The rest were either total failures or failed to meet business requirements.[5]

- The Standish Group also estimated that of the $382 billion spent in 2003 on IT projects in the United States, $82 billion was a total waste. One-third of the projects that either failed or did not meet business requirements had overruns of 200 to 300 percent.[6]

- Robert Cooper's studies on new-product development showed that about 46 percent of all resources were allocated to projects that were canceled or failed to yield an adequate financial return. Only one of four products that entered development became a commercial success.[7]

- A study conducted in 1998 by the Bull Computer Corporation in the United Kingdom found that 75 percent of IT projects missed their deadlines, 55 percent exceeded their budgets, and 37 percent did not meet project requirements.[8]

For fifteen years we have collected data on more than six hundred projects in the business, government, and nonprofit sectors in various countries and have documented hundreds of project case studies. (See appendix 1 for a description of our research. Later appendixes include some of our research instruments.) Some 85 percent of the projects we studied failed to meet time and budget goals, with an average overrun of 70 percent in time and 60 percent in budget.[9]

Why Even Well-Managed Projects Fail

You may think that projects fail because of poor planning, lack of communication, or inadequate resources; but as the evidence suggests, failure is often found even in well-managed projects that are run by experienced managers and supported by highly regarded organizations. Consider the following:

Denver International Airport was initiated in 1989 to take over Denver's Stapleton Airport, which had outgrown its maximum capacity.[10] But the project suffered an extensive delay of sixteen months and an enormous cost overrun of $1.5 billion. As it turned out, one component—the automatic bag-handling system—had a higher risk than the project's other elements, but it was treated as a standard, well-proven subsystem, just like any other part of the project.

The Segway personal transportation system was expected to change the way people traveled, particularly in big cities.[11] With high sales expectations, its builders prepared a substantial infrastructure for mass production. Although the product was well designed and fun to ride, it did not fulfill its business forecasts; sales were short of predictions and, in retrospect, the extensive investment in production capabilities seemed unjustified.

NASA's Mars Climate Orbiter (MCO) was supposed to circle the planet Mars and collect weather data as well as act as a relay communication station to a second vehicle, Mars Polar Lander. MCO was launched by NASA as planned on December 11, 1998, but after nine and a half months in space, its signal was lost just as it began its final insertion maneuver. The failure was later described as a technical error due to a failure to use metric units in the coding of one of the ground software files.[12]

These projects took place in different industries, were aimed at different markets, and used different technologies. Yet they had one thing is common. They all had highly talented and dedicated managers, the best professional teams, the latest project management tools, and total support from top management. It seemed that each of these projects had every ingredient needed to succeed, but all of them failed to meet their expectations; when managers finally understood what went wrong and why, it was too late to fix the problem. The common theme to all of these failures was that executives as well as project teams failed to appreciate up front the extent of uncertainty and complexity involved (or failed to communicate this extent to each other) and failed to adapt their management style to the situation. The full story of these projects will be told later in the book.

These projects are not unique. We can find similar situations in every organization, where well-managed projects fail to deliver on their promises and end up in disappointment.

Why We Need a New Framework and a New Approach

Many executives believe that if they come up with the right strategy or business plan, their project teams will "get it done" and execute the strategy as directed. As we have observed, top managers frequently look at project budgets as a cost, not an investment, and see project activities as part of operations. They rarely appoint a "chief project officer" or vice president of projects, and their project teams are left on their own with little guidance or help from the top.

Project teams often try to follow a well-established set of guidelines that has become standard in the discipline of project management (see "The Evolution of a Discipline"). Although the conventional project management body of knowledge forms a good foundation for basic training and initial learning, it may not suffice for addressing the complex problems of today's projects. Simply asked, if you apply the standard tools and follow the rules and processes as prescribed, will your project be successful? As we have found, the answer is, not always. Often, even if you do everything by the book of conventional project management, you may still fail.

Most project problems are not technical but managerial. When technical errors cause projects to fail, it is usually management that failed to put the right system in place so that these errors would be detected in time. Such problems stem from the framework and the mind-set that drive the traditional approach to project management, rather than from a

The Evolution of a Discipline

When you look at the Pyramids, the Great Wall of China, the Greek Pantheon, and even Stonehenge, you realize that projects have been an important part of every civilization. Yet not until modern times did companies begin organizing work around projects; and when tools, techniques, and methods became standard across industries, a new discipline—project management—emerged.

As a formal discipline, project management as we know it was born in the middle of the twentieth century. The Manhattan Project, which built the first atomic bomb during World War II, exhibited the principles of organization, planning, and direction that influenced the development of standard practices for managing projects. During the cold war, large and complex projects demanded new approaches. In programs such as the U.S. Air Force's intercontinental ballistic missile (ICBM) and the Navy's Polaris missiles, managers developed a new control procedure called program evaluation and review technique (PERT). This approach evolved simultaneously with the critical path method (CPM), which was invented by DuPont for construction projects. These methods led to current network scheduling charts, which became the standard planning and control tools.[13] Such charts describe the project plan as a logical network of sequential activities, with allocated times for each activity.

Like any discipline or profession, project management includes rules, procedures, and tools used by all practitioners around the world. Accordingly, professional associations have been formed to disseminate and share the knowledge and experience of the profession. The premier organization, the Project Management Institute (PMI), was

lack of process or practice. The critical questions are these: Can we help project teams make the right assessment before presenting their project proposals to top management? Can we show executives how to ask the right questions and foresee danger before they make a commitment to a project and before it is too late? And can we guide project teams in adapting their project management style to the circumstances, environment, and task? It seems that managers at all levels need a new framework and a new language to communicate with each other about projects. Our goal in this book is to offer such a framework, which represents a new and more realistic approach to project management.

founded in 1969 and has since done a remarkable job in building the guide to the Project Management Body of Knowledge (PMBoK), which has become the de facto standard of the discipline.[14] Other associations, such as the International Project Management Association (IPMA) of Europe, have done similar things in other parts of the world.

The Traditional Way to Manage Projects

Typically, you begin project planning by creating a scope statement, which defines the work that needs to be done. The scope is then divided into elements of work, called *work packages,* which are built hierarchically in a tree structure called a *work breakdown structure* (WBS). From there, you build an *organizational breakdown structure* (OBS) and a network scheduling chart; then you allocate the required resources, develop the budget, and lay down many other parts of the project plan.

Every project plan must include, at a minimum, a scope statement, a WBS, an OBS, a schedule, and a budget. Some also include a risk management plan to assess what can go wrong and plan what to do about it. The ultimate objective of a conventional project plan is to complete the project on time, within budget, and according to requirements.

But project management is also a process, and so the PMI has defined nine major knowledge areas or managerial processes: scope, integration, cost, time, quality, risk, procurement, human resources, and communication. Those processes are then divided into forty-one subprocesses.[15] The PMI has recently developed a model of organizational project management maturity (OPM3), built according to these areas to assess an organization's level of standardization in project management.[16]

Why Traditional Project Management Often Fails

The standard, formal approach to project management is based on a predictable, fixed, relatively simple, and certain model. It is decoupled from changes in the environment or in business needs; once you've created the project plan, it sets out the objectives for the project, and the project manager must execute the plan using a "management-as-planned" philosophy.[17] After the project is launched, progress and performance are assessed against the plan, and changes to the plan should be rare and, if possible, avoided.[18] Consider the following two major drivers of project management:

- **The triple constraint.** Project managers see their jobs as successful when they are able to complete the project on time, within budget, and within performance goals (or requirements). This has famously been named the *triple constraint* (or "iron triangle") of project management. Deviations from the triple constraint are seen as negative signals that must be prevented or corrected.

- **One size fits all.** Many executives and managers assume that all projects are the same, thus suffering from the "project is a project is a project" syndrome.[19] They expect to succeed by simply following a standard set of activities as outlined in conventional project management books, none of which currently includes guidelines for distinguishing among projects and for selecting the right approach for a project.[20]

In their struggle to keep projects on track, executives and teams get frustrated when they try to fulfill unrealistic expectations of stability. Worse, in their effort to focus the project on the triple constraint, project teams often lose sight of the business rationale behind their projects: that they must satisfy a customer and achieve business results, and not just meet project requirements. And when they try to follow a standard set of rules for all projects, they often employ the wrong approach for their specific project.

The classical drivers of project management are no longer sufficient in the current business environment. The traditional model fits only a small group of today's projects. Most modern projects are uncertain, complex, and changing, and they are strongly affected by the dynamics of the environment, technology, or markets. Virtually every project we studied underwent unpredictable changes, and none of the projects was completed exactly as planned. Furthermore, as we found, projects differ in many ways, and one size does *not* fit all. To succeed, you must adjust your project to the environment, the task, and the goal, rather than stick to one set of rules.

In most projects you can no longer assume that your initial plan will hold until the project ends. Changes *will* take place and plans will have to be adjusted to the change. Sometimes you cannot even build a complete plan for your entire effort. Instead, you must establish a small pilot program to create small-scale prototypes, and include interim milestones to resolve important unknowns before you can commit to the full project, or you must separate an unpredictable component from the rest of your project and treat it completely differently than the bigger, more reliable task. The extent of unpredictability, contingency, and change will be different for different kinds of projects. None of these realities is included in the classic project management textbooks or guides.

A Better Way to Manage: Toward an Adaptive Project Management Approach

Based on our research, we suggest changing the paradigm of project management and accepting things as they are. In this book we develop a new approach and a new formal model to help managers understand what project management is all about. The new approach is based on a success-focused, flexible, and adaptive framework. We call it the *adaptive project management approach*, and it differs from the traditional approach in several ways, as shown in table 1-1.

According to the adaptive approach, projects are not just a collection of activities that need to be completed on time. Instead, projects are business-related processes that must deliver business results. Many projects are not predictable or certain. Rather, they involve a great deal of uncertainty and complexity, and they must be managed in a flexible and adaptive way. Planning is not rigid, fixed, or shaped once and for all; instead, it is adjustable and changing, and as the project moves forward, replanning is often appropriate or even unavoidable.[21] And project management styles must adapt to the specific project and its requirements.

Although this approach represents a shift in thinking, it is inevitable if you want to meet today's organizational challenges. While no framework

TABLE 1-1

From traditional to adaptive project management

Approach	Traditional project management	Adaptive project management
Project goal	Getting the job done on time, on budget, and within requirements	Getting business results, meeting multiple criteria
Project plan	A collection of activities that are executed as planned to meet the triple constraint	An organization and a process to achieve the expected goals and business results
Planning	Plan once at project initiation	Plan at outset and replan when needed
Managerial approach	Rigid, focused on initial plan	Flexible, changing, adaptive
Project work	Predictable, certain, linear, simple	Unpredictable, uncertain, nonlinear, complex
Environment effect	Minimal, detached after the project is launched	Affects the project throughout its execution
Project control	Identify deviations from plan, and put things back on track	Identify changes in the environment, and adjust the plans accordingly
Distinction	All projects are the same	Projects differ
Management style	One size fits all	Adaptive approach; one size does *not* fit all

can provide all the answers, we believe that every organization can significantly improve its business results and achieve more home runs from its projects if it applies the approach described in this book.

We do not suggest, however, that you should eliminate the traditional approach. Rather, the adaptive approach builds on it. Many elements of traditional project management will continue to be essential. Together, this book's chapters present a theoretically sound, research-based, broadly valid, and practical approach for dealing with today's dynamic and uncertain projects. Following we summarize its major principles.

Creating the Business-Focused, Success-Oriented Project

This book presents a new multidimensional model for assessing and planning project success beyond the triple constraint.[22] It is based on the idea that "what you measure is what you get" and on investment benefit analysis. It also assumes that the project leader is responsible for achieving all the metrics of project success.

Our model considers the strategic as well as the tactical aspects of project performance in the short *and* the long term, and it considers the points of view of different project stakeholders, including customers and businesses. Once adopted, the new model will affect the planning and execution of projects and will focus everyone's attention on more than just meeting time and budget goals.

Specifically, the new success criteria involve at least five dimensions (or metrics):

- Project efficiency: meeting time and budget goals

- Impact on the customer: meeting requirements and achieving customer satisfaction, benefits, and loyalty

- Impact on the team: satisfaction, retention, and personal growth

- Business results: return on investment, market share, and growth

- Preparation for the future: new technologies, new markets, and new capabilities

Each metric may have several submeasures, and it may differ from project to project in detail, intensity, importance, and other aspects. In some cases you will have to define other specific criteria for your project, but overall these metrics provide a workable framework for dealing with organizational and business needs. This framework is presented in detail in chapter 2.

The Diamond Approach: Adapting to a Project's Risks and Benefits

To address differences among projects, we present a diamond-shaped framework to help managers distinguish among projects according to four dimensions: novelty, technology, complexity, and pace (NTCP). If you think of the diamond as a baseball field, then each dimension can be seen as a base that represents three or four possible project types.

The diamond is designed to provide a disciplined tool for analyzing the expected benefits and risks of a project and developing a set of rules and behaviors for each project type. If you visit each base during project planning in a methodical way, you will be able to consider the uniqueness of your project on each dimension and select the right managerial style for this uniqueness. The diamond analysis is also helpful in assessing a project in midcourse, identifying possible gaps in a troubled project, and selecting corrective actions to put the project back on track. Finally, and perhaps most importantly, it provides a common language for discussion among executives, managers, teams, and customers during the project approval, contracting, and monitoring process.

The four bases of the diamond are defined as follows (see figure 1-2):

- **Novelty.** This base represents the uncertainty of the project's goal, the uncertainty in the market, or both. It measures how new the project's product is to customers, users, or to the market in general and thus how clear and well defined the initial product requirements are. Novelty includes three types: derivative, platform, and breakthrough.

- **Technology.** This base represents the project's level of technological uncertainty. It is determined by how much new technology is required. Technology includes four types: low-tech, medium-tech, high-tech, and super-high-tech.

- **Complexity.** This base measures the complexity of the product, the task, and the project organization. Complexity includes three types: assembly, system, and array (or system of systems).

- **Pace.** This base represents the urgency of the project—namely, how much time there is to complete the job. Pace includes four types: regular, fast/competitive, time-critical, and blitz.

Each dimension affects project management in its own way. Novelty affects the time it should take to freeze product requirements and the accuracy and reliability of marketing data. Technology affects how long it should take to get the design right and freeze it, the intensity of the technical

FIGURE 1-2

The diamond model—assessing a project's risks and benefits and selecting the right management approach

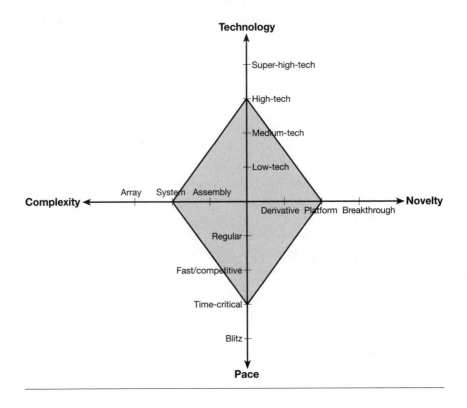

activities, and the technical skills required by the project manager and team. Complexity affects the project organization and the level of bureaucracy and formality needed to manage it. Pace affects the planning and reviews, the autonomy of the project team, and the involvement of top management, particularly in the most urgent projects.

In the unsuccessful projects we studied, we often found gaps between the diamond shape of the project's required characteristics and the diamond shape of the actual management style that was used. In retrospect, these gaps explained why the project failed or did not fulfill its full expectations. As an illustration, consider how the diamond analysis can help us understand the failure of the Denver International Airport project.

Denver International Airport

Denver International Airport was perceived as a typical, although complex, construction project. As is common in construction projects, its technology level can be classified as low-tech. If you analyze its management style using the diamond's four dimensions (novelty, technology, complexity, and pace), you will conclude that the project was managed as a platform, low-tech, array, fast/competitive project. But the automatic bag-handling system was a different kind of project. It required a totally new technology that had never been applied on such a large scale. That part of the program had to be handled as a platform, high-tech, system, fast/competitive project, but it was managed just like all other components (see figure 1-3). Thus, the project's failure to assess the uncertainty level of one of its most sensitive and new components caused the excessive delays and enormous cost overruns. A simple diamond analysis would have identified this gap ahead of time.

FIGURE 1-3

Denver International Airport project

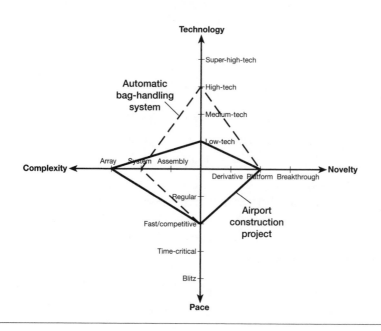

A Road Map to This Book

This book is organized as follows:

Part 1: A New Model for Managing Projects. This first part provides the motivation for, background of, and description of the main approach and framework.

- **Chapter 1: Why Your Business Success Depends on Projects.** This chapter has introduced the reasons managers should focus on the opportunity that exists in project management and why they need a new framework and language for managing projects.

- **Chapter 2: What Makes a Project Successful.** This chapter discusses the transition from the classic triple constraint paradigm to the new business-focused model for using multiple dimensions of project success. It features the following cases:

  - The Sydney Opera House

  - Los Angeles Metro subway

- **Chapter 3: The Diamond Framework.** This chapter discusses the diamond model in detail. It shows how a diamond analysis can serve as an up-front assessment of benefits and risks and as a disciplined planning tool. Chapter 3 discusses these cases:

  - FCS, a military fire control system

  - Sony's Walkman

  - The BMW Z3 automobile

  - The federal response to Hurricane Katrina

  - The World Trade Center construction project

Part 2: The Four Bases of Successful Projects. The second part outlines the NTCP bases of the diamond model. It devotes a chapter to each base (or dimension).

- **Chapter 4: Novelty.** How new is the product to the customers and users? With a newer product, market research is less reliable and requirements are less clear. Chapter 4 analyzes three cases:

  - The creation of the *Toy Story* movie

  - The Segway personal transportation system

  - A financial middleware software program

- **Chapter 5: Technology.** What is the project's level of technological uncertainty? Greater technological uncertainty requires an extensive design effort, more testing, and later freezing of the design, and managers with greater technical savvy. Chapter 5 analyzes the story of these projects:

  - Denver International Airport

  - The SR-71 Blackbird reconnaissance aircraft

  - NASA's Apollo moon landing program

  - NASA's space shuttle program

- **Chapter 6: Complexity.** How complex is the product or the organization (or both)? This measure is based on a hierarchy of systems and subsystems. Higher complexity requires bigger organizations, more interaction, and increased formality. Chapter 6 discusses these cases:

  - The Ford 2000 restructuring effort

  - The English Channel tunnel, or Chunnel

  - The Harmony project, a telecommunications collaborative software network

- **Chapter 7: Pace.** How much time is available to complete the project? Increased pace requires careful time management, more autonomy for project teams, and more support from top management. Chapter 7 cites these examples:

  - NASA's Mars Climate Orbiter

  - The Y2K problem: A rush to comply

Part 3: Putting the Diamond Approach to Work. The third part of this book illustrates the practical application of the diamond model in various contexts and environments.

- **Chapter 8: Managing Projects for Business Innovation.** This chapter discusses the business needs behind projects and explains how they can affect project selection as well as specific project management practices. We also discuss the relationship between project management and innovation, including "the innovator's dilemma" and the customer adoption cycle. Chapter 8 discusses four cases:

  - Selecting IT projects in a large media corporation

- The Market Watch software project

- The invention of flash memory

- The history of the microwave oven

- **Chapter 9: Managing Projects Within the Existing Organization.** This chapter shows you how to apply this book's models in your organization and how to include the adaptive approach as part of your *existing* project management procedures. It then discusses in detail how to perform project planning and handle project uncertainty and risk. We also describe how to improve overall project activity efficiency and how to deal with project outsourcing dilemmas. This chapter features the following story:

  - The Quadrant model (for project efficiency)

- **Chapter 10: How Markets and Industries Affect Project Management.** This chapter shows how various kinds of customers and markets require various project management styles. It also outlines the differences in project management among major industries. It features one case:

  - The wire coating project

- **Chapter 11: Reinventing Project Management for Your Organization.** This chapter explains what executives and managers need to do to take full advantage of the new approach for the benefit of their organizations. The chapter concludes with predictions about the future evolution of project management.

Key Points and Action Items

- In modern organizations the share of project activities is constantly growing, whereas the percentage of effort devoted to operations is decreasing.

- Most projects fail to meet time and budget goals and business objectives. Projects are the next significant unexploited candidate for achieving excellence and gaining competitive advantage.

- Managers at all levels can take advantage of this opportunity by paying greater attention to the way their businesses are handling projects. Project management is not the business only of project managers or team leaders; it is everyone's business.

- Traditional project management is based on a predictable, stable, certain, and linear model. It is focused on a plan that is prepared once up front to meet the project's time, budget, and performance goals, and it is mostly detached from environmental changes during project execution. It also assumes that all projects should follow a standard set of rules and processes.

- Traditional project management is no longer enough to ensure success in today's dynamic projects. Even if you do everything by the book, you may still fail. There is a need for a new approach and a new language for managers to understand what project management is all about.

- Looking at your organization, you may ask yourself a number of questions. Do your projects get the same or more attention as operations? Do project managers get enough support from the organization and top management? Do you treat projects as costs or as investments?

- You should assess project success by using five dimensions: efficiency, impact on the customer, impact on the team, business success, and preparation for the future.

- The diamond framework offers a disciplined tool for assessing a project's benefits and risks and for selecting the right project management style. It also gives you a model for assessing a project at midcourse and for putting a troubled project back on track. The diamond model includes four dimensions (bases) to distinguish among projects: novelty, technology, complexity, and pace.

WHAT MAKES A PROJECT SUCCESSFUL

The Sydney Opera House

One of the world's greatest tourist attractions is the Sydney Opera House, an architectural wonder visited every year by millions of travelers.[1] The original project plan, as envisioned by the New South Wales government in the 1950s, included an estimated budget of about 7 million Australian dollars and a schedule of five years. But getting there was tough. The construction project experienced enormous difficulties—extensive delays, bitter conflicts, and painful budget overruns. Sixteen years passed before the opera house opened its doors, and its final price tag was more than 100 million dollars.

Judging it purely on time and budget performance, you might conclude that the Sydney Opera House project was a textbook example of project failure. But no one really cares any more how the project was managed, and almost everyone sees the Opera House as a success story. It provides continuous income and fame to the city of Sydney, and it remains one of the most fascinating buildings in the world.

We have seen similar projects that did not meet their time and budget goals or did not follow the standard project management procedures and yet, with time, were judged to be successful. And we have seen projects fail despite being well managed according to the traditional rules. Some were completed on time and within budget, yet they did not bring much value to their organizations or customers.

But if meeting time and budget goals is not the only criterion, what else is there? In an era when projects are among the most widespread phenomena in modern organizations, it is not so easy to answer this simple question. The traditional mind-set maintains that project success depends on satisfying the triple constraint—on time, within budget, and according to specifications. In the dynamic world of business-related projects, however, abiding by the triple constraint is no longer sufficient, and a new model is needed.

No matter what the motivation for a project, any assessment of project success must be linked to the parent organization's success and to its well-being in the long run. However, despite numerous arguments, there is still no universal way to measure and assess project success.[2] This chapter suggests a business perspective on project success. Our aim is to help executives and managers better define their expectations during a project's planning phase and later assess real project success.

Beyond Time, Budget, and Performance

What does project success mean? Should the same rule apply to all projects? Although time to market may be critical to a company's current competitive position, many other issues may have an impact on project success in the long run. Consider the following famous cases.

When the first generation of the Ford Taurus was introduced in 1986, it quickly became the best-selling car in America and one of the most successful cars in Ford's history. Its revolutionary design and exceptional quality created a new standard in the U.S. automobile industry, and customers simply loved the car. Yet when the development project was completed, its project manager was demoted because the project was completed three months later than scheduled.[3]

The first Windows software launched by Microsoft suffered enormous delays, with continuous redirection of resources and people. But Windows turned out to be one of Microsoft's most profitable products and an enormous source of revenue.[4]

Before introducing its big hit, the Macintosh, in 1984, Apple Computer completely failed with its predecessor, the Lisa computer. Apple's managers acknowledged later that without the lessons learned and technologies developed on the Lisa project, the Mac's success would not have been possible—bringing into question whether Lisa was indeed a complete failure.[5]

When it comes to project success, the key question is this: what do organizations need to consider before they launch a new project, and how should they assess a project in retrospect?

Meeting time and budget goals is only a small part of the picture. Having achieved such goals suggests that the project was managed carefully and efficiently and that the project team did a good job of planning, monitoring, and executing the plan. But adhering to a project plan tells us nothing about achieving the long-term business goals for which the project was initiated in the first place.

Most projects are part of the strategic management of their organizations, and they should be assessed based on their contribution to overall business results, and not only on their ability to meet time, budget, or performance goals. Furthermore, project benefits can have many forms; some may be immediate, and others may be realized only later. An organization must therefore set project goals in advance to reflect its expectations, both in the short term and in the long term. Consequently, all project activities must be aligned with these expectations.

A Multidimensional Strategic Concept

Some scholars have suggested distinguishing between the success of the project and the success of the product. They argue that we should first assess the efficiency of project execution (was it completed on time and within budget?) and then later look at the product's success and its impact on the business (did it create the expected market impact and bring in the anticipated revenues?).[6]

We believe, however, that project and product success should not be separated. They are two sides of the same coin, and both must be addressed by the project team during project execution. It all boils down to a simple question: how did the project contribute to the organization's success and effectiveness?

Who Is Responsible for a Project's Success?

This perspective requires project managers to view project success in a wider sense and to take the responsibility for making it happen. Executives, for their part, must convey to project teams the overall business perspective, define the business expectations in advance, and ask the questions pertinent to business expectations before a project plan is approved and while a project's progress is reviewed.

With this mind-set, project managers manage their projects from day one in a different way. They are constantly aware of the business environment and make sure that the team's activity is focused on the project's short- *and* long-term goals. The emphasis and importance of project goals may differ from project to project, but the total responsibility for overall project success rests on the shoulders of the project manager, the one who is running the project day-to-day.

Note, however, that some companies separate the role of the project "owner" from that of project manager. The owner takes care of meeting the business needs, and the manager is responsible for timely delivery. Yet even in this case, you cannot remove the team and its leader from their responsibility to make sure that their day-to-day work leads to the long-term success of the end result.

Success: Multiple Dimensions, Multiple Viewpoints

We see project success as a multidimensional, strategic concept.[7] Every project needs more than one dimension for assessing success, and those dimensions vary in importance and significance, depending on the project.

Measuring organizational effectiveness on different dimensions is not new. It has evolved in recent years at the corporate level, as companies have realized that assessment based on traditional financial and accounting measures is not enough. Kaplan and Norton developed the corporate Balanced Scorecard concept to address these issues. It includes four major dimensions: financial measures, customer-related measures, internal measures, and innovation and learning measures.[8] Typically, organizations choose fifteen to twenty submeasures that reflect their specific needs and environments. Other studies have suggested adding yet another dimension, for a total of five: financial, market related, process quality, people development, and preparing for the future.[9]

But how does all this apply to projects and their success? Clearly, any collection of measures should address more than one need and should represent the concerns of more than one stakeholder group. But above all, success measures must reflect the strategic intent of the company and its business objectives, for three reasons. First, if a project does not serve the organization, why do it at all? Second, it should encompass success at different times: what may seem well done in the short run may end later in disappointment, and short-term setbacks may turn into long-term rewards. Project success should therefore be observed with different time frames in mind. Finally, success measures should reflect the interests of various stakeholders who will be affected by the project's outcome.

Consider, for example, the construction of a new office building. An architect may consider the project a success in terms of its aesthetics; an engineer, in terms of technical competence; an accountant, in terms of money spent under budget; a human resources manager, in terms of the team's satisfaction. Finally, a CEO will rate the building in terms of its effect on the stock price, and an owner, in terms of return on investment.[10] What may seem a great project to one community may not be appreciated by another. The following example represents a case that was considered world-class by the traditional project management mind-set, only to end up as a failure because it did not address the needs of its major stakeholders, the customers.

The Los Angeles Metro: A Subway System in an Automobile City

In January 1993, the Red Line—the first 4.4 miles of the Los Angeles Metro—opened its doors to passengers in downtown Los Angeles. This line had been commissioned as the first segment of a subway system that had been planned for years.

An underground railway in Los Angeles was first suggested in 1925, but city voters rejected it. In the urban environment of the 1980s, voters finally mandated funding for an integrated railway system. It would be implemented in stages, and, when completed, the planned twenty-three miles of the Red Line would fan out from downtown in three directions (east, west, and mid-city), creating the backbone of a new transportation system designed to serve the city for the next thirty years.

The project faced numerous technical and management challenges: hydrocarbon gases in the ground, abandoned oil wells, contaminated underground water, and high seismic activity. But the greatest challenge was changing the attitudes of citizens by convincing them to leave their cars at home and use a subway system.

The Rail Construction Corporation (RCC), the construction arm of the Los Angeles Mass Transportation Authority, set several yardsticks for assessing project success according to the project mission and vision: to build a world-class subway system for the Los Angeles community and become the model of excellence in public works design and construction. Success would mean completing the first segment ahead of time and within budget, maintaining construction safety records that were 50 percent better than the national average, hiring local and minority businesses, maintaining on-time train operations at 98 percent, achieving formal industry recognition, and winning distinguished industry awards.

By all these measures, the project was successful. It was completed eight months ahead of schedule, with no budget overruns. It was even selected as "Project of the Year" by the Project Management Institute in 1993.[11] However, the remaining phases of the project were dropped a few years later when the city realized that train usage was significantly lower than expected. The challenge of changing the citizens' attitudes about leaving their cars at home and using the subway system was never met. The most important part of the project's mission—building a world-class system that will be used by the community—was ignored in favor of "becoming a model of excellence in public works design and construction."

The Five Main Dimensions of Project Success

Based on our research, we suggest that a comprehensive assessment of project success in the short and the long term can be defined by five basic groups of measures:[12]

- Project efficiency

- Impact on the customer

- Impact on the team

- Business and direct success

- Preparation for the future

Other dimensions may also be relevant, but these groups represent a wide spectrum of project situations and cover a great majority of cases and time horizons. Each dimension includes several possible submeasures, as listed in figure 2-1. (Appendix 2 shows the research questionnaire used in our study.)

FIGURE 2-1

Specific success measures

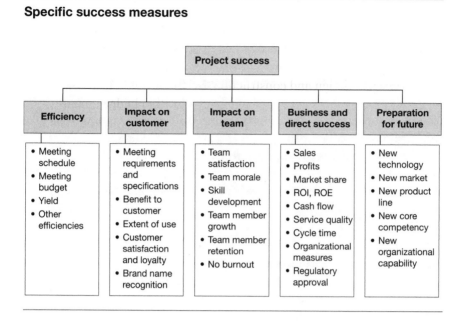

The first dimension, *project efficiency* (or meeting planned goals), represents a short-term measure: whether the project has been completed according to plan. Was it finished on time? Was its spending within the budget? As we mentioned, meeting resource constraints probably indicates a well-managed, efficient project, but it may not guarantee that the project will ultimately succeed and will benefit the organization in the long term. However, with increased competition and shorter product life cycles, time to market may be a critical competitive component that cannot be ignored.

The second dimension, *impact on the customer,* represents the major stakeholder whose perception is critical to the assessment of project success. This dimension should clearly state how the project's result improved the customer's life or business and how it addressed the customer's needs. For example, if the customer is a service provider, success in this dimension might be defined as follows: "The product will enable the customer to cut in half the response time to its own customers, and reduce errors by 60 percent."

As figure 2-1 shows, this (and not project efficiency) is the dimension that includes product performance measures, functional requirements, and technical specifications. Who, after all, is most affected by product performance, if not the customer? This dimension typically also includes the level of customer satisfaction, the extent to which the customer is using the product, and the extent of customer loyalty: whether the customer is willing to purchase or order the next product.

The third dimension, *impact on the team,* reflects how the project affects the team and its members. Good project leaders energize and inspire their team members and make the project a memorable, exciting experience. Other projects may be remembered as demanding and exhausting experiences. This dimension assesses the cumulative impact: team satisfaction, morale, the overall loyalty of the team to the organization, and the retention of team members after the project is completed. But this dimension also assesses the indirect investment the organization has made in team members. It measures the extent of team learning and team growth and of team members' newly acquired skills and new professional and managerial capabilities.

The fourth dimension, *business and direct success,* reflects the direct and immediate impact the project has on the parent organization. In the business context, it should assess sales levels, income, and profits, as well as cash flow and other financial measures. In short, this dimension should relate to the project's commercial success and answer one simple question: did it help build the bottom line?

In many cases, this dimension is represented by a typical business plan that outlines future expected sales, growth, and profits from the resulting product. In other cases, this dimension may involve an investment benefit analysis plan, which ties the investment to expected returns. However, this dimension might also include business-related measures for internal projects not aimed at new products for external markets, such as reengineering projects for restructuring business work flows. In such cases, this dimension often includes measures of costs saved, improved production time, cycle time, yield, and quality of process.

This dimension may also apply to nonprofit organizations. For example, when a charity foundation initiates a project to improve its services, shorten its processes, and serve more customers more cost-effectively, assessing the success of such an improvement project should include measures designed to reveal the direct impact of the project on benefits to the public.

The final dimension, *preparation for the future,* addresses the long-range benefits of the project. It reflects how well the project helps the organization prepare its infrastructure for the future and how it creates new opportunities. Future infrastructure may include new organizational processes and additional technological and organizational competencies. Typical measures might include creating a new market, creating a new product line, or developing a new technology.

As with Apple's Lisa, projects without immediate business benefits may still provide critical stepping-stones for future opportunities. To analyze this dimension, you can ask a number of questions. Did your project test new ideas that will result in further markets, innovations, and products? Did you develop new technologies and core competencies? And are you prepared to initiate change and create the future in your industry or to adapt quickly to external challenges, unexpected moves of competitors, and surprises in markets and technology?

The five measures presented here provide a universal framework for assessing project success in most cases and environments, but sometimes it may be necessary to define additional success dimensions for specific projects. For example, in the pharmaceutical industry, one of the clear tests of project success is getting FDA approval for a new drug or treatment; in election campaigns, winning defines ultimate success.

Similarly, in public and government projects, success may be assessed by the image and perception of the government by the citizens, for which special measures may be developed, whereas in battle, success is not only winning the war but also minimizing casualties and civilian suffering.

Project Success as a Dynamic Concept

When using these main dimensions, project success becomes a dynamic concept with both short- and long-term implications. The first dimension, efficiency, can be assessed in the very short term—during project execution and at the moment of project completion. The second and third dimensions begin to take shape while the project is in progress, in the form of assessments of the aptness of the specifications for customer needs and of the quality of the team's interactions. They typically become clear within the first few months after project completion, after the product has been delivered to the customer and the impact on the team shows up in the larger organizational context.

The fourth dimension, business and direct success, can be assessed only after a substantial sales level has been achieved and when project returns break even, usually after one or two years. And finally, the fifth dimension can be assessed only much later, probably after three, or even five, years, when the long-term benefits of the project start to pay off. In practice, these assessments overlap, but the dimensions' time frames change, as illustrated in figure 2-2.

The Impact of Time

Which of our five dimensions is most important? As the nature of the dimensions suggests, their relative importance also shifts depending on when you look at them. In the short term, and particularly during project

FIGURE 2-2

Time frames of success dimensions

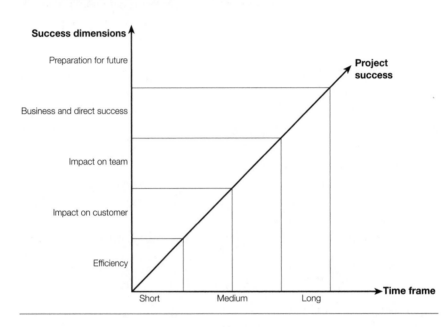

execution, the project efficiency dimension is critical. In fact, it is the only one that can be measured in concrete terms at this stage. Meeting resource constraints, measuring deviation from plans, and looking at various efficiency measures may be the best ways to monitor project progress and control its course.

After the project is complete, however, the importance of this dimension diminishes. As time goes by, it matters less and less whether the project has met its resource constraints, and in most cases, after about a year it is almost irrelevant. While the second and third dimensions—impact on the customer and team—become relevant after project completion, the time to think about them (as well as all the other dimensions) is during the project itself, when you have the power to influence them.

The fourth dimension, business and direct success, becomes significant only later. It usually comes to the foreground after a while, when sales of the project's product start to bring in profit or establish market share. And finally, preparation for the future, which expresses the long-term benefits of the project, affects the organization only after years have passed. The relative importance of the five dimensions as a function of time is shown in figure 2-3.

FIGURE 2-3

Relative importance of success dimensions: A matter of time

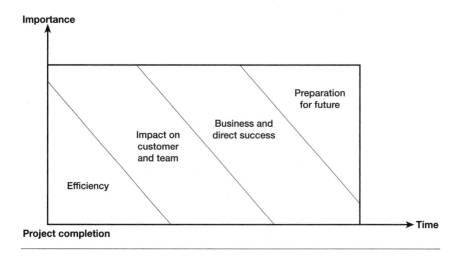

Types of Projects and the Success Dimensions

Later chapters address the issue of various project types, discussing in detail how to adjust your management approach. For now, note that risk and opportunity typically vary together by project type—the higher the risk, the greater the opportunity—and success measures should reflect this situation. Low-risk, low-uncertainty projects normally create limited opportunities, and most such opportunities can be pursued with a high level of confidence.

It follows that for low-risk projects, meeting resource constraints may be more critical and relevant than for higher-risk projects. The immediate success of low-risk projects relies on meeting time and budget constraints, and their expected profits can usually be determined in advance. In contrast, for high-risk, high-uncertainty projects, poor performance in the short term, budget overruns, and even limited business success may be offset by longer-term benefits, such as creating new markets, developing expertise in new technologies, and preparing the infrastructure for more advanced products in the future. Clearly, customer and team satisfaction and direct success are important to all types of projects.[13] The relative importance of project success measures changes, therefore, with levels of risk and uncertainty, as shown in figure 2-4.

FIGURE 2-4

Relative importance of success dimensions is project dependent

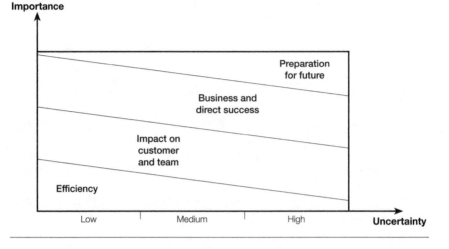

In summary, we must note again that although the dimensions of success may vary in importance over time and with project type, they nonetheless need to be addressed throughout the life of the project. Next, we discuss how companies and managers can apply this approach.

Applying the Success Dimensions Framework to Your Projects

Companies need to establish a success-focused project environment that employs a multidimensional, flexible measurement approach and that pays attention to each success dimension during project planning and execution. If no one cares during project execution whether the customer will buy the product, the chances of coming up with a profitable product are much lower. Organizations can therefore take several key steps from the outset to ensure a project's success.

Adapt Your Expectations to the Project Type

Managers' and team members' attention must be focused as early as possible on the project's objectives, as specified by the company. If organizations are planning to achieve strategic benefits from projects, managers should incorporate these benefits as predetermined measures of project success. They must look both at the short-term and the long-term benefits of the project and judge its performance along all dimensions.

Since no given set of dimensions can serve all projects, managers need to adapt their expectations to the project type and weight the various success dimensions based on the project. For example, a high-uncertainty, high-risk project will be assessed mainly on its business and long-term effect, rather than on short-term measures of time and budget performance. Conversely, it is unlikely that a low-uncertainty, low-risk project, such as construction of a new building, will help the organization develop new technology or create new opportunities.

Make Project Success Dimensions Part of Project Planning

Project success dimensions must therefore become an integrated part of project planning, and a standard component in the strategic management of the organization. You should incorporate success measures into the decision-making process of top management when you initiate the project, and you should include them in the project team's charter. Management must commit the organization's resources to meet these measures. You need to document them in detail and make them a part of the project plan, and you need to monitor them during project reviews. Are they still relevant? And how is the project doing in achieving them?

Managers and project teams should be evaluated based on their performance in all dimensions, rather than only the short-term ones. Any specific project should be focused on the appropriate dimensions. Is it a short-term, low-risk project whose benefits are based on efficiency? Or is it a high-risk project, in which the organization is ready to suffer some overruns and even live with less satisfactory business success in the short run in order to enjoy the long-term benefits and infrastructure built for creating the future?

The adaptive and flexible project management style also applies to project success. If necessary, you should be ready to adapt your project's success dimensions in response to new information and changes in the environment. During project reviews, executives should look at these success dimensions and the progress that has been achieved and, if needed, approve changes in the measures according to the changes in the circumstances.

Accept Greater Responsibility

In our view, project managers are responsible for achieving success in all dimensions—first and foremost, for customer satisfaction and business results. When we presented these ideas to managers or other scholars, the typical response was supportive and enthusiastic. From time to time, however, we have heard another opinion—one best represented by the words of an anonymous reviewer of one of our research papers: "A project manager must make sure the project is completed in time, within budget, and it should meet its specifications. Everything else is irrelevant. If these are not congruent, it can be argued that there was a failure *outside* of the project, not within it, and the project can be considered a legitimate success."

We hope that such long-held beliefs are fading away. No one outside the project knows the project better than its manager, and no one can do more to guarantee its success. The extended and continuous period of work on the project should be devoted to creating a success-focused environment, beyond the triple constraint, in which each team member knows clearly what success means and acts purposefully to achieve it.

But what about rewards? How do we reward a project manager for a job well done when the business results will come (or not come) long after project completion? A portion of these rewards may come naturally during project execution in the form of customer reaction or initial business response. Ultimately, however, the adaptive approach will cause a culture change in organizations. Projects will be tied more closely to business results, executives will be more attuned to project processes, and in the long run reward systems will become more flexible and adaptive to multiple indicators of project performance.

Dealing with the Possibility of Failure

Most of this chapter has focused on project success—how to measure it and how to plan your project for the greatest success possible. But what about failure? Unfortunately, as we have seen, failure is common in projects, and project teams must deal with it during planning, just as they deal with planning for success. Many teams indeed use a risk management plan for their projects; however, we argue that you should define the success *and* failure criteria on various dimensions at the same time. Failure criteria state in advance what can go wrong with a project and form the basis for your detailed risk management plan. Projects may fail to meet their time and budget goals, fail to meet requirements or satisfy the customer, fail to meet the business objectives, cause harm or hazard, or even endanger human life. We provide more details on project risk in later chapters and deal specifically with risk management in chapter 9.

Now that we've examined what determines a successful project, chapter 3 outlines the framework through which the adaptive project management approach can be applied to various kinds of projects in various situations and environments.

Key Points and Action Items

- Project success cannot be judged by the triple constraint alone. Time, budget, and performance are short-term dimensions that do not reflect longer-term success. Project success is a multi-dimensional, strategic concept that should consider both the short- and long-term success of the project and its product. It should focus on business success as well as the efficiency with which the project is run, and it should consider different stake-holders' points of view.

- Five dimensions are typically sufficient to plan and assess project success: efficiency, impact on the customer, impact on the team, business and direct success, and preparation for the future. Each of these dimensions is then reflected in detailed measures for each project. Additional dimensions may be needed in specific cases.

- Different projects have different success measures. These measures depend on the point of view, the time frame, the project uncertainty, and other variables. The relative importance of success dimensions depends on the time of the observation and the type of the project.

- Success dimensions are determined as part of the project plan and should drive project execution. They should be defined together with possible failure criteria for "what can go wrong." It is the responsibility of the project manager and team to make sure that a project is executed so that it meets all the success dimensions.

- Success dimensions may also change during the project's life cycle, as new information is gathered and as the environment changes.

- Executives should implement a system in which all projects, as a first step, define the relevant success dimensions in the project plan. Project reviews should include progress reviews along all success dimensions and, if needed, approve changes in success measures.

- Your organization's culture should reward project managers and teams for more than meeting time and budget goals. Give greater responsibility to project managers, and make sure that they are rewarded when the product performs well in the market and when customers are really happy with the outcome.

◆ 3 ◆

THE DIAMOND FRAMEWORK

TO GO BEYOND the conventional practices of project management, we must begin by recognizing that one size does not fit all. Unlike operations, which are repetitive, each project by definition is unique. Every project represents a new experience, addressing a new problem with a new constellation of management challenges, and the management process is never a matter of repeating known steps and procedures.

Because individual projects are unique, managers and executives need to understand the ways in which projects differ from one another and the importance of fitting the right organization to the right project. Not understanding these differences, in fact, can often endanger a project and even lead to failure. Consider the following story.

The FCS Project

FCS was a third-generation fire control system developed by a well-known defense contractor in Israel. The main challenge for the FCS project was to improve the hit accuracy of weapons mounted on moving vehicles.[1] Because the contractor was experienced in building components and subsystems for similar previous generations, its executives assumed that they had the capability to compete for an entire system. After a competitive bidding process, the company won the contract.

The major technical innovation in the FCS was a new stabilization technique, which promised to improve performance substantially.

However, it would also require the use of technology that was totally new to the company, as well as an entirely different operational doctrine.

Nevertheless, company managers assumed that they could manage the development of this new system in the same way as their previous, less comprehensive projects. They also assumed they could use existing modules, with minor modifications, as building blocks for the new system. In addition, they assumed that once they had developed, tested, and validated all the subsystems, it would be a straightforward matter to assemble them into a functioning integrated system. Based on these assumptions, they put together a team in the way they always had, and they set about the new project with the same general mind-set and methodology to which they were accustomed.

However, most of the engineers working on the program had no experience with the crucial new stabilization technology. Furthermore, none of the team members had built entire systems, with responsibility for overall performance to meet the system's end-user expectations. On top of that, the whole project was new to the customer, and this meant that the ultimate performance objectives (and minimum requirements) were somewhat uncertain. The plan was to start delivering initial units after sixteen months and to begin full-scale production in three and a half years.

It soon became clear that the original project schedule was unrealistic. The project plan was therefore rewritten—twice. Still, the project steadily fell behind. After the first year, the company initiated emergency procedures and started to funnel additional resources to the program. Yet it took two full years for company managers to realize that the whole program needed to address two major problems, which lay outside the scope of the original plan altogether. By this time the crisis was full blown.

The first problem was that developing the stabilization technology would require much more time, because the new units needed additional design cycles to accommodate greater technological uncertainty.

The second problem was more profound: a complex system does not simply function as a collection of subsystems. The program needed an extensive period of system integration, together with the development of a new combat doctrine. Those activities were not part of the original project plan.

A drastic change in project management style was needed. After the intervention of top management, new systems engineering and integration groups were added to the team. In addition, the company mobilized specific hand-picked experts, including external consultants, to help the team in its efforts. And top management involvement became much more extensive, with daily briefings and almost instant reporting of new problems and solutions. This change resulted in a breakthrough, and it led, after thirty-eight months, to the delivery of the first fully functioning system. Production started after five years, with a final delay of twenty-one months and cost overruns of almost twice the original budget.

Why Organizations Need a Framework

The executives of the FCS project had to learn a painful lesson. In retrospect, if they had correctly assessed the project difficulties ahead of time, they would have instilled the right approach from the start. What the project managers lacked was a model for systematically assessing project uniqueness and understanding the key dimensions by which the new project differed from those in their previous experience.

But how can we refer to a framework, a model, or a common template if each project is unique? Are we not condemned to telling idiosyncratic stories about each new undertaking? Is there any way of establishing a coherent methodology that can be applied systematically to a wide range of projects?

The answer is yes: each project *is* unique, but not in every respect. When we survey a wide range of projects, we may find considerable variability—but also quite a number of common features. Indeed, as you will see, the variability itself follows certain patterns, and this means that we can develop general methods for handling various types of projects. This characteristic variability has not been captured so far in the current project management literature and is not part of the common body of knowledge.[2]

Project managers are often among the most creative leaders in an organization, perhaps explaining why they have gravitated to this role. They have learned that they must solve their own problems, often without guidance from higher-level executives, and they still must get the job done within a limited time frame. When they don't find a solution in the textbooks, they invent their own.

But what practitioners often lack is a perspective of sufficient generality; any given manager will participate in only a small number of projects in the course of a career. The contribution of scientific discipline is therefore to extend and generalize the relevant principles beyond the scope of limited individual experience. In our experience, what managers need most is a model to help them identify differences among projects, classify their own projects, and select the right approach for the project.

This chapter presents the NTCP diamond model that is used throughout the book as a practical framework for addressing the variability among projects. Although the diamond model may not be the only way, it provides a workable solution and a starting point for most projects, organizations, and managers. Let's begin with a look at how to assess and classify the project at hand.

How to Distinguish Among Projects

Projects differ from one another in many ways. They can be distinguished by technology, size, location, risk, environment, customer, contract, complexity, skills, geography, and many more aspects. But projects also have a lot in common. Every project has a goal, limited time and other resources, and a project manager or leader, and projects typically develop budgets, schedules, and organizations to determine who does what. The question is how to combine the common *and* the different elements into one model that allows managers to classify their projects and choose the right approach for each project.

To classify a project, you can employ three leading drivers: the goal, the task, and the environment.

- **Goal.** What is the exact outcome or product that this project needs to achieve? What does the end product do? The project's end product should be seen in a broad sense: it can be tangible or intangible, a process, a business, an organization, a system, a marketing campaign, or even an educational program.

- **Task.** What is the exact work that needs to be done? How difficult is it? How well known is it? Have similar tasks been done before? How complex is it, and how much time is available?

- **Environment.** The project's environment includes the business environment, the market, the available technology, or the specific industry. It may also involve the external economic, political, or geographic environment, as well as the internal environment in the company: the culture, the people, the skills, the procedures, and any other projects competing for the same resources.

Our objective was to build a context-free framework that would not depend on the industry, technology, or specific organization and would be universal enough to capture the wide spectrum of projects. In our research we tried to understand the underlying dimensions that make one project different from, or similar to, another in ways that can tell us how to manage projects more effectively.

Drawing on classic contingency theory, we concluded that we can define three dimensions that characterize each project: uncertainty, complexity, and pace. (Appendix 3A discusses how classic contingency theory can be applied to projects and how these dimensions emerged. Appendix 3B includes our research questionnaire on classification and appendix 3C discusses the conceptual basis for classification systems.[3]) *Uncertainty* refers to the state of our information about the project's goal, its task, and its environment; often this information is sketchy and incomplete, especially at the outset. *Complexity* is a measure of the project scope, reflected in characteristics such as the number of tasks and the degree of interdependency among them. And, of course, *pace* relates to the time dimension and the existence of "soft" or "hard" deadlines that drive the work.

In practice, we have found it helpful to expand this model, recognizing that there are really two major sources of uncertainty: market (or goal) uncertainty, and technological (or task) uncertainty. Thus the NTCP (novelty, technology, complexity, and pace) diamond model emerged. The uncertainty dimension is now split into two parts: novelty is determined by goal or market uncertainty, and technology by technological uncertainty.

Perhaps the best way to explain and explore this model is by looking at well-known examples.

The NTCP Dimensions: Some Famous Examples

One advantage of the NTCP model is that the dimensions are fairly easy to identify. The FCS story, presented earlier, illustrates the difficulty of a project that faced a high degree of new technology and the complex problem of integrating many subsystems into one functioning system. Specifically, the new technology required extensive time for technical design, building, and testing, and the complex nature of the product required a special organization and an extensive period of system integration and systems engineering. These represent the roles of the technology and complexity dimensions. The following story illustrates the impact of the dimension of novelty.

A Market Revolution Created by Sony

The first Walkman was born out of frustration.[4] Masaru Ibuka, the cofounder and honorary chairman of Sony in the 1970s, told some of his subordinates, "I wish it was easy to listen to recorded music on an airplane. Whenever I fly on business I take a heavy tape deck and headphones onto the airplane." To please their boss, a team of Sony employees removed the recording components from an existing handheld Sony tape recorder, making it lighter and smaller, and added a set of earphones. What was left became a prototype for the first Walkman—small enough to carry onto an airplane or listen to music while taking a walk.

Even though he had no marketing research support, CEO Akio Morita decided in 1979 to develop and market the Walkman as a commercial product. As Morita put it, "The market research is all in my head; we *create* markets!" With no clear specifications, the development team worked for months, with two objectives: good sound quality and small headphones that felt like you weren't wearing them at all.

Although the technology was not new, the product represented a new-to-the-world concept. Initial customer reaction was lukewarm. Of thirty thousand units produced, only three thousand were sold, and Sony managers understood that they needed an innovative marketing strategy. But how could they convince people they needed a product that they'd never seen, owned, or even thought of before?

The first step was to get the word out to people who influence the public, such as celebrities and music industry people. Sony sent free Walkmans to Japanese recording artists and to TV and movie stars. Targeting younger people and active folks, Sony employees rode the trains, wearing their Walkmans and listening to music. On Sundays, they walked around in Tokyo shopping centers and cultural and sports events. Each employee wearing a Walkman became a walking sales demonstration.

Some people were skeptical at first, but when they tried out the new music system they were amazed. This was an entirely new experience. Japan was swept up in the Walkman wave, and soon visiting tourists were going home with these made-in-Japan souvenirs. Within a year, sales reached a million units and the Walkman revolution began. No wonder its brand name became generic and was admitted to the *Oxford English Dictionary* in 1986.[5]

This almost classic story illustrates the difficulty organizations may encounter with market uncertainty. In projects having this kind of uncertainty, a company cannot rely on common marketing research, nor can it precisely predict expected sales. Market uncertainty is based on how new (or novel) the product is to the market it serves.

Let's look now at the idea of complexity, illustrated by the story of another well-known product.

The BMW Z3

In the late 1980s BMW struggled with slowing sales imposed by new Japanese luxury car competitors.[6] The company also suffered from the decline of worldwide motorcycle markets. In an effort to reverse this trend, BMW decided to reposition itself as a producer of quality-oriented luxury vehicles having a unique and definitive identity in the marketplace. It defined its product as "the ultimate driving machine," built for people seeking excitement and a unique expression of individuality. Among other things, BMW needed a product that would satisfy the same needs that motorcycles do and would represent an exciting, aesthetically pleasing product. Several alternatives were considered, among them race cars, dune buggies, sport utility vehicles, and roadsters. The roadster concept was finally adopted in 1992 because it allowed BMW to maintain its goal of producing superior and exciting vehicles. The vehicle was dubbed Z3.

BMW understood the complexities of car production. It was accustomed to overcoming the difficulties associated with the design, development, and production of new cars as complex systems, a process involving the integration of many subsystems produced by numerous internal and external subcontractors. However, the Z3 presented additional levels of complexity. The first was the decision to launch the Z3 as the first BMW car designed in Germany but produced in the United States (in a new plant in Spartanburg, South Carolina), thereby aligning with a long-term company objective of becoming a truly global brand. This decision required adapting to a different culture of concurrent cross-functional teams in a matrix organization. The goal was to use a new lean and flexible manufacturing environment, a lesson learned from Honda.

Second, BMW decided to leverage the buzz of the Z3 and invest 60 percent of its marketing efforts in nontraditional venues. The goal was to generate interest in the Z3 two years before product launch. The nontraditional approach included, among other things, launching a tie-in with the new James Bond movie, *Golden Eye*, featuring the Z3 as a gift item in the Neiman Marcus catalog, and featuring the car in an interactive BMW home page on the Web.

To cope with these complexities, managers attempted to make the design as simple as possible. They used an existing 3-series car platform and very few new components. However, to make sure everything went right, BMW produced 150 integration and testing prototypes. This number was much higher than with any previous project. Parts for initial units were made in Germany, but integration took place in the United States, and when completed, these cars were put in U.S. showrooms before product release. This action gave joint German and U.S. teams the opportunity to identify and resolve design and manufacturing problems early in the product's life cycle. It also enabled redesign work without the need to shut down production, and it created market interest before the official launch.

When all bugs had been removed, and in spite of supply delays, the Z3 captured 32 percent of the estimated target market in its first year of sales, exceeding revenue forecasts by 50 percent. Featuring the Z3 in the James Bond movie and other nontraditional marketing techniques resulted in nine thousand preproduction orders and caused a marketing paradigm shift at BMW.

The Z3 project is an example of how a company managed an unusual degree of project complexity. Its success resulted from BMW's detailed attention to building the right organizational structure and extensive integration efforts, with a great many integrated prototypes. The project reflected a massive and successful change in BMW's culture and structure—a change to a modern, global company that employs an integrated design, marketing, and manufacturing team to produce cars that communicate pure driving enjoyment, to sell all over the world.

Our next story illustrates the pace dimension of the diamond by recalling the painful events of Hurricane Katrina.

Hurricane Katrina

Katrina hit the coasts of Louisiana and Mississippi on August 29, 2005, causing the greatest devastation from a natural disaster in the history of the United States. The storm was a reminder that even the most developed society in the world is as vulnerable as other societies, and in some ways more vulnerable. But it was also a wake-up call for government as the sector responsible for the safety and well-being of its citizens. Katrina's magnitude and scope were beyond the comprehension and perhaps the capacity of a city or state to handle. It demonstrated that when catastrophe strikes, it is the responsibility of the federal government to act swiftly to save lives and property and to get life back to normal as quickly as possible.

Yet the Federal Emergency Management Agency (FEMA) and other U.S. government agencies were slow to respond and act. Critical time passed before any government help was evident in New Orleans, while people, desperate for help, clung to rooftops or scavenged food and shelter. For three days looters and criminals took advantage of the chaos and added terror and fear to the devastated city. It took the government four days to begin acting. At that point, finally, a convoy of military trucks drove through the floodwaters, and the first supplies of water and food reached victims who had waited for days. Thousands of armed National Guard troops also streamed into the city to help restore order.

Anyone looking at Katrina's relief efforts as a project would conclude that the failure was caused by the government's inability (or unreadiness) to respond immediately to the crisis at the most critical time, when thousands of people were seeking help and chaos took over. In retrospect, the government learned too late about the extent of the disaster and waited too long to hear from local authorities about what help they needed.[7] In the absence of information, the federal government did not take action; yet during a catastrophe, the first few hours are the most critical. That is when you can save the most lives and have a significant impact on the outcome. The reality is that during those fateful moments there is no time to wait for information or prepare plans.

The story of Hurricane Katrina shows that you cannot treat a crisis like any other project. Typical projects start by making a plan and then taking action to implement it. But in crisis, plans are often useless. On one hand, it would be helpful to think of possible scenarios ahead of time and build contingency plans for any imaginable disaster; it would also help to prepare equipment and people who are ready to respond. On the other hand, when crisis strikes, it is often unimaginable, and you must be ready to act *without* a plan.

The most important thing is to be there, to take action, and to give local leaders the authority to respond on the spot; above all, you must adopt the habit of improvisation, which means you must start doing instead of waiting until you have a plan. These kinds of projects, which we call blitz, represent the highest level of pace in the NTCP model. Also, however, Katrina relief was the most complex project possible, because it involved an entire city and its people. In the complexity dimension, then, it would be called array, representing the highest end of the spectrum.

The NTCP Model: An Introduction

The NTCP model is a structured framework that managers can use when making decisions about projects and about how they should be run. These decisions may involve such things as selecting the right projects and their managers, allocating resources, planning, assessing risk, selecting the project management style, selecting the project's structure, building processes, and choosing tools. Each dimension includes three to four levels along a spectrum in which a project might fall, as shown in figure 3-1.[8]

In chapters 4 through 7 we examine each dimension (or each base) of the diamond in detail. For now let's briefly walk through them.

Novelty: How New Is Your Product in the Market?

Product novelty is defined by how new the product is to its markets and potential users. This dimension represents the extent to which customers are familiar with this kind of product, the way to use it, and its benefits. It also represents the uncertainty of your project goal—that is, how clearly you can define the requirements and customer needs up front.

Product novelty includes three types: derivative, platform, and breakthrough.[9] These categories determine which marketing approach is best and how much impact the product will have on project management. In essence, product novelty will affect three major issues: the reliability of marketing research, the time it takes to define and freeze product requirements, and the specific marketing strategies for the product. The levels of novelty are defined as follows:

- *Derivative* products are extensions and improvements of existing products.

- *Platform* products are new generations of existing product lines. Such products replace previous products in a well-established market sector. A typical example is a new car model.

FIGURE 3-1

The NTCP model

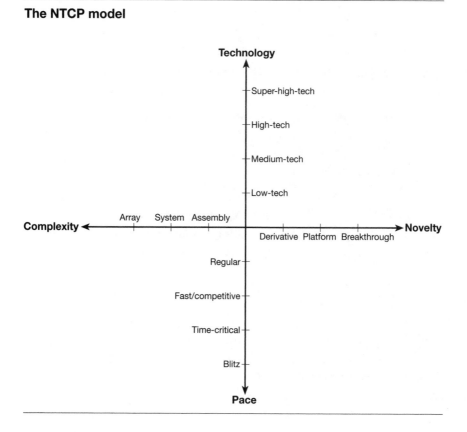

- *Breakthrough* products are new-to-the-world products. They transform a new concept or a new idea into a new product that customers have never seen before. The first Sony Walkman and the first 3M Post-it notes are typical examples.

Technology: Technological Uncertainty

The major source of task uncertainty is technological uncertainty. (Other sources might be the lack of team experience or tight budget constraints.) Technological uncertainty has an impact on, among other things, design and testing, communication and interaction, the timing of design freeze, and the needed number of design cycles. It also affects the technical competence needed by the project manager and project team members. Four levels comprise technological uncertainty.[10]

- *Low-tech* projects rely on existing and well-established technologies. The most typical examples are construction projects.

- *Medium-tech* projects use mainly existing or base technologies but incorporate a new technology or a new feature that did not exist in previous products. Examples include products in stable industries, such as appliances, automobiles, or heavy equipment.

- *High-tech* projects represent situations in which most of the technologies employed are new to the firm but already exist and are available at project initiation. Most computer and defense development projects belong to this category.

- *Super-high-tech* projects are based on new technologies that do not exist at project initiation. Although the mission is clear, the solution is not, and new technologies must be developed during the project. A good example is the moon-landing program.

Complexity: The Complexity of Your Project (System Scope)

A simple way to define various levels of complexity is to use a hierarchical framework of systems and subsystems. We call it *system scope,* and in most cases a lower scope level can be seen as a subsystem of the next higher level. Project complexity is directly related to system scope and affects project organization and the formality of project management. Three typical levels of complexity are used to distinguish among project management practices: assembly, system, and array.

- *Assembly* projects involve creating a collection of elements, components, and modules combined into a single unit or entity that performs a single function. Assembly projects may produce a simple stand-alone product (such as a CD player or a coffee machine) or build a subsystem of a larger system (such as an automobile transmission). They may also involve building a new organization that is responsible for a single function (such as payroll).

- *System* projects involve a complex collection of interactive elements and subsystems, jointly performing multiple functions to meet a specific operational need. System projects may build products such as cars, computers, or buildings, or they may deal with the creation of entire new businesses that include several functions.

- *Array* projects deal with a large, widely dispersed collection of systems that function together to achieve a common purpose (sometimes they are called "systems of systems" or "super systems"). Examples of arrays include national communications networks, a mass transit infrastructure, or regional power distribution networks, as well as entire corporations.

Pace: How Critical Is Your Time Frame?

On this scale, projects differ by urgency (or how much time is available) and by what happens if time goals are not met. Pace impacts the autonomy of project teams, the bureaucracy, the speed of decision making, and the intensity of top management involvement. We have identified four levels of pace: regular; fast/competitive; time-critical; and blitz.[11]

- *Regular* projects are those efforts where time is not critical to immediate organizational success.

- *Fast/competitive* projects are the most common projects carried out by industrial and profit-driven organizations. They are typically conceived to address market opportunities, create a strategic positioning, or form new business lines.

- *Time-critical* projects must be completed by a specific date, which is constrained by a definite event or a window of opportunity. Missing the deadline means project failure. Examples might be the launch of a space vehicle based on a specific cosmic constellation, or the Y2K project.

- *Blitz* projects are the most urgent, most time-critical. These are crisis projects. Solving the crisis as fast as possible is the criterion for success.

The Adaptive Diamond Model

Combining the specific project categories on each dimension creates our adaptive diamond model. The diamond shape provides a graphical illustration of a project according to its levels of novelty, technology, complexity, and pace. Figure 3-2 shows, for example, the diamond of a platform, high-tech, system, time-critical project.

The diamond model serves several purposes in coming chapters. First, it shows clearly what type of project is at hand. To communicate in writing a specific diamond of project classification, we use a language that translates the diamond to letter notations (in a vector format). Thus, the diamond in figure 3-2 is noted as D = (Pl, HT, Sy, TC). Similarly, a breakthrough,

FIGURE 3-2

The NTCP diamond

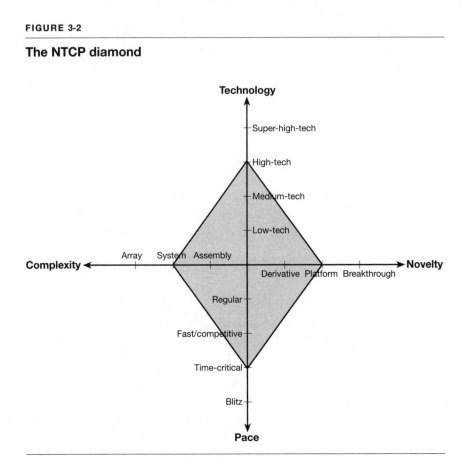

medium-tech, array, fast/competitive project would be noted as D = (Br, MT, Ar, FC).

Second, as you'll see next, you can use the diamond as a tool for analyzing the fit between the required and the actual project management styles. It is also useful for two-way communication between management and project teams.

Required and Actual Management Styles: The Fit and the Gap

The level of fit between the required and the actual management style often provides an explanation for project troubles or failure. It also gives you an opportunity to analyze the problem and offer recommendations for getting a project back on track.

We thus use the diamond as a graphical tool to demonstrate gaps between how a project should be managed and how it was actually managed. We call it the *required* style versus the *actual* style. We use a solid-line diamond for the required style, and a dotted-line diamond for the actual style. For example, in the FCS project story that opened this chapter, the required style was platform, high-tech, system, fast/competitive. Analyzing the events and managerial actions, we conclude that the project was initially managed as a platform, medium-tech, assembly, and fast/competitive project (see figure 3-3).

The third purpose for the diamond is for use by management to identify the major benefits and risks associated with the project. As everyone knows, risk and opportunity go together. The greater the opportunity, the higher the risk. The same is true for projects.

Project Selection: Balancing Benefit and Risk

With the diamond model, managers can select the right project manager, assign team members, and identify how much management attention is needed. Thus as managers make decisions on project selection, initiation, and resource allocation, they can look at the diamond as a tool for discussing the potential benefits and risks of each project proposal. In real

FIGURE 3-3

The FCS project

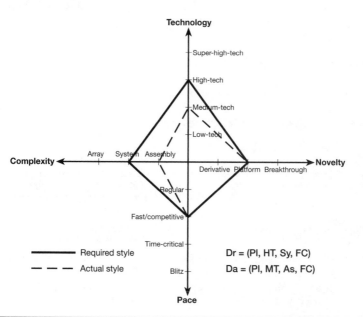

Dr = (Pl, HT, Sy, FC)
Da = (Pl, MT, As, FC)

life, bigger diamonds are more precious but more prone to be stolen. Bigger diamond models represent projects having higher potential payoffs and benefits, but they also portend higher risk.

Each of the NTCP dimensions represents a different type of risk and benefit to the project. Table 3-1 and the following discussion summarize these benefits and risks for each of the four dimensions. (Chapter 9 includes a detailed discussion about project risk management and how to apply the diamond analysis to quantify the risk in real-life projects.)

- **Novelty.** Derivative projects produce improvements to existing products, which typically are well defined in advance. Platform projects, however, produce new generations of existing products, which represent a significant change in performance. But this change involves increased risk of product performance under- or overkill, something customers may not like. Breakthrough, new-to-the-world products may create outstanding opportunities for businesses, but they present the greatest risk to companies of hitting the right product, recovering the investment, or attracting faster competitors.

- **Technology.** Higher technology may produce more-advanced products with increased performance and functionality. But they obviously create increased risk of technology that is incomplete or immature or simply fails. At the highest level of super-high-tech, customers may expect a quantum leap in performance and benefits (such as in space programs), but because technologies need to be developed during the project, such projects are far riskier than those that adopt known technologies.

TABLE 3-1

Benefits and risks of high NTCP levels

Dimension	Expected benefit	Potential risk
Novelty	Exploiting new market opportunities; leapfrogging competition; gaining first mover advantage	Having difficulty predicting exact market needs; missing sales targets; attracting competitors to copy your ideas
Technology	Improving performance and functionality	Experiencing technology failure; lacking needed skills
Complexity	Bigger programs, bigger payoffs	Having difficulty in coordinating and integrating
Pace	Gaining early market introduction, mounting quick response	Missing deadlines; making haphazard mistakes

- **Complexity.** Complexity presents both an opportunity based on the level of investment and a risk associated with complexity (or size). The risks involved with complexity are both organizational and technical. As complexity grows, the number of components grows and the need for interaction and coordination increases. System projects have difficulty in integration and configuration management, and array projects must deal with political, environmental, and economic issues.

- **Pace.** Increasing pace creates faster response. The risk of rushing things increases, however, as pace becomes faster. In time-critical projects, for example, missing the end date means project failure, and in blitz projects immediate reaction is necessary; otherwise, the crisis will not be resolved.

The Impact of the NTCP Dimensions on Project Management

Once the project has been selected and the expected benefits and risks assessed, how should various projects be managed? Each of the NTCP dimensions affects project management in a different way (see figure 3-4). In the coming chapters we explore all these aspects in more detail. Here is a summary:

- Novelty affects the accuracy of market predictions, the ability to determine requirements, and the timing of requirements freeze. The higher the novelty, the less you can depend on marketing research. At the highest level, breakthrough, market data is virtually non-existent, because customers have never seen your product and cannot tell you how they will use it or even whether they like it. You need to obtain customer feedback quickly using early prototypes before final product requirements are set.

- A higher technology level requires increased design and development activities, more design cycles, later design freeze, and better interaction among team members. A high technology level also requires that team members have higher technical skills and that you hold frequent technical reviews in addition to the usual managerial reviews.

- Complexity affects your organization and its procedures. The greater the complexity of a project, the more complex the organization will be and the more formal the procedures you will need.

FIGURE 3-4

The impact of the NTCP dimensions on project management

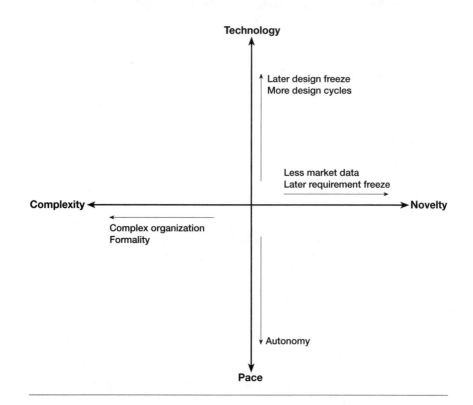

- Pace requires increased attention to time deadlines. The faster the pace, the greater the autonomy you need to give your project teams and the more support they will need from top management.

Remember, however, that no model can apply to all situations. Organizations may therefore need to develop their own way of classifying projects.[12] For example, organizations may face other kinds of uncertainty, not only in the market or technology. They may need to pay specific attention to uncertainties associated with politics, economics, geography, and funding. Each of these uncertainties may have its own impact on project management.

Similarly, some projects may face other types of complexity, regarding everything from vendor groups and customers to local or global network complexity. Or projects may also be distinguished by cost constraints; for example, a project's cost may depend on the requirements and the plan, or a project may be given a cost constraint of "not to exceed" a certain amount.

In sum, there are many ways to distinguish projects, and it is beyond the scope of this book to outline all possibilities. However, once project managers accept and internalize the concept that different projects require different management styles, companies can find the specific way they need to adapt particular projects to their unique circumstances.

We conclude this chapter with the story of the World Trade Center (WTC). The World Trade Center will always be remembered for the tragic terrorist attack of September 11, 2001. However, here we want to remember how the WTC came to be built: through a unique project that realized the dream and vision of its leaders. The project, which began construction in the 1960s and was completed in 1973, represented project management at its best. If we apply the model of this book to this project, we see that its builders correctly identified the risk and opportunity of this task and knew how to select the right approach for this unusual project. We offer this story as a tribute to great project management.

The World Trade Center Project

The World Trade Center was conceived in the 1960s to revitalize lower Manhattan. It was one of the first visible signs that New York's economy was transforming from manufacturing to services. The Port Authority of New York and New Jersey (PA) undertook the project—the only organization that had both the political autonomy and the financial resources to pull it off.

Austin Tobin, the executive director of the PA, put Guy Tozzoli in charge of the WTC project. Tozzoli, a young Navy veteran who specialized in radar engineering, had previous experience in smaller port projects in New Jersey and New York but no experience in construction. Still, to his credit Tobin saw qualities in Tozzoli that led to the decision to put the young engineer in charge, in spite of all the odds.[13]

Early in 1964, after considering a few less ambitious architectural proposals the Port Authority announced that it would create the tallest building in the world. Minoru Yamasaki, the chosen architect, was ordered to aim higher than the Empire State Building. Adding twenty more stories, the PA hoped, would favorably tip the economics of this real estate venture. But the PA also wanted to focus the project on a single, powerful idea: encouraging world peace by promoting international business.[14] Construction took eight years and involved more than ten thousand workers in various stages, with an average of four thousand on a daily basis. The PA's World Trade Department coordinated and administered more than seven hundred contractors.

To characterize the project's diamond components, we will start with novelty. Combining a shopping mall with wide office spaces and transportation systems was not a breakthrough idea, but certainly it was not a derivative of existing similar commercial complexes. That made the project a platform. As for complexity, the World Trade Center comprised seven buildings on sixteen acres of prime land, totaling more than 12 million square feet of high-quality office space. The center encompassed a collection of systems, including elevators; heating, venting, and air conditioning (HVAC); and transportation, utilities, communications, sanitation, and other elements. Lower Manhattan's largest shopping mall was located in the WTC basement, along with a seven-level parking garage. Its interface with public transportation systems and other facilities in the neighborhood clearly placed the project at the top of the complexity classification, into the array category (see figure 3-5).

FIGURE 3-5

The World Trade Center project

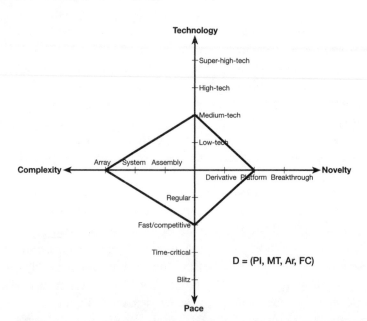

$$D = (Pl, MT, Ar, FC)$$

In contrast to most standard construction projects, the World Trade Center was more technologically challenging than anything that had been done before. The first major advance in technology was the "reverse bathtub" system, which solved the problem of reaching bedrock through the water table of the Hudson River. Although this technique used an existing technology developed by an Italian firm, it had never been tried on such a large scale.

Second, to transport the fifty thousand people working in the towers, the design included more than one hundred elevators of a new high-speed, high-capacity type; their doors opened to both sides to allow the first-entering passengers to be first out. Third, the exterior structural column design was also revolutionary, taking advantage of newly developed high-strength steel. An additional concern was the ten- to fifteen-foot sway the tall towers would experience and to what degree the occupants could tolerate it. These and other technological challenges categorize this effort as a medium-tech project.

Initially, many changes made for economic and political reasons extended the planning more than fifteen years. However, once construction started, the pace approached the fast/competitive category, in which time-to-completion has business and economic consequences. Timetables of the WTC project had to be checked daily to avoid the potential $1 million daily cost of work delays. From the moment construction began, progress remained on pace with only a few small glitches.

Project managers understood well the extent of uncertainty and complexity posed by this project and had prepared the right means and processes to deal with them. For example, although it is common in construction projects to freeze the design before the beginning of construction, management was ready to support changes, which were perceived as critical to the long-term success of the WTC. For instance, management decided to modify the window design for the WTC rooftop restaurant to give visitors a breathtaking view of the city.

As a large array project, the WTC needed a well-run bureaucratic central system of coordination. Work was divided among hundreds of subcontractors by the office of engineering and architecture. To solve system integration problems, the PA employed a large construction company, together with an advisory board of architects and real estate personnel. The group of twenty engineers and architects had direct channels of communication, enabling the complex integration of all subunits. Meetings with the Board of Directors of the Port Authority were conducted monthly, and lower-level review meetings took place weekly and even daily.

In retrospect, throughout the entire project its leadership managed the project with a strategic, long-term perspective in mind. They did not focus only on finishing the project on time and within budget but were constantly concerned with the business and long-term effects of the end result. They were also ready to face the economic, environmental, social, and political aspects of the WTC. Although no theoretical classification existed at that time, management clearly took the right action to deal with project risk by understanding implicitly the extents of novelty, technology, complexity, and pace (as shown earlier in figure 3-5).

The construction of the World Trade Center had a dramatic long-term effect on the well-being of the great city. Described as the biggest construction project in the world, the WTC became a symbol of world trade and peace. After its completion, construction boomed in lower Manhattan, creating extremely valuable real estate. A service economy blossomed, with financial services and insurance leading the way.

The first three chapters of this book have shown why organizations need a new model to deal with the challenge of projects. These chapters form the conceptual basis for the rest of the book. In the next four chapters, part 2, we discuss in detail the four dimensions of project distinction and provide the rules for how to adapt project management to your project's type.

A common theme in all these chapters is the idea of viewing a project as a temporary organization and a process. In reality, however, you can distinguish a project's effort by three different, though not disjointed, processes in the project life cycle. The first is the requirements definition process, which involves defining the customer needs and translating them into product requirements. Second is the technical process, which involves translating the requirements into technical specifications and then designing, building, and testing the product. The third is the managerial process, which involves controlling the first two processes, collecting information about their progress, and making decisions about them.

In our search for project contingencies we use this view of a project in each of the following four chapters to ask a key question: how do the various project types affect the project organization as well as these processes? We begin with novelty in chapter 4.

Key Points and Action Items

- The theory of contingency suggests a context-free distinction based on the uncertainty, complexity, and pace of projects. We expand this theoretical perspective by using two types of uncertainty: market and technology. This leads to the project adaptation diamond (the NTCP model), which includes four dimensions: novelty, technology, complexity, and pace.

- A project's novelty refers to how new the product is in the market and how certain the goal is; technology refers to how much new technology is used on the project; complexity refers to how complex the product is in a hierarchy of systems and subsystems; and pace refers to how urgent the time frame may be. Each dimension is divided into three to four specific project types. A single project is represented by its own diamond.

- The NTCP diamond model enables managers to identify project risks and opportunities as well as the gap between the required management style and the actual management style employed on an ongoing project. The model is also useful for selecting the right approach to the project during planning and initiation.

- Although the NTCP model provides a context-free framework for most projects, in some cases you may need a specific model for your project or organization. It can be based on other types of uncertainty or complexity, or other environmental variables.

Part Two

THE FOUR BASES OF
SUCCESSFUL PROJECTS

◆ 4 ◆

NOVELTY

N OVELTY, THE FIRST DIMENSION of our adaptive project management model (and the first base to be visited by managers), is determined by the nature of the project's product—how new the product is to the market, the customers, and the potential users. Novelty represents the extent to which buyers and users are familiar with this kind of product—its benefits and the way they can use it. It indicates the level of uncertainty in the market, or external uncertainty, and it also reflects the project's goal uncertainty—how well the end result or the project goal can be defined.

The classification we use is not new. For example, Wheelwright and Clark, in their extensive studies on new product development, used three categories of products to describe the company's project portfolio and create an aggregate project plan: *derivatives, platforms,* and *breakthroughs*.[1] We adopted these categories for the novelty dimension. As we show later, they affect managerial behavior, marketing activities, and other tasks of project management. Table 4-1 defines the three levels of novelty and lists typical examples.

How Novelty Affects Projects

The level of a product's novelty affects the process of defining the product's requirements and market-related activities. Specifically, product novelty affects how easy it is to know what to do or what to build and how to market your product to customers. These tasks involve at least four aspects of project management:

TABLE 4-1

Definitions and examples of project novelty

Level of project novelty	Definition	Examples
Derivative project	Extending or improving existing products or services	Developing a new version of a personal computer using the same technology; upgrading a production line; streamlining organizational procedures
Platform project	Developing and producing new generations of existing product lines or new types of services to existing or new markets and customers	Building a new automobile generation; developing a new aircraft; creating a new generation of a cellular system
Breakthrough project	Introducing a new-to-the-world product or concept, a new idea, or a new use of a product that customers have never seen before	The first enterprise resource planning (ERP) package; the first microwave oven; the first Walkman; the Segway personal transportation system

- How well you can rely on market research data

- How well you can define product requirements and project goals

- How long you should wait to freeze product requirements

- Which marketing techniques and market penetration strategy you should use

Note that although new-to-the-market products may involve new technology, this is not always the case. Product novelty and the newness of the technology you're adopting are two different things. You can often find products of high novelty that use existing, well-established technology. As discussed in chapter 3, the Walkman was a new concept in the market, but the product was based on well-known technologies found in portable radios and tape recorders. Although the technical solution was easy, other decisions were difficult: marketing research was inconclusive, and the decision to launch the product was based on managerial intuition. Similarly, the famous 3M Post-it notes did not use advanced technologies, but the product was not well supported by marketing predictions. Only after initial market testing did the product begin its journey as one of the most successful products in the history of office supplies.

Let's look at another famous story: the first full-length computer-animated movie.

The *Toy Story* Story: A New Platform in the Movie Industry

In 1991, Walt Disney Company and Pixar Animation Studios entered into a collaborative effort to create *Toy Story,* the first full-length computer-animated film. The film required the combined effort of two creative and completely different companies.[2]

Disney was well known for its animated films. From its first full-length film, *Snow White and the Seven Dwarfs* (1937), the company's Feature Animation division had set an unprecedented standard in animated films. Since then it had made thirty-eight feature films using essentially the same method of production: animators drew each scene on plastic frames, which were shown at twenty-four frames per second.

Pixar—founded by George Lucas, later acquired by Steve Jobs, and years later bought by Disney—had up to that time produced several computer-animated short films, which were the company's main source of revenue. But Pixar was looking beyond making short movies.

For Disney and its customers, *Toy Story* was a new generation of an existing product line in a well-established market. The movie gave Disney an opportunity to use new software technology that later would serve as a platform for a stream of animated movies such as *Shrek, Finding Nemo,* and *The Incredibles.*

To produce *Toy Story,* each company focused on what it knew best. Having the drive and capabilities to create computer-animated films, Pixar was responsible for the movie's production technology, and Disney for the artistic content and marketing. By using Disney's experience in producing full-length films, Pixar learned for the first time to stockpile digital characters, sets, props, and scenes to be reused, saving the partners significant cost in these labor-intensive tasks of animated film production.

Throughout the four years of the project, executives from Disney and Pixar met regularly to assess the film's progress, reviewing both the production and the storyline. The movie opened in U.S. theaters in 1995, one day before Thanksgiving, which is among the busiest weekends for movie attendance. *Toy Story* was an immediate success, and not only in financial terms. It also set a new standard and established a technological platform for many animated movies in the years to come.

When building platforms, you often build not only a new product but also the infrastructure for future products. Making *Toy Story* opened up a new spectrum of business opportunities for both companies. However, the lessons of the film as a project extend beyond product novelty. In fact, the project is relevant to other dimensions of our model. It was also a system project on the complexity dimension, and a high-tech project on the technology dimension, as we discuss in detail in the next two chapters.

For now, let's explore in more detail the elements of platform projects like *Toy Story,* together with the other two types: derivatives and breakthroughs.

Distinguishing Projects Based on Novelty

Projects at the various levels of novelty possess their own unique elements that strongly distinguish them from one another. Managers must understand these differences and adapt their managerial activities to the project's novelty level.

Derivative Projects: Modifications, Extensions, and Improvements

Derivatives are extensions and improvements of existing products and may include cost reduction efforts, product improvements, product modifications, or additions to existing lines. Think, for example, of a new version of Post-it notes based on different colors or shapes. Previous products are well established, and market research data is readily available. The "what to do" question is easy to answer.

For this kind of derivative product, predictions about product cost, as well as other product requirements, can be fairly accurate, and there is no need for market experimentation. Product requirements can therefore be frozen as early as possible, most likely at project launch, and the design should ensure fast execution for timely completion. Moreover, marketing of derivatives is focused on product advantage in comparison to previous models and is aimed at serving existing customers, as well as potential new customers, with added product features and varieties.

Platform Projects: New Generations

Platform products are new generations of existing product lines for new or existing markets and customers. New aircraft or automobile designs are typical platform examples, as were the tools used to create *Toy Story.*

Projects to build platform products typically create new families of products and form the basis for derivatives.

Such products replace previous products in a well-established market sector. Although some platforms may involve completely new technologies, product usage by customers is predicted fairly well. Still, a new platform development can take more time than derivative product development.

For platform projects, companies should perform extensive market research, study the data of previous generations, and carefully plan product prices. The final setting of product requirements will therefore be made well into the project execution period. However, there is a trade-off: you should freeze requirements fairly early so that you can ensure timely product introduction and reasonable profitability. Marketing efforts for platform products should focus on creating the product's image, emphasizing product advantages, and differentiating it from its competitors.

Breakthrough Projects: Creating New-to-the-World Products

The literature on innovation has traditionally distinguished between incremental and radical innovation.[3] Radical innovation represents a diversion from known markets and known solutions or technologies, whereas incremental innovation seeks to build on, complement, and extend existing products. Radical innovation does not build and extend what exists, but rather seeks to overturn it. It is sometimes destructive to the skills, practices, product forms, and social relationships that exist within an organization.[4]

Breakthrough products represent radical innovations in the market. Often called *new-to-the-world* products, they make almost everything you know about the market irrelevant. The projects that create them are transforming a new concept or a new idea into a product that customers have never seen before. One example was the first Segway two-wheeled personal transportation system; others were the first personal computer, the first microwave oven, and the first Internet browser. Breakthrough projects can also be identified in industries that have no customers in the usual sense, such as outer space. Thus, it is appropriate to classify many space missions as breakthroughs, because no similar programs have been done before.

Although breakthrough products may use new or mature technologies, their expected market does not exist. Customers do not know anything about the new product, nor do they know how to use it until they see and try it. Marketing research studies are therefore ineffective, and product definition must be based on best guesses, intuition, and market trial and error.[5] Requirements must thus remain flexible until first market introduction is made and until customer feedback is available. Fast proto-typing is necessary before final requirements are set and is much more crit-ical than extensive market research. Companies that manage breakthrough projects must work closely with customers, who test initial prototypes and help the company shape final product requirements. When you manage breakthrough projects, you must therefore realize that product definition will most likely change after initial market trials and feedback from early users.

Marketing of breakthrough products is different from marketing of the other two types. It is focused on getting the attention of customers, which Jeff Moore called "innovators and early adopters."[6] Its goal is to educate customers about the potential of the new product and often to articulate hidden customer needs. Marketing of new-to-the-world prod-ucts often involves selling products below production cost, or even giving them away. Another method may be to bundle the new product with well-known existing products so that customers can learn and appreciate the breakthrough benefits.

Breakthrough products often create new directions in the industry or even create new industries. New-to-the-world products introduce new concepts of design, and that often prompts entry of followers. Often, the new product design becomes the industry standard. The ability of a firm to establish its technology as an industry standard is a critical element in its long-term competitive position and success. (We return to this prob-lem later in the chapter.)

Product Novelty and Project Success

Clearly, different levels of novelty may have different market and business objectives. A derivative product is typically aimed at gaining additional cus-tomers and extending the life of an existing cash cow. In contrast, you might introduce a breakthrough product to create a new market and a new use for customers that have never used a similar product. Therefore, as described in chapter 2, your project planning should include setting expectations in ad-vance. This means deciding what will constitute project success *or* failure. Table 4-2 summarizes these expectations for different levels of novelty.

Making It All Work: Combining Product Novelty and Project Management

How should you treat different novelty levels in real-life projects? Think back to our example of *Toy Story*, which illustrates a typical problem of a platform project: how to build the infrastructure for future derivatives.

TABLE 4-2

Project novelty and project success: What to expect

Success dimensions and possible failure	LEVEL OF PROJECT NOVELTY		
	Derivative	*Platform*	*Breakthrough*
Efficiency	High efficiency is critical; no room for overruns	Time to market is important for competitive advantage	Efficiency is difficult to achieve and may not be critical (unless competitors work on the same idea); overruns likely
Impact on customer	Gaining additional customers and market segments	Having high strategic impact on customers; retaining previous generation customers	Outstanding improvements in customer's life and work
Impact on the team	Team members extend their experience in quick product modifications	Team members gain technical and managerial experience in introducing new generations	Team members explore new fields and gain extensive experience in unknown markets
Business and direct success	Extends life of existing products; additional revenues and cash cow current products	High strategic impact on the business; expectation of years of revenues and building of additional derivatives	Long-term, significant business success; may come later, after initial products have been tested and refined
Preparation for the future	Almost none	Maintaining a strategic position in the market	Creating new markets and establishing substantial leadership positions
Possible failure and risk	Low risk; risk may involve being late and gaining only marginal value	Medium risk; risk may involve failing to make enough progress compared with the previous generation, or even missing a generation in the market	Highest risk; risk involves failing to address a real need of customers, failing to sell the idea to customers, or failing to assess real market size

The technology required to create the movie was new (high-tech), novelty was at the platform level, and complexity was at the system level. In figure 4-1, we use the notation $D = (Pl, HT, Sy, -)$ to describe part of the *Toy Story* diamond shape (except for the pace dimension, which is discussed in chapter 7).

Table 4-3 lists the major impact that levels of novelty have on project management in terms of product definition, managerial decisions, and market-related activities. Appendix 4 describes how different levels of product novelty can affect the traditional processes of project management characterized by the nine major PMBoK knowledge areas.

FIGURE 4-1

The *Toy Story* project

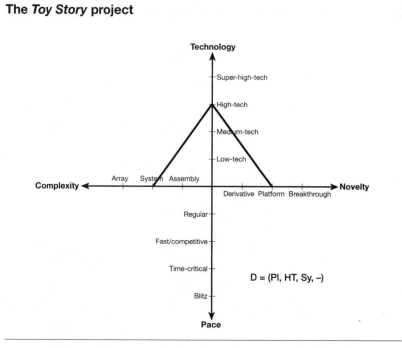

Now let's look in more detail at the most difficult and least understood level of novelty: breakthrough projects.

The Risk and Opportunity of Breakthrough Projects

Breakthrough projects involve the highest risk in the market, but they may potentially carry the greatest business opportunity. By introducing a new concept to customers, companies can create new markets and dominate them for years. But as history shows, early innovators often fail, leaving the battlefield for competitors and imitators to claim the benefits. How can companies protect their invention when bringing a breakthrough product to the market?

The first and perhaps most difficult barriers to promoting break-through projects are internal. Unfortunately, research has shown that it is often difficult to get support for radical projects in large firms, where internal cultures and pressures push efforts toward lower-risk projects, incremental projects, and those that promise immediate reward.[7] To promote and gain approval for such projects, you need strong internal champions who are not afraid to speak up and to stake their personal reputations on

TABLE 4-3

Impact of project novelty levels on project management

Managerial aspect	LEVEL OF PROJECT NOVELTY		
	Derivative	*Platform*	*Breakthrough*
Market data	Accurate market data exists from previous products and market research	Need extensive market research and careful analysis of previous generations, competitors, and market trends	Unreliable market data; market needs unclear; no experience with similar products; customer base not defined
Product definition	Clear understanding of required cost, features, functionality, etc.	Need to invest extensively in product definition, involve potential customers in process	Product definition based on intuition and trial and error; need fast prototyping to obtain market feedback; many changes in product definition
Timing of product requirements freeze	Early freeze of product requirements, usually before or immediately after project launch	Freeze requirements later, usually at mid-project	Very late freeze of requirements, often after prototype feedback
Marketing	Emphasize product advantage in comparison to previous model; focus on existing as well as new customers, based on product features and modifications	Create product image; emphasize product advantages; differentiate from competitors	Create customer attention through new and innovative marketing techniques; educate customers about potential of product; sometimes give away products free or at reduced price; articulate hidden customer needs; extensive effort often needed to create industry standard

what they believe. The fact that marketing research is not reliable makes it even more difficult to get such projects off the ground.

As Michael Tushman and Charles O'Reilly have shown, to increase the chances of success of breakthrough projects, organizations need to separate the breakthrough activity from the activities of the rest of the organization. Developing novel projects side by side with less novel projects often hurts the novel project because powerful existing activities generate extensive sales, albeit in mature markets.[8]

The External Risk of Market Uncertainty

Two influential books by Clayton Christensen (*The Innovator's Dilemma* and *The Innovator's Solution*) focus on the disruptive nature of breakthrough innovations and on the lack of market data about radical ideas.[9] As Christensen puts it, "Markets that don't exist cannot be analyzed." Furthermore, current customers never direct companies to create breakthrough products, and in fact their advice usually keeps companies away from the next revolutionary big thing.

The solution? Start with small trials, and play with ideas that do not threaten the existing organizational establishment. Instead of using market research, a project manager should use judgment and intuition to create fast prototypes and test them quickly in the market to obtain customer feedback as soon as possible. Only then can you finalize product characteristics and freeze requirements. No market research could have predicted the enormous success of the Walkman or Post-it notes. Only when first users tried these products were the companies able to learn what the products should look like, where they were going, and what else they could be used for.

The Battle for Industry Standards

Establishing a company's breakthrough product design as the industry standard—often called *dominant design*—largely determines the product's long-term competitive success.[10] As experience shows, when a breakthrough idea is copied by others, often the leader's design does not become the standard, even if it represents a better product. Think of Sony's superior Betamax VCR cassette standard, which lost the battle to JVC's VHS standard, or Apple's Macintosh design, which lost the monopoly to the PC Windows standard in spite of early advantages in performance, ease of use, and user friendliness.

During the battle for industry standards, companies must focus project activity on capturing market share rather than earning large margins. Apple's focus on high margins, and its refusal to allow cloning of its Mac design, quickly made the IBM PC and its low-cost compatibles the industry standard for many years. Thus you should make your breakthrough product attractive, as much as you can, by lowering prices and offering other entry incentives. Once the product is established as the standard, you can shift your focus to things such as increases in price and margin.

A breakthrough product can become an industry standard by other means, such as licensing, entering into strategic alliances, adopting an appropriate positioning strategy, and diversifying to complementary products. Key factors that affect the scale of these outcomes include the height of barriers to imitation, the capabilities of competitors, your own resources and skills, and the availability of complementary products.[11]

The story of the Segway personal transportation system is a classic example of a breakthrough project.

The Segway Story

Formerly known as "Ginger," Segway was developed by entrepreneur Dean Kamen, whose company, DEKA, also invented the first portable insulin pump, Baxter's HomeChoice dialysis machine, and the iBOT, a wheelchair capable of climbing and descending stairs.[12] One day a DEKA employee surfed past Kamen on an iBOT proof-of-concept prototype consisting of a platform balanced on a single axle and driven by two servomotors; a joystick was used for steering. In a flash of inspiration, Kamen envisioned a new-to-the-world product that could change the way people get around.

The story of Segway is the tale of a breakthrough product development project that excelled in almost every possible way. Kamen hired some of the brightest and most innovative engineers. They designed and perfected each element of Segway; they even paid attention to minor details such as the audible tones the vehicle would generate, making them as pleasant as possible. When the product was ready, the marketing, too, was unusual, resulting in unprecedented awareness with virtually no advertising budget. Dean Kamen and Segway appeared on almost every morning TV program, were photographed with every possible celebrity, and were even seen with the president of the United States. However, although Segway was an elegant product, it did not flood the market as expected; its creators had misassessed the market need.

From the beginning, the Segway team was not allowed to obtain feedback from real customers as needed in breakthrough projects (see figure 4-2). Kamen's fear that others would steal his ideas prevented the team from testing early prototypes with customers.[13] The project went into a Catch-22: without access to real market reaction, no one could determine the final requirements that would best fit customer needs.

If DEKA had established a robust requirement-setting process in which customers were involved, the project would not have proceeded into final design until customer feedback was analyzed and product requirements were frozen. To Kamen's credit, he recognized that he could not rely on customers to provide specific design direction. He had learned long ago that customers didn't always know best: "They hadn't thought about the problem deeply enough to envision innovative solutions."[14]

However, even though customers cannot always find solutions, they can at least identify their problems. When presented with a new solution, they can typically tell you how good it is and how you can improve it. That part was clearly missing in Segway's development.[15] When a semimarket test was finally conducted, it revealed for the first time an unexpected issue: "Some riders had said that their commutes to work were too long for Ginger, or that they preferred to walk for short errands."[16] Rather than take this finding as a warning signal and investigate it further, the company continued to move the Segway project forward as planned.

Kamen wanted not only to design Segway but also to manufacture it. Although a manufacturing plant was built to produce forty thousand units per year, DEKA sold only six thousand Segways in the first eighteen months after launch. Undoubtedly, the product has not revolutionized the world, as Kamen suggested, nor has it met his business expectations.

FIGURE 4-2

The Segway project

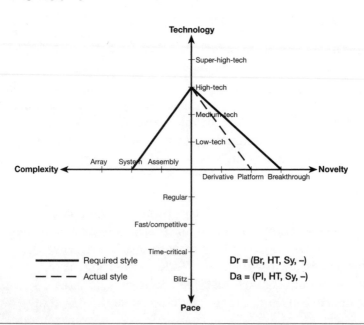

Dr = (Br, HT, Sy, –)
Da = (Pl, HT, Sy, –)

Segway's story offers valuable lessons to companies dealing with break-through projects, especially lessons about the inability to predict real market expectations and the need to use real customer feedback early on. Such practices in DEKA's case would have focused the company on initial market segments such as package delivery or helped it move faster to off-shore lower-cost manufacturing. DEKA might have considered licensing the product to other manufacturers in exchange for royalty fees, or per-haps producing a sitting model for longer trips. These ideas could have made the Segway a greater success story. Still, who knows? Perhaps one day Segway will change the way the world gets around.

The Impact of Misclassifying a Product's Novelty

Novelty affects project management mainly in product definition and market activities. To manage projects effectively, you must identify the level of your product's novelty early and quickly determine its impact on project planning and organization. Product novelty also affects the people you choose for the project and the management style you adopt. Manage-ment style should be more rigid at the lower levels and more flexible at the higher end, with greater creativity needed as the level of novelty increases.

The following software platform development case illustrates the im-portance of the correct assessment of novelty—in particular, what can happen when a platform project is treated as a simple derivative.

The Financial Middleware Software Project

The client for this software project was an investment management company looking to lower its costs by creating a straightforward format for processing its customers' buy and sell orders. The tradi-tional business process involved making investment decisions on behalf of clients, such as pension funds or wealthy individuals. The decisions to trade were made internally and involved three systems: trading, accounting, and communication. The external process in-volved sending the trade details (stock name, quantity, price, and fee) to the respective bank within a prescribed amount of time. Be-fore this project, most of these activities were preformed by hand.

The company was a small organization that had no prior experi-ence in monitoring complex software projects. The project was con-tracted to an external vendor, which claimed to have developed similar systems previously for the health care industry. The vendor suggested that this project would be a modification to its generic off-the-shelf middleware. At first, it appeared a perfect fit. The investment company needed a simple computerized platform, and the vendor was looking to expand its client base to financial institutions.

The new system consisted of three software components: middleware software to transfer trade information automatically, database software, and enrichment software, which receives the information from the database and sends it to an external bank.

All went well for the first four months; however, about midway through the project, things began to deteriorate. The modified systems did not function as expected, and the vendor had to allocate more resources to deal with the problems. When a first prototype was eventually delivered, the customer was unable to test it in due time. In the end, the vendor simply handed the source code to the customer and walked away. The investment firm was left to struggle with the software installation and testing on its own. The project was under constant review and change; deliverables were either altered or canceled. Finally, after long delays and additional cost, a workable version of the first mock-up was approved.

In retrospect, both parties miscalculated the extent of the risk and difficulty associated with this project. As it turned out, in comparison with medical systems, building a financial system containing complex business logic was a major leap. The customer did not possess the knowledge and expertise needed to manage or even define such a complex project. For its part, the vendor did not estimate the extent of change in the market that this product would introduce, assuming that it was simply an extension of a previous product for a different industry.

Using the diamond model, we can conclude that the vendor perceived the product's novelty as a derivative of a previous product, rather than a platform product—an assumption that turned out to be wrong (see figure 4-3). Introducing a product into a new industry must be treated as a platform project—a new generation for a new customer.

Similarly, as you will see in chapter 5, although the vendor had experience in this kind of technology, for the customer the project represented a high-tech project. However, it was treated as a medium-tech project and it was assumed that no technical reviews were needed.

Had the parties correctly assessed the project's level of novelty, many things would have been done differently. The vendor would have invested more time in understanding the uniqueness of the financial industry and

FIGURE 4-3

Financial middleware software project

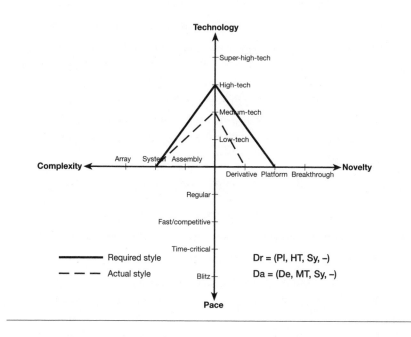

Dr = (Pl, HT, Sy, –)

Da = (De, MT, Sy, –)

understanding the company's decision-making process, distribution of data, and interaction between customers, vendors, banks, and other financial institutions. The customer and its project manager would have spent much more time in specifying the system, writing testing procedures, and performing design reviews to reduce technical risks. All these activities would have been included in the project plan and would not have been added on an emergency basis when trouble appeared.

Now that we've examined novelty, we turn in chapter 5 to the second dimension of the NTCP diamond model: technology, or technological uncertainty.

Key Points and Action Items

- Product novelty is determined by how new the product is to the market, customers, and potential users. There are three levels of novelty: derivative products, platform products, and breakthrough products. Derivatives are extensions and improvements of existing products. Platforms are new generations of existing product lines for new or existing markets and customers. Breakthroughs are new-to-the-world products.

- A product's novelty level affects requirements definition and product marketing—that is, how easy it is to know what to do or what to build, and how to market the product to the expected buyer and user. These tasks involve four aspects of project management: how well you can rely on market research data; how well product requirements can be defined; how long you should wait until you freeze product requirements; and which marketing techniques and market penetration strategy you should use.

- For derivatives, the "what to do" question is relatively easy to answer, and product requirements must be frozen as early as possible. For platform projects, it takes longer to define the product's requirements, based on extensive market research and cumulative data on previous generations.

- For breakthrough projects, marketing research typically is ineffective, and product definition must be based on best guesses, intuition, and market trial and error. Requirements must remain flexible until market introduction is possible and customer feedback is available.

- The ability of a firm to establish its design of a breakthrough product as an industry standard is a critical determinant of its long-term competitive position and success.

- Each project should assess product novelty up front and should determine the managerial implications during the planning phase: how you can use marketing research, when to freeze the requirements, and what marketing strategy will be best for the product.

◆ 5 ◆

TECHNOLOGY

I N THIS CHAPTER we explore one of the most important dimensions for distinguishing among projects: technology—or, more accurately, technological uncertainty—and its four levels: low-tech, medium-tech, high-tech, and super-high-tech. As you will see, assessing a project's technology level can be tricky, even in low-risk industries such as construction. To illustrate this situation, we return to the story of Denver International Airport, which badly missed its completion date and target budget.[1]

Misjudging a Construction Project:
The Case of Denver International Airport

By the early 1980s, Denver's Stapleton Airport had outgrown its maximum capacity levels because of the city's rapidly expanding economy. In 1989, Denver voters approved the construction of a new modern airport. Construction began in November of that year, with a scheduled completion date in fall 1993.

Despite the huge size of the project, the four-year time frame seemed adequate. The mission was clear, funding was available, studies indicated great economic benefit, and the project had the necessary political backing. What was expected to be a standard, although large, construction project with no apparent problems, however, became a nightmare for its stakeholders and resulted in enormous delays and excessive costs.

One of the new airport's largest tenants, United Airlines, was planning to use the airport as its second-largest hub. To turn aircraft around in less than thirty minutes, United required an automated baggage system. The planned state-of-the-art, integrated system would improve ground efficiency and decrease time-consuming manual baggage sorting and handling. In December 1991, it commissioned BAE Automatic Systems, Inc., to design and implement an automated baggage system with an estimated schedule of 2.5 years. This project was a first of its kind and bigger than anything similar done before.

From its inception, the baggage-handling project faced an uphill battle. Several problematic issues—such as a lack of communication, unrealistic time frames, insufficient planning, and misuse of human resources—plagued the project from the start. By August 1994, the project was eleven months late and had hampered airport operations. To avoid further consequences, management decided to sign an alternative $50 million contract for building a more traditional baggage system as a backup. The plan was that United would use the BAE system only for its own terminal concourse. Comprehensive and intensive testing of the system culminated in a successful, three-hour full-scale practice run in January 1995. The airport finally opened for business in February 1995, sixteen months late and $1.5 billion over budget.

The airport's late opening and excessive cost resulted from insufficient attention to project uncertainty. Although the airport as a whole was a low-tech project, the baggage-handling system needed to be treated differently. Being the first of its kind, the system had all the elements of a high-tech project, which requires several design cycles and extensive testing (see figure 5-1). Project managers failed to fully understand the risks and the need to decouple the baggage-handling system project from other parts of the airport construction. BAE was familiar with building automated baggage-handling systems, but typically at a much smaller scale. The newness of the technology, the large number of entities to be served by the system, the high degree of technical and project uncertainty, and the short time span for completion were the critical factors that made the difference.

In retrospect, up-front understanding of the technological uncertainty involved would have allowed managers to consider a backup system from the start, enabling the airport to open on time even when one relatively small component was not ready.

FIGURE 5-1

Denver International Airport project

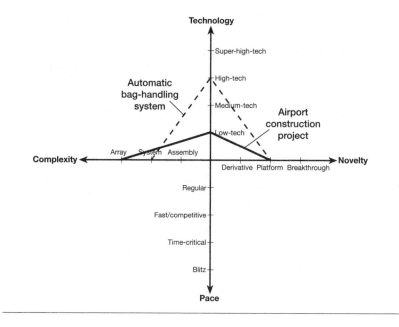

We define *technology* as the knowledge, capability, and means needed to create, build, manufacture, and enable the use of a product, process, or service.[2] Technology may be embedded in tangible or intangible products and may involve software or hardware, and its know-how may be rooted in various disciplines such as mechanics, electronics, biotechnology, ergonomics, and so on. Most modern projects employ technology (or multiple technologies) as part of the final product or in the process of building the product. A small handheld PDA may include software, electronics, display, and packaging technology, whereas larger products, such as aircraft, may involve hundreds of technologies. And technology may be young or mature, well established or recently developed.

What Is Technological Uncertainty?

In our model, the technology dimension indicates the project's level of technological uncertainty. This level depends on the extent to which the project is using new or mature technology.[3] The project's technological uncertainty level is not universal but subjective, because it depends on the technological know-how that exists or is accessible to the company. It is therefore a measure of how much new, versus mature, technology exists for use in the project.[4] Because most projects employ a mixture of technologies, we base our classification on the share of new-to-the-company technology within the product or process. Although the technological uncertainty measure can be seen as a continuum, we found that four levels cover the entire spectrum of projects (see table 5-1 for a summary of the distinctions among the four types of technological uncertainty). The four types are defined as follows.

Low-Tech Projects: Low Technological Uncertainty

This type of project involves implementing existing technologies—that is, mature, well-established technologies to which all industry players have equal access. Such technologies are sometimes called *base technologies* and typically offer little potential for competitive advantage.[5] Although the effort may be very large in scale, the technology is easily obtained and does not carry any difficulty or uncertainty in execution. Typical projects in this category are construction, road building, bridges, and utility installation. Another example is *build-to-print* projects, in which one contractor is required to rebuild a product previously designed and developed by someone else.

Medium-Tech Projects: Medium Technological Uncertainty

These are the most common industrial projects. Such projects rest mainly on existing and mature technologies; however, they may involve a limited

TABLE 5-1

Project types based on levels of technological uncertainty

| | LEVEL OF TECHNOLOGICAL UNCERTAINTY | | | |
	Low-Tech	*Medium-Tech*	*High-Tech*	*Super-High-Tech*
Definitions	Uses only existing, well-established, and mature technologies	Mostly existing technologies; limited new technology or a new feature	Uses many new, recently developed, existing technologies	Key project technologies do not exist at the time of project initiation
Examples	Construction, road building, utilities, build-to-print	Derivatives or improvements of products; new models in established industries (e.g., appliances)	New systems in a fast-moving industry (e.g., computers, military systems)	New, unproven concepts beyond the technological state of the art (e.g., Apollo moon landing program)

amount of new technology (often one or two types, but never a critical technology for project success). Some projects incorporate a new feature that has not been tried and that provides the product's competitive advantage, serving as what's often called its *key* technology.[6] Typical projects may include the development of a new model in a well-established industry (e.g., automobile or consumer electronics) or improvements, modifications, and upgrades of existing products.

High-Tech Projects: High Technological Uncertainty

These projects constitute the first use of new, but existing, technologies. Specifically, in such projects many of the central technologies involved are new. Such technologies are often called *pacing* technologies because they have the potential to change the basis of competition.[7] Although not yet embodied in a product or process, these technologies have been developed before the actual project effort. Incorporating existing but new technologies for the first time typically leads to products that did not exist in the past, or are even new to the industry. Many defense development projects can be included in this category, as can projects in high-tech or high-velocity industries.[8]

Super-High-Tech Projects: Very High Technological Uncertainty

Although many organizations do not distinguish between high-tech and super-high-tech projects, there is a big difference. Super-high-tech projects require the development of new technologies that do not exist at the time of project initiation, and this development is part of the project effort. Sometimes these technologies are called *emerging* technologies, meaning that they seem to have the potential to become pacing technologies.[9] But typically, the technologies to be used are still unknown.

Super-high-tech projects may have a clear mission and well-known customers. Yet the need to develop nonexistent technologies results in very risky and relatively rare projects. In many cases such projects are carried out by large organizations or government agencies. Famous examples are the Apollo moon landing program, the Strategic Defense Initiative (often called "Star Wars") and NASA's Hubble space telescope.[10] Such projects can also be found in start-up companies that explore a nonexistent technology for commercial use.

We must emphasize, however, that super-high-tech projects are not necessarily technology development or pure R&D projects. They may have a real customer and a clear mission, but the technology to carry out the mission is still unknown at the time of project launch.

Technological Uncertainty and Project Success

As we mentioned, the level of technological uncertainty depends on the specific technological base of the firm and the industry. For example, a low-tech firm developing a new type of product might confront difficulties if it uses new technologies it hasn't previously tried. Such a project is considered high-tech to this firm but is seen as medium-tech in a more technology-savvy firm. Similarly, different levels of technological uncertainty produce different project results and different effects on a company's performance. For example, a low-tech project in a traditional industry such as construction typically delivers a standard level of profit in a slow-moving environment. On the other hand, a high-tech or super-high-tech project may represent an opportunity to achieve exceptional business results and to create a leadership position for the company.

But technological uncertainty also involves risk. The risk of failure increases with each level of uncertainty, starting with low and moderate and moving up to the highest levels in high-tech and super-high-tech projects. At these levels, technology may not fulfill expectations, may cause projects to overrun, or may even cause unknown safety hazards. As mentioned, project planning should set the expectation in advance by defining what project success means, based on several success dimensions. Moreover, it should consider the risks and failure factors up front. Table 5-2 summarizes the expected results on various success dimensions for different levels of technology, as well as the possible risks.

In the sections that follow, we describe the effects of technological uncertainty on the design of new products or services. We also look at the managerial implications of technological uncertainty for various types of projects.

How Technological Uncertainty
Affects Project Management

The differences between lower-tech and higher-tech projects may have a substantial impact on project management activities, especially on the technical activities that shape the product's configuration and specifications.[11] But technological uncertainty also influences the levels of communication and interaction, the managerial attitude, the review processes, and even the required capabilities and skills of the team and its manager.

A project's technical activities typically include engineering, building, assembling, testing, reviewing, and approving the design and product specifications. As technological uncertainty increases, the design, devel-

TABLE 5-2

Technological uncertainty and project success: what to expect

Success dimensions and possible risk	LEVEL OF TECHNOLOGICAL UNCERTAINTY			
	Low-Tech	*Medium-Tech*	*High-Tech*	*Super-High-Tech*
Efficiency	High efficiency is critical	Efficiency is important	Overruns may happen; don't expect them, but accept them when they happen	High probability of overruns
Impact on customer	Standard product	Functional product; adds value to customers	Significantly improves customer capabilities	Quantum leap in customer effectiveness
Impact on the team	Extends team experience in the industry	Extends team experience in quick designs and product modifications	Extends team learning in applying new technologies	Builds technical leaders of unknown technology development
Business and direct success	Reasonable profit	Moderate profit; medium return on investment	High profit; high market share	Outstanding business results in the long run; market leadership position
Preparation for the future	Almost none	Gains additional organizational capabilities	New product line; new market	Leadership position; new core technologies
Possible failure and risk	Low; no specific risk from technology used	Moderate risk from technology	High risk of delays, overruns, and undesirable performance from using new technologies for the first time	Extensive risk from unknown technologies; excessive delays and cost overruns, with possible product failure or failure to achieve its expected performance

opment, and testing activities become more intense. In low-tech projects no development or testing is needed, because usually the product is built from its blueprints as designed. With higher technology, more development activity is needed, more testing is conducted, and more prototypes are built until the final product is shaped. And as we found, at the highest end, all successful super-high-tech projects built a small-scale prototype to test the newly developed technologies before a final selection of technologies was made.[12]

Design Cycles and Design Freeze

The completion of a product often requires several iterations of design, building, and testing. These iterations, part of the development activities, are called *design cycles*.[13] A technical project can therefore be seen as a multistage process of design cycles that are performed to reduce uncertainty.[14] A low-tech project needs only one cycle, whereas projects at the medium-tech level typically have two; a high-tech project requires at least two or three design cycles, and a super-high-tech project requires about three cycles after final technologies have been chosen. Figure 5-2 shows the number of design cycles for each project type, with *n* representing the number of cycles needed to select the final technologies.

Completing the sequence of design cycles is marked by an important event called *design freeze*. This event does not mean that no further changes can be made; it indicates, however, that the product has reached its final expected form and that additional changes can be made only if essential. Importantly, the higher the level of technological uncertainty, the later you should schedule the freeze decision. For low-tech projects, this decision typically is made even before the start of project execution; for medium-tech projects, during the first quarter of project execution; for high-tech projects, at about midpoint; and for super-high-tech projects, during the third or fourth quarter (see figure 5-2).

Defining the level of technological uncertainty at project initiation enables managers to include these decisions as part of the project plan and allocate the budget and other resources to carry them out successfully.

FIGURE 5-2

Possible time ranges for design freeze, number of design cycles, and risk areas for project outcomes

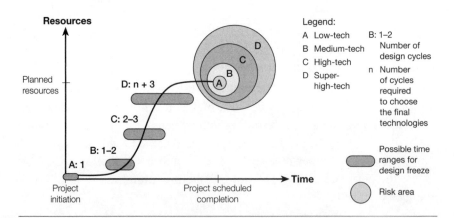

(For more detail and empirical data on design cycles and design freeze, see appendixes 5A and 5B.)

Finally, as technological uncertainty increases, you must devote more time in project reviews to technical issues. At the lower levels, formal managerial reviews of progress and milestones may be sufficient. However, for high-tech and super-high-tech projects, managerial reviews alone are not enough. Projects must conduct technical reviews with teams of objective experts in relevant disciplines who are not involved in the project on a day-to-day basis. These *peer reviews,* which guarantee that the team receives ample feedback during the development period, are critical, and their absence is often the major reason a project fails.[15]

Management Style, Communication, Attitudes, and Contingencies

Because greater technological uncertainty increases the need to delay the design freeze and conduct more cycles of design, build, and test, it requires a more flexible management style and increased tolerance for ambiguity and uncertainty. In addition, the transition period after design freeze is characterized by an abrupt shift in the project manager's attitude toward change. A high level of flexibility and tolerance for change characterize the project during the initial stage, followed by low or almost no flexibility once the design is frozen.[16]

In low-tech projects, managers must be firm and stick to the initial plan. In medium-tech projects, they should be ready to accept some changes early on, but after design freeze they should make every effort to get the product out the door as soon as possible. Highly flexible styles are needed at the higher levels of technological uncertainty. High-tech project managers must be ready to accept many changes and must wait longer for the final product design; and managers of super-high-tech projects must be extremely patient, must live with continuous change, and must make sure that all alternative technologies have been tried. They must also develop an attitude of "look for trouble," since the sooner they can identify problems, the earlier they can fix them.

Technological uncertainty also affects project communication and interaction. At lower levels, a formal process of communication and pre-scheduled meetings is typically sufficient. As technological uncertainty increases, the formal process must be complemented with informal interaction and unscheduled meetings. At the highest levels, managers must install and provide ample opportunities for informal interaction—meeting stations, joint sessions, and after-hours activities—so that people can share recent work experience and problems.

Finally, although no one expects delays, when they happen managers need to be prepared to cope with them, especially in high-tech and super-high-tech projects, where the uncertainty and the associated risk are great and delays often occur. Many projects therefore allocate contingent resources to respond to unexpected difficulties and delays. Our measure of technological uncertainty enables you to make these allocations in a rigorous way. At the low-tech level, 5 percent is a typical number, for medium-tech, 5–10 percent, high-tech, 10–25 percent, and for super-high-tech, 25–50 percent may be needed. For example, NASA's successful Apollo program had a contingency reserve of about 50 percent in its initial budget.

Project Manager and Team Skills

Project managers must of course be good administrators, planners, and leaders. Although these skills are required for all projects, high technological uncertainty requires, in addition, project managers who have strong technical skills. Managers must be able to assess the technical work of others and make technical decisions about design as well as judge interfaces between disciplines and project teams. They must have the intuition to understand what their technical people are talking about and must be able to grasp the project as a whole. Similarly, as technological uncertainty increases, project team members must be highly educated and technically savvy, with exceptional top experts at the highest level of uncertainty.

Summarizing the Technology Impact

Table 5-3 summarizes the major differences among the levels of project technology. It also includes the industries where these project types are typically found and lists the typical products for the various levels. (See appendixes 5A and 5B for descriptions of empirical research results that relate to technological uncertainty and for the impact of technological uncertainty on traditional project management according to the PMI PMBoK knowledge areas.)

The Special Case of Super-High-Tech Projects

You may question the reason for adding a fourth type of project—super-high-tech—rather than simply designating such projects along the common spectrum of low, medium, and high. The super-high-tech level is needed to distinguish between "routine" high-tech projects, which use many new-to-the-firm technologies, and super-high-tech projects, which

TABLE 5-3

Project characteristics and technological uncertainty levels

Variable	LEVEL OF TECHNOLOGICAL UNCERTAINTY			
	Low-Tech	*Medium-Tech*	*High-Tech*	*Super-High-Tech*
Technology	No new technology	Some new technology	Most technologies are new	Key technologies do not exist at project initiation
Typical industries	Construction, production, utilities, public works	Mechanical, electrical, chemical, some electronics	High-tech and technology-based industries; computers, aerospace, electronics	Advanced high-tech and leading industries; electronics, aerospace, biotechnology
Type of products	Buildings, bridges, telephone installation, build-to-print	Nonrevolutionary models, derivatives, or improvements	New, first-of-its-kind family of products, new military systems (within state of the art)	New, unproven concept, beyond existing state of the art
Development, testing, and prototypes	No development; no testing	Limited development; some testing	Considerable development and testing; prototypes usually used during development	Need to develop key technologies during project effort; must have intermediate small-scale prototype to test concepts and select new technologies
Design cycles and design freeze	Only one cycle; design freeze before start of project execution	One to two cycles; early design freeze, no later than first quarter project of execution	At least two or three cycles; design freeze usually at mid-point during second or third quarter	Typically three cycles after the final technologies have been selected; late design freeze, usually during third or even fourth quarter
Project reviews	Formal progress and status reviews	Formal progress and status reviews; some technical reviews of final design	Technical reviews with experts in addition to formal progress reviews	Extensive peer reviews by technical expert teams critical to success
Management style and attitude	Firm style; sticking to the initial plan	Less firm style; readiness to accept some changes	More flexible style; many changes are expected	Highly flexible style; living with continuous change; "looking for trouble"
Communication and interaction	Mostly formal communication during scheduled meetings	More frequent communication; some informal interaction	Frequent communication through multiple channels; informal interaction	Many communication channels; informal interaction instituted and encouraged by management
Project manager and project team	Manager with good administrative skills; mostly semiskilled workers	Manager with some technical skills; considerable proportion of academicians	Manager with good technical skills; many professionals and academicians on project team	Project manager with exceptional technical skills; highly skilled professionals and many academicians
Project contingent resources	5%	5%–10%	10%–25%	25%–50%

need to develop nonexistent technologies to meet project goals. The need to develop new technologies as an integral part of a project represents a distinct level of uncertainty and risk, and it requires a unique managerial approach.

First, super-high-tech projects must involve a highly flexible atmosphere that allows the introduction, evaluation, and testing of new, sometimes radical, ideas. Second, such projects need an extended period of development. During this time, previously unknown technologies are developed and tested until the final technology and configuration are selected. Third, in these projects a small-scale prototype must be built on which the newly developed technologies are tried and tested. Such a prototype must be tested and approved before a final selection is made and the chosen technology is included in the full-scale product.

To illustrate the uniqueness of a super-high-tech environment, we turn to one of the most famous aerospace projects: the building of the SR-71 Blackbird reconnaissance aircraft by Lockheed (now part of Lockheed Martin) in the late 1950s. Even today this program stands as an icon of project management excellence in the face of enormous technical and managerial challenges.

The SR-71 Blackbird: A Super-High-Tech Revolution in Aviation History

The SR-71 Blackbird, one of the most successful aircraft ever built, was the only operational aircraft to fly at Mach 3.2 speed at an altitude of 80,000 feet.[17] Initiated in the 1950s, the SR-71 had as its goal to replace the U-2 reconnaissance aircraft employed by the U.S. Air Force and the Central Intelligence Agency.

Lockheed's development division (headed by Clarence L. "Kelly" Johnson) designed the Blackbird (then called the A-12). To meet the aircraft's challenging requirements, Lockheed engineers struggled with daunting technical challenges, many of which were the first of their kind. For example, initial proposals involved liquid hydrogen-propelled engines, something that later proved impracticable because of high fuel consumption. The design was therefore changed to two conventional, but still unique, afterburner turbine engines, which use special jet fuel. The engines had to operate across a huge speed range, from a takeoff speed of 207 mph to more than 2,200 mph at the highest altitudes.

The airframe was built almost entirely of titanium alloys to withstand heat generated by sustained Mach 3 flight. The airframe design was optimized to exhibit a low radar profile and coated with a special radar-absorbing black paint, which also helped dissipate the intense frictional heat resulting from flight at extreme speed. It gave the plane its distinctive "blackbird" appearance.

From the novelty perspective, SR-71 was only at the medium level of platform, because it replaced a previous generation, the U-2. However, given the extent of the mission and the technologies that were needed to achieve it, we categorize the project in retrospect as super-high-tech (see figure 5-3). It required development of new technologies that did not exist at project initiation. Without formally using any classification framework, Johnson managed a dedicated team of only 135 engineers, essentially adopting the management style of super-high-tech projects.

This structure came to be known as the "skunk works."[18] Working as a stand-alone operation with minimal bureaucracy and a very high level of communication, the team initiated and tested many innovative ideas and used advanced engineering approaches to circumvent the problems typical of the harsh environment of high-altitude, high-speed flying. The group worked hard on cost reviews, made frequent changes, and operated in continuous and

FIGURE 5-3

SR-71 Blackbird project

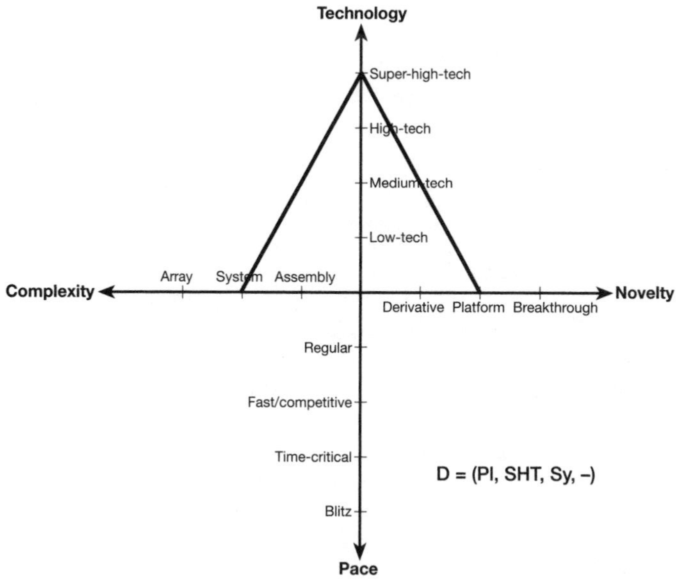

$$D = (Pl, SHT, Sy, -)$$

close cooperation with the customer. But above all, the success of
the project can be attributed to Johnson's way of managing the
project: being highly flexible, living with great ambiguity over
extended periods, freezing the design very late after testing the
unexplored technologies, using many prototypes, and demonstrat-
ing strong technical expertise and technical leadership.

The Low and High Ends of Technology

Technological uncertainty is perhaps the dimension that matters most in
planning, engineering design, resources, and risk. In this section we address
the differences between the low and the high ends of the technology spectrum by comparing low- and medium-tech projects to high- and super-high-
tech projects. (Table 5-4 summarizes these differences.)

The major difference between the low and high ends of the technological uncertainty spectrum is the managerial approach that best fits the situation. At the low end (low-tech and medium-tech projects) managers
are better off using a rigid, "stick to the plan and get it done" approach.

TABLE 5-4

Low- and medium-tech versus high- and super-high-tech projects

Managerial issue	PROJECT TYPE	
	Low- and Medium-Tech	High- and Super-High-Tech
Managerial style	Rigid, no-nonsense, "get it done" approach	Flexible, ready to accept many changes and tolerate long periods of uncertainty
Project reviews	Formal, top management approval of major phase completion	Formal executive reviews plus technical peer reviews by experts to assess the design and provide professional feedback
Saving time by overlapping phases	Phase overlaps possible	Phase overlaps not recommended
Best contract type	Fixed-price	Cost-plus; fixed-price is possible at a later stage of development
Development approach	Linear development	Spiral development
Additional concerns	Lower cost, on time	Risk management, systems engineering, quality management

The specifications are fairly well known and are frozen early, and managers should not allow changes to distract the project from timely delivery. Rather, they should focus the team's effort on finishing the project at the earliest time and the lowest cost possible.

At the higher end (high- and super-high-tech projects), the best approach is different. At these levels of uncertainty, managers should adopt a flexible attitude, allowing changes in the product's specifications and design late in the project. And they should be ready to live with a high degree of uncertainty for a very long time.

Project reviews at the lower end are mostly formal, when members of the executive team (often called the *executive review board*) review the project's progress and performance and provide go-ahead decisions for the next steps. At the higher end, formal top management reviews are often not enough to detect problems ahead of time and guarantee successful completion of the project. At this level, most projects are better off mobilizing the help of professional experts who serve as a peer review board to examine the project's technical progress, review the design, and provide professional feedback on open technical problems and possible risks.

Management sometimes tries to shorten a project by overlapping project phases—that is, starting the next phase before the current one is completed. This practice (sometimes called "crashing") may be possible at the low end of technological uncertainty but typically is less successful (or even impossible) at the high end. The level of uncertainty and risk in high- and super-high-tech projects is so high that the risk associated with overlapping is unacceptable. Typically, the next phase depends too much on the results of the current one, and overlapping may result in so many changes that the practice fails to save any time or money.

Another major question is what type of contract to use. Often, the dilemma is between a fixed-price contractual commitment and some form of cost-plus contract. In fixed-price contracts, the contractor takes on all the risk but also has a chance to earn considerable profit. We found that a fixed-price contract may work well at the lower level of technological uncertainty but may be deficient at the higher end, where it creates an unacceptable risk to both sides. The contractor may lose money because of unexpected project difficulties, and the customer may get an inadequate product when the contractor tries to stay within the price range and builds a solution that is less than optimal. In this case both sides may be better off with a cost-plus incentive fee contract, in which risk and opportunity are shared by the parties. The customer bears the cost of development, avoiding shortcuts and less-than-optimal solutions, and the contractor has an incentive to produce the best result and still maintain his profits.

In some projects, however, a combination of the two methods can work. In the early phases of development a cost-plus contract is used. Later, when the uncertainty level is reduced, the contract is replaced with a fixed-price contract.

From an engineering standpoint, technological uncertainty typically is reduced by using a phased design, prototypes, and testing. Phased design takes two typical forms: one is a linear, phase-after-phase format, and the other is a spiral or agile development model, which has become popular in recent years. In the spiral model, only core requirements are satisfied by the first product prototype. To enable rapid improvement of the product, the basic design is modular, supporting future add-ons and improvements with each cycle.[19] The spiral development model is made up of sequential design cycles (definition, design, build, test, definition, design, and so on) that constitute a spiral-like shape of ever-enlarging circles.

The linear model works best for low- and medium-tech projects, and the spiral model for high- and super-high-tech projects. Increasing technological uncertainty requires longer design, build, and test periods before the final design can be frozen. In addition, the high risk involved in high- and super-high-tech projects requires the use of various methods to reduce its impact, such as evolving development, systems engineering, or risk management.

We conclude this chapter with the stories of two of the most ambitious technological projects of our time: the Apollo moon landing mission and the space shuttle program. Both represented enormous scientific and engineering challenges, and both required the most advanced project management capabilities. Although their events have been well documented before, it is intriguing to examine their stories in the context of our framework since both their management styles and outcomes were so different.

The Apollo Moon Landing: A Triumph of Science, Exploration, and Management

Initiating the Apollo program in the early 1960s, President John F. Kennedy set the goal of landing the first American on the moon before the end of that decade. It was clear that this program involved unusual new unknowns. NASA's engineers had to struggle with, among other things, radiation as well as meteoroid hazards. The lunar surface environment was largely unexplored, presenting numerous potential threats, such as lunar dust and extreme temperature differences between the shaded and the sunlit areas. At that time, there was no available technology to control such differences or to protect the astronauts from them. In addition, there was no clear concept of how to launch a lunar module into space; it could have been an earth orbit, a lunar orbit, or a combination of the two.[20]

The Apollo program adopted a unique development and testing approach. In NASA's risk-averse environment, everything was tested and retested, with numerous safety mechanisms in place to make sure nothing could go wrong. For example, NASA launched ten Apollo flights before the first moon landing was attempted.

In retrospect, we can categorize the Apollo program as a breakthrough, super-high-tech, array, fast/competitive project (see figure 5-4). The final configuration and the design freeze were considerably delayed until all unknowns were resolved. NASA had used Gemini, which sent two astronauts into orbit, as an intermediate program and a small-scale prototype. This less ambitious program helped resolve many of the unknown factors and helped the organization develop and select the new technologies that would later be integrated

FIGURE 5-4

Apollo program

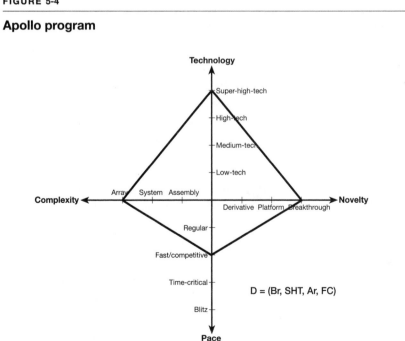

$$D = (Br, SHT, Ar, FC)$$

into Apollo. The successful moon landing of *Apollo 11* in July 1969 symbolizes a victory, not only in exploring unknown space territories but also in pioneering new and far-reaching technologies.

Now contrast the *Apollo 11* project with the space shuttle program.

The Space Shuttle Program: A Story of Overoptimism

The idea of the space shuttle was to enable human beings to function in an extraterrestrial environment by using the same vehicle on repeated flights. The program was first proposed in 1969, when the nation was still excited by the success of Apollo. As a natural extension to the moon landing, NASA proposed the shuttle as an element in an interplanetary transportation system that would enable the United States to land a crew on Mars in the 1980s. At that time, however, the enthusiasm and space competition that characterized the Apollo era had evaporated, and the shuttle's initial high-cost proposals received little support.

NASA officials discovered that their main hope of winning congressional support for the shuttle in the atmosphere of indifference and skepticism was to emphasize its cost effectiveness—namely, its reusability and its low development price tag. The notion was that this innovation could be built almost entirely within the state of the art, largely from off-the-shelf parts or ones that could readily be fabricated. The space agency's projection of the shuttle was simply that of a "space-adapted airplane."[21] Eventually, the project to build a moderate, low-cost, reusable space shuttle was approved, and its final configuration was selected in 1972.

It is now clear that NASA's initial attitude toward the shuttle project constituted what we would classify as that of a platform, high-tech, system, fast/competitive project. However, the belief that this space vehicle could be built quickly and almost entirely within the state of the art, based on existing technologies, turned out to be unrealistic. The problem of building such a huge vehicle that could function effectively both in space and in the atmosphere was too difficult under the optimistic, "success-oriented" attitude adopted by NASA.[22] Eventually the program suffered extreme overruns amounting to almost three years in time delays and 60 percent in unexpected costs, all accumulated even before the tragic *Challenger* accident in 1986.

Developing the space shuttle turned out to be one of the most difficult (if not the most difficult) and exasperating engineering challenges of the space age. Engineering and design problems during the development phase were enormous. For example, the newly developed main engines failed fourteen times in less than two years.[23] The famous thermal protection system, which consisted of thirty thousand hand-glued tiles, proved to be an unstable add-on to the orbiter structure, causing many disruptions and numerous delays.[24] Had the agency built a small-scale prototype and run earlier technology and flight tests, it might have chosen different solutions from those initially selected.

The *Challenger* accident in January 1986, which took the lives of seven astronauts, shocked the world. Suddenly, the agency that once had been described as capable of doing the impossible had to freeze space flight for more than two years and take a good look at itself. The presidential commission that investigated the accident (the Rogers commission) concluded that the failure was the result of faulty design of an aft field joint, which was unacceptably sensitive to factors such as temperature, physical dimensions, properties of materials, and the effects of reusability.

The 2003 *Columbia* accident, which took the lives of another seven astronauts, reminded the public of the risk and uncertainty of space flight. The Columbia Accident Investigation Board (CAIB) identified the technical cause as foam debris that hit the left wing's thermal protection. However, the board in its report also addressed the managerial and organizational causes of the accident:

> *Too often, accident investigations blame a failure only on the last step in a complex process, when a more comprehensive understanding of that process could reveal that earlier steps might be equally or even more culpable. In this Board's opinion, unless the technical, organizational, and cultural recommendations made in this report are implemented, little will have been accomplished to lessen the chance that another accident will follow.*[25]

CAIB provided a detailed analysis of the program's history and decision making, often citing the risk and compromises that NASA had taken early to get the program approved. It also pointed to years of resource constraints, fluctuating priorities, schedule pressures, mischaracterization of the shuttle as operational rather than developmental, and lack of a consensus national vision for human space flight.[26]

In retrospect, based on the program's initial risk and uncertainty, it seems that from its inception the program needed a different management philosophy. In this context, a breakthrough, super-high-tech project management style was probably more appropriate than the platform, high-tech style that was used (see figure 5-5). In addition, the increased pressures to launch the shuttle set the pace at a fast/competitive level, whereas a regular pace perhaps would have better fit the high level of risk and uncertainty.

Hindsight is always easier than foresight. We must remember that when the shuttle program was approved and its budget set, NASA was under extreme pressure by the administration to prove the system's cost effectiveness and to considerably cut development expenses. Under such circumstances, NASA abandoned its well-intentioned plan to build a small-scale test vehicle to make certain it had thoroughly tested all the technology before embarking on a full-scale vehicle.[27] Perhaps if NASA had presented to the administration a formal framework for the classification of program risk characteristics along different dimensions, it would have been able to make a better case for an increased budget and less pressured

FIGURE 5-5

The space shuttle program

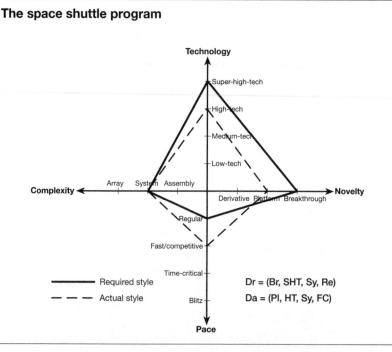

time line.[28] Such a framework also would have been helpful in guiding the internal debate between engineers and management to assess program risk ahead of time and secure the appropriate safety mechanisms to manage program uncertainties in a different way.

The two space programs will quickly become history, but their lessons are still fresh and relevant. Approaching technological uncertainty with the right mind-set and understanding its risks up front are critical to success in many current programs. Assuming that all projects need the same level of attention to technology, or underestimating the real risk, may lead to project failure and, as with the shuttle, even the loss of human lives.

The next chapter deals with another critical dimension for project distinction—complexity. When projects become very complex—for example, when they involve building large systems—they may also involve a large number of technologies. For this situation some companies, such as NASA and other government agencies, have recently adopted a framework called technology readiness level (TRL). According to this framework, each technology is assessed based on nine levels of maturity.[29] The combination of new technology and high complexity makes managing these projects a unique challenge, as we will see in the next chapter.

Key Points and Action Items

- Technological uncertainty is the extent of new versus mature technology used in a project. Based on technological uncertainty, there are four types of projects: low-tech, medium-tech, high-tech, and super-high-tech. The level of technological uncertainty is subjective and depends on the company's experience in technology.

- Technological uncertainty affects a project's expected success. The use of higher technology may create greater value for the customer and the company, but it also increases the risk of time and budget overruns.

- Technological uncertainty affects project management in technical activities such as design, prototyping, and testing. The higher the technology, the later you should freeze the design and the more design cycles the project will need. Higher technology also requires increased communication and interaction, greater flexibility, and the ability to live with longer periods of uncertainty.

- The use of higher technology requires that the project manager and project team have advanced technical skills in addition to their administrative and managerial skills.

- Super-high-tech projects are special cases that entail building nonexistent technologies during the project's effort. This task requires outstanding technical leadership, extended periods of development and testing of new technologies, the use of small-scale prototypes, and very high flexibility.

- Managers should assess the level of technological uncertainty in major projects and should allocate resources and people according to the projects' levels of risk and opportunity. Managers should also be tolerant of and be ready to accept delays in high-tech and super-high-tech projects because of higher levels of risk.

- Managers should consider a project's level of technological uncertainty during the planning and organizing phase. They should schedule the design freeze and the number of design cycles based on technological uncertainty, as well as contingent resources, technical peer reviews, and the technical competence of the team.

◆ 6 ◆

COMPLEXITY

IMAGINE YOURSELF managing an organizational reengineering project. The project involves streamlining the operational processes of the
organization and installing new information technology (IT) software
to control these processes, manage the databases, and offer online information to managers and decision makers.

Although these tasks seem basic, they differ greatly depending on the
organization. For example, in one kind of organization you might be
dealing with the work flow of only one department, one functional group,
or a single process within a local unit (such as a bank's branch office). In
these cases the effort would be relatively modest; people know each other
well, the processes are simple, and the IT involved is limited.

Now suppose your reengineering project involves an entire business,
with various integrated functions such as design, manufacturing, marketing, sales, and distribution. This project would be bigger, or perhaps more
complex, than the preceding one. In this case, coordination would be much
more critical, and you would need to employ formal tools, extensive documentation, and more sophisticated software.

Now suppose your task is to manage the reengineering project for a
large multinational corporation spread all over the world. It would be an
enormously complex project. Most people involved wouldn't know each
other, and their work would have to be coordinated in a coherent way. This
project would have to be carried out in a highly formal and bureaucratic
way, with many subprojects devoted to various parts of the company.

The difference among these three projects is their degree of complexity.
In this chapter we discuss such differences and explore the *C* dimension—

complexity—of our NTCP model. As before, because one size does not fit all, different levels of project complexity require different project management styles—and applying the wrong style may lead to project failure. You have seen this situation illustrated in chapter 3 with the FCS project, which treated a complex system using a management style better suited to a subsystem. This chapter further conceptualizes the notion of complexity and describes in detail its impact on project management.

Although project complexity depends greatly on the complexity of the product (or outcome) of the project, note that this chapter focuses on the complexity of the *project*, not the product. Note too that even though people often tend to confuse complexity with uncertainty, these concepts are not the same. You can find highly complex projects with low levels of uncertainty, and vice versa.

What, then, is the best way to define and distinguish between levels of project complexity? One option might be the size of the project (measured, for instance, in terms of budget, people, etc.). But size alone may not be enough. A very large and expensive project in one industry—say, construction—might be less complex than a smaller project in another industry, such as biotechnology. Complexity also depends on, among other things, the various elements that make up a project—their number, their variety, and the interconnections among them.

The idea is to find a simple, universal way to conceptualize complexity in a context-free framework, regardless of the industry or technology involved. To address this problem we choose to differentiate between the outcome of the project (the product) as a whole and the product in its parts; we use a hierarchy of systems and subsystems as a natural way to distinguish among the various project complexities.[1]

How Product Complexity Affects Project Complexity

Every project has a product, which may be composed of components, systems, and subsystems.[2] For example, a computer system's major subsystems are its keyboard, processor, internal memory, power supply, and display device. The keyboard's components are the case, the keys, the connectors, and other electronic parts.[3] We must emphasize, however, that projects' products are not always artifacts, or pieces of hardware. The products of the reengineering projects mentioned previously are new processes and new software to support these processes. Project outcomes, therefore, can be tangible or intangible, can consist of hardware or software, and can include services, marketing campaigns, political campaigns, or new organizations. Table 6-1 presents a hierarchy of six levels of *prod-*

TABLE 6-1

Levels of product complexity

Product com- plexity level	Definition	Examples (hardware, software, organizations)
Material	Physical substance, matter	Silicon, plastic, fabric
Component	A fundamental element of a subsystem that never works alone	Light bulb, case, bearing, electronic component, software code paragraph
Subsystem or assembly	A collection of components and modules combined into one unit and performing a single function of a limited scale	Power supply, car transmission, TV set, word processor application, one organizational department
System	A complex collection of units, subsystems, and assemblies performing multiple functions	Radar, communications link, HVAC system, office software package, manufacturing line
Platform of systems	A single structure used as a base for other installed systems that are serving the platform's mission	Aircraft, building, boat, ERP system, computer operating system, manufac- turing plant, a division in a corporation
Array or system of systems	A large, widespread collection or network of systems function- ing together to achieve a common mission	National air traffic control, interstate highway, a city, the Internet, a large multinational corporation

uct complexity. As you will see shortly, however, *project* complexity types consist of only three levels.

Products of different complexity levels have different design and managerial implications for the projects that create them. As organizational theory has shown, the complexity of products may lead to descriptions of different typologies in terms of organizational and structural variables.[4]

As mentioned, we use the product complexity level to define the hierarchy of project complexity. However, as we have found, several levels of product complexity are managed in similar ways, and therefore project complexity shows less variability than product complexity. This finding led us to conclude that the six levels of product complexity can be addressed by three typical levels of project complexity.[5] We title these types (1) assembly projects, (2) system projects, and (3) array projects. To be specific, we found that projects that deal with materials or components are very similar in nature to projects that deal with assemblies and that systems are built in a similar way to platforms of systems (see table 6-2).

TABLE 6-2

The three levels of project complexity

Project complexity	Product complexity	Examples of projects
Assembly	Material, component, subsystem, assembly	Development of a PDA, Post-it notes, design of a single service
System	System, platform of systems	Missile development, new computer development, new automobile model, a single building construction, restructuring a production plant
Array	Array, system of systems	English Channel tunnel, national missile defense system, new neighborhood construction, nationwide cellular network

The Three Types of Project Complexity

The major distinction between the three types of projects has to do with the way they're organized. Increased project complexity implies a more complex organization, increased interaction among its parts, and increased formality in managing the project.

Assembly Projects

Assembly projects deal with a single component or device or with a complete assembly. An assembly product either performs a well-defined function within a larger system (such as a car transmission) or is an independent, self-contained product that performs a single function of its own (such as an LCD projector). Therefore, the development of a radar receiver, a new model of a VCR, or a computer hard drive is an example of an assembly project. Similarly, the design and testing of a new service, such as mortgage loan processing, is also an assembly project.

An assembly project is usually performed within one functional unit by a small team working in one location, with intensive communication among the members. Team members usually know each other well and communicate daily, with limited formality and documentation.

System Projects

System projects deal with systems such as computers, missiles, or communication equipment. However, they may also deal with the next level of product complexity: entire platforms, such as aircraft, vessels, automobiles, buildings, or the creation or improvement of a complete business unit. Such projects may also create large, intangible products, such as a complex software application or the reorganizing of a business unit that includes many functional groups.

Because system projects are more complex than assembly projects, they entail the creation not only of the product itself but also of the collateral supply of training means and facilities, testing equipment, maintenance tools, logistics support, spare parts, and a great deal of documentation. In previous chapters we mentioned examples of system projects, such as the creation of *Toy Story* in the 1990s and the development of the SR-71 Blackbird reconnaissance aircraft in the 1960s.[6]

System projects are rarely performed within a single organization. They require a central project (or program) office that coordinates the efforts of numerous subgroups and subcontractors, with an increased level of formality and bureaucracy. The central office is responsible, at minimum, for defining customer requirements, product definition, system design, systems engineering, and system integration and testing.

Array Projects

An *array project* deals with a dispersed collection of systems that function together to achieve a common purpose, sometimes called a "system of systems." Array projects are never performed at a single site (e.g., in one building); rather, they are spread over a wide geographical area and typically consist of a variety of system subprojects. Array projects are large in scale, and in most cases they are built in an evolutionary form, in which additional systems are gradually appended.

Projects at this level often deal with modifying, improving, or adding components to an existing array rather than building an array from scratch. A well-known example of an array project is the New York City Transit Authority's program of modernizing the city subway infrastructure in the early 1990s. This program consisted of more than 350 separate efforts, including constructing and rebuilding tracks, stations, and bridges.[7] Similarly, the English Channel tunnel project was an array project connecting two countries, with numerous systems such as stations, tracks, three tunnels, and so on.[8]

Array projects (often called "programs") are typically structured under an umbrella organization that deals mainly with the financial, logistical, and legal issues and is responsible for contracting and controlling the offices of the system projects that make up the array.

The following case illustrates a project at the highest level of complexity. It tells the story of Ford Motor Company, which initiated in the mid-1990s its Ford 2000 restructuring and reengineering program. The project spanned two continents, multiple design, development, and engineering centers, and worldwide distribution and marketing facilities, thus qualifying as an array project.[9]

The Ford 2000 Project

In 1994, although sales topped $128 billion and profits were up 110 percent compared with 1993, Ford executives were worried about future problems with product development and productivity. The company simply could not design and build new cars and trucks as quickly as competitors were.

Concerned about its ability to compete in the twenty-first century, Ford launched a bold restructuring effort designed to change the company's business process and organizational structure. The vision of Ford 2000 was to transform the company from its mind-set of regional operation to a global corporation with worldwide processes and systems of product development, manufacturing, supply, and sales. Executives also believed that these activities should be based on the use of high technology and advanced data management and communications systems.[10]

The Ford 2000 restructuring effort was initiated without the threat of recession or corporate raiders, and without mass layoffs, divestitures, or wrenching disruptions.[11] Here are some of the activities and changes that Ford undertook:

- Three separate operations on two continents were combined into a single operating unit.

- The company established five Vehicle Program Centers, each with worldwide responsibility for the design, development, and engineering of the vehicles assigned to it.

- Ford's white-collar automotive workforce of some eighty thousand was regrouped into half as many organization-chart boxes as before.

- The company involved hundreds of employees in the process. The principle was simple: "Involve the people who will have to live with the change, in making it happen."

- Ford published a weekly faxed newspaper, ran an electronic bulletin board, broadcast a weekly in-house TV show, and convened meetings attended by thousands of employees to keep them up-to-date on developments.

This effort, which illustrates nicely the complexity aspect of our model (see figure 6-1), paid off, at least in terms of productivity. The company's productivity in 1998 was the best among the Big Three U.S. automobile corporations. Ford required an average of 22.85 hours of labor per vehicle, which was virtually even with Toyota's 21.3 but much better than GM's 30.32 hours and Chrysler's 32.15 hours, and Ford leapfrogged its U.S. rivals in per-car profitability.[12]

The Impact of Complexity on Project Management

The typical managerial process in project execution involves planning, scheduling, budgeting, contracting, organizing, staffing, and controlling activities, as well as information gathering and sharing, decision making, negotiation, and other coordination activities.[13] As you may recall from classical project management, project planning usually starts by breaking the project work into a work breakdown structure (WBS) in a treelike

FIGURE 6-1

The Ford 2000 project

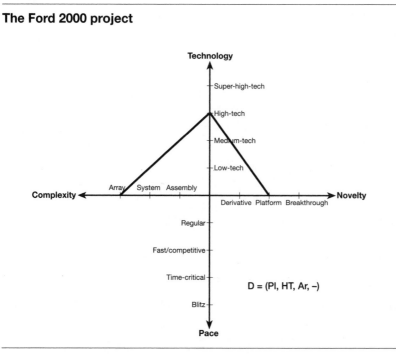

form.[14] The WBS serves as the basic tool for integrating the separate parts into one operational system, establishing the project schedule, and controlling its progress through the project's life cycle.

The level of project complexity affects activities associated with project planning: project contracting, project execution and control, and documentation. As complexity increases from assembly to system and then to array, many things change in a project. In addition to different types of organizations, projects of differing complexity involve different types of customers, contracts, planning and controlling techniques, documentation, and managerial focus. We discuss these changes in the following sections.

Typical Organizational Structures

The major difference among projects along the complexity dimension relates to the organizational structure, the formality of processes, and the way in which project activities are coordinated and integrated. At the lower end, assembly projects are performed within one organization and very often within one functional group, with, however, help from other technical functions.

At the system project level, projects typically have a main contractor that is responsible for the delivery of the final product. The entire effort is divided among several subcontractors, either in-house or external. The main contractor is in charge of the final product integration and is accountable for meeting performance, quality, time, and budget goals. Work is typically led by a program management office, interacting with various functional departments in assorted professional areas and dealing with outside organizations through separate contracts. In addition, a full- or part-time customer representative is usually present on the project site.

Array projects are organized differently from projects at the other levels. Managing an array program requires the administration of many separate projects, each devoted to a segment or system. It is therefore organized as a central umbrella organization, which is often set as a separate entity or company and formally coordinates the efforts of all other subprojects. Given the evolutionary development of many arrays, the array project organization typically is established as an ongoing program, to which more segments are continuously added.

Degree of Formality and Bureaucracy

The second major difference along the complexity dimension is the project's degree of formality and the managerial emphasis. Formality tends to increase with complexity. Assembly projects are typically characterized by an informal, family-like, mostly technical atmosphere. People know each other well and often do not bother dealing with formal documentation or detailed planning. Any formal documentation is imposed on the project team by higher management or by the client. In many cases planning is done manually, and there is very little bureaucracy. Project managers of assembly projects focus on questions of cost, quality, and delivery of their product to the customer or to manufacturing.

At the system level, the style is more rigid and formal. Because system projects require integration of the final product, project management must be concerned with a mixture of technical and administrative issues. System project managers often tend to "bureaucratize" their projects and adapt tools for managing, controlling, and coordinating.

You can often find at least ten kinds of formal documents relating to various technical and managerial aspects of the project. A notable example is the *earned value* report. This document expresses the combined status of budget spent and the actual work achieved in terms of financial figures. You might also find a *termination price* report, which continuously assesses the cost in case the customer decides to terminate the project, and a *level of effort* document, which classifies all activities into those that directly affect the program and those that do not. This document enables management to concentrate its efforts on activities that directly affect the probability of success and avoid wasting time on less important activities. In addition to the cost and quality focus found in assembly projects, system projects are faced with the challenge of defining, designing, and integrating a system. This is a particularly difficult task, and we will return to this question later in this chapter.

At the highest level of array projects, formality is maximized. The dispersed nature of the end product and the extent of subcontracting make it necessary to manage these programs in a very formal way and to put a lot of effort into the legal aspects of the various contracts. Such projects, however, involve much less of an integration problem. Project management is therefore occupied mainly with financial, control, and legal issues, and technical matters are left to the managers of subprojects. The ordinary tools for planning and controlling projects seem less relevant, and the management of each project often must develop its own system of contract coordination and program control.[15] The usual project management tools (such WBS, PERT, or Gantt charts) are useful only to a limited extent. Consequently, the project manager and team must develop an entirely new system for planning, controlling, reporting, and configuration management.

Such programs cannot use typical industry standards, such as Department of Defense (DoD) standards. Because of their size and complexity, each program must develop its own standards and policies to guide its system contractors.

Leaders of array projects also must be aware of the social and environmental impact of their projects and must take into account the views of political decision makers. No array project can survive if it loses its political support.

Let's look now at the English Channel tunnel project (or as it is often called, the Chunnel project), which shows the importance of correctly assessing a project's complexity level.

The Chunnel Project

The Channel tunnel linking Britain with the European continent was a dream that went back to Napoleon.[16] In 1985, the "Invitation to Promoters" issued by the British and French governments called for a link that would last 120 years, be resistant to terrorist attacks, and be impassable or fatal to rabid animals.

Earlier ideas, from the first proposal in 1802 to initiatives of the 1970s, had been knocked down by the frailty of political windows of opportunity or by economic downturns. The new Chunnel promoters of the 1980s were aware of these vulnerabilities and thus planned for seven years of design and construction. Most engineers, however, felt that a project of this magnitude would need fourteen years for proper design and construction. The Chunnel project consisted of building three tunnels, each 50 kilometers long: one main rail tunnel in each direction, and a smaller service tunnel in between.

The project required a treaty between Britain and France, which was signed by the two countries' leaders in 1987, authorizing an Intergovernmental Commission and a Safety Authority to oversee the project. The Eurotunnel Company was established as the owner-operator of the venture, and Transmanche Link, a consortium of ten French and British construction firms, was formed as contractor.

In addition to the complexities of building a tunnel of this magnitude, Eurotunnel had to deal right away with creating a functioning organization, building a company, negotiating a multibillion-pound contract, and raising enough money to pay for the enormous project. The project encountered complexities that might have killed most other projects. These involved cultural differences, political and financial complications, conflicts of interest, lack of leadership at the highest level, a poorly written contract, and conflicting health and safety concerns.

The British government required that the project be financed entirely by the private sector. Private financing raised about £1 billion, and a worldwide consortium of banks ultimately loaned £5 billion to the project. However, the lenders were also shareholders, and this proved an obstacle for the international banks in charge of reviewing the contract.

The two new companies had different agendas. Eurotunnel felt that the tunnel should reflect a technological state of the art. With a poorly written contract that allowed conflicting interpretations, Eurotunnel introduced numerous changes in scope and design that greatly affected costs. The contractor, Transmanche Link, on the other hand, felt its role was simply to supply a tunnel that met the demands of the contract. Disagreements between these two organizations over scope festered through the life of the project.

The construction companies lost more than $1 billion during the project, and an additional loss of $3.2 billion was accumulated during the first three years of operation. Eurotunnel narrowly escaped bankruptcy in 1997, when its creditor banks finally agreed to restructure $14.8 billion in debt and accept 45 percent of Eurotunnel's equity.

The Chunnel is a typical example of an array platform project. However, although its builders were aware of its political aspects, they underestimated its complexity, treating it perhaps primarily as a system project (see figure 6-2). The tunnel was an all-or-nothing proposition. No part of the project could operate until all phases were completed. Most of the problems encountered during its execution were a result of its enormous scope and geographical spread, two governments with conflicting needs, two different cultures, and a complex consortium of companies coming from different countries. In terms of technology, we can classify the project as medium-tech, because the uncertainty and the equipment involved in digging such a tunnel made it much riskier than a regular construction project.

In retrospect, had project complexity been assessed correctly, things might have been easier. A detailed binding policy written carefully by a central body with higher authority might have prevented cultural and coordination difficulties.

Nevertheless, despite all its construction troubles the Chunnel is operational and will continue to transport people and goods for many years. In the long run it may even bring economic value to those who had the vision and the means for building this phenomenal project.

As the Chunnel project demonstrates, the need for properly assessing a project's complexity can't be overestimated. Array projects are the most complicated of all. Treating an array project as a system project may result in unnecessary delays, poor coordination, and conflicts among participants.

However, similar misjudgments also can be made at lower levels of complexity. As mentioned in chapter 3, the FCS project had all the ingredients of a system project but was treated as an assembly project. The project managers underestimated the complexity of the system, and that required an extensive period of system integration and a proper system engineering design process. In contrast, the *Toy Story* project, described in chapter 4, demonstrated a careful attention to project complexity and a successful integration of two companies having different cultures and expertise.

FIGURE 6-2

The Chunnel project

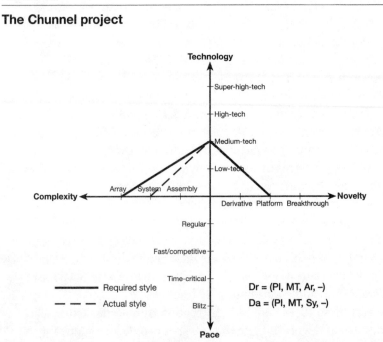

Summarizing the Impact of Complexity

Table 6-3 (page 114) summarizes the major differences that are found in the three project complexity levels, including possible risks at each level. Appendix 6A includes a collection of empirical research results that relate to project complexity. Appendix 6B summarizes the impact of complexity on traditional project management PMBoK areas.

The Weak Link: System Projects

Most projects undertaken by organizations are small assembly projects. In contrast, array projects are rare and costly, and they require long-term commitments. Many are initiated by governments after long periods of initiation, planning, and conceptualization. Famous recent examples include the International Space Station, the Strategic Defense Initiative (SDI), and the reconstruction of Kuwait after the Gulf War.[17]

System projects, on the other hand, often seem to get lost in the middle. They are the least understood and often cause the most difficulties. This section devotes a special discussion to these projects.

Typical Difficulties of System Projects

System projects create or modify systems and platforms of systems. The end result is an integrated system that has multiple functions and operates under a wide range of conditions and environments. System projects typically have many things in common.[18]

First, system projects deal with a complex collection of functions under a variety of environments. They include a complex collection of subsystems and assemblies. These subsystems work together with a great degree of interaction and influence on one another. Furthermore, many of these subsystems are very different from one another; they involve different technologies and require different skills, different methods of designing and building, and different cost and quality considerations. And many of these subsystems are being built by other, sometimes remote organizations through complex contracting and business engagements.

Second, subsystems usually interfere with one another and compete for the system's resources. In physical systems the trade-off may relate to space, electric power, computer memory, or frequency usage. In service systems the trade-off relates to managerial attention, IT resources, or even office space. A change in one subsystem may have a substantial impact on other subsystems and on the system as a whole, and may put the whole system out of balance.

TABLE 6-3

Project characteristics according to project complexity

	LEVEL OF PROJECT COMPLEXITY		
Characteristic	*Assembly*	*System*	*Array*
Customers	Consumers or the main contractor of a larger project	Consumers, industry, public, government, or military agencies	Public organizations, government or defense agencies
Form of purchase and delivery	Direct purchase or a simple contract; contract ends after delivery of product	Complex contract; payments by milestones; delivery includes logistical support	Multiple contracts; evolutionary delivery as various segments are completed and paid for
Project organization	Performed within one organization, usually under a single functional group; almost no administrative staff in project organization	A main contractor, usually organized in a matrix or pure project form; many internal and external subcontractors; various technical and administrative staff	An umbrella organization, usually a program office to coordinate subprojects; many staff experts: administrative, financial, legal, PR, etc.
Planning	Simple tools, often handled manually; rarely more than 100 activities in the network	Complex planning; advanced computerized tools and software planning packages; hundreds or thousands of activities	A central master plan with separate plans for subprojects; advanced computerized tools; total program may include up to 10,000 activities
Control and reporting	Simple, informal, in-house control; reporting to management or main contractor	Tight, formal control on technical, financial, and schedule issues; reviews with customers and management	Master or central control by program office; separate additional control for subprojects by contractor; many reports and meetings with contractors
Documentation	Simple, mostly technical documents	Many technical and formal managerial documents	Mostly managerial and legal documents at program office level; technical and managerial documents at lower level
Management style, attitude, and focus	Mostly informal style; family-like atmosphere; typical focus on cost, quality, delivery, and manufacturing (when relevant)	Formal and bureaucratic style; some informal relationships with subcontractors and customers; sometimes dealing with political and interorganizational issues; major focus needed on system requirements, system design, and system integration	Formal, tight bureaucracy; high awareness of political, environmental, legal, and social issues; strong focus needed on program policy coordination and political decision makers
Policies, standards, and guidelines	Typically no particular standards or policies used	Industry or corporate standards are followed	Program must develop its own policies and standards; no common industry standards exist for programs of this size
Possible risk	Low risk of missing requirements	Medium to high risk; risk involves difficulty in integrating all subsystems as an optimal functioning system; difficulty with complex configuration and mutual influences between subsystems, or risk of recovering the investment	Highest risk; risk involves weak coordination between the systems that make up the array and failure to accomplish its mission; misalignment with the environmental, political, or economic climate, or extensive spending of resources in case of overruns

Third, the operation of system projects is a complex activity. It requires specifically trained personnel, maintenance, repair, upgrades, documentation, and contractor support. And rarely do customers of systems buy only the system. They are concerned with the entire life cycle of the system: the ease of getting the system running, the need to train the operators and service people, and the cost of operation, as well as the system's serviceability, reliability, and maintainability.

Many system projects therefore suffer from similar difficulties (failure factors) that may risk project success.[19] For example, managers of system initiatives often have great difficulty identifying actual users' needs and translating these needs into system requirements. It is often difficult to foresee the final system, its complex functionality, and its expected risk. As a result, final system capabilities are often less than promised and expected; maintenance and support are complex and error prone; and final system reliability, maintainability, and serviceability levels are lower than expected. And even in successful systems, it is often difficult to identify suitable performance metrics or determine real system life-cycle cost and operational effectiveness.

Thus, managing successful system projects is a serious challenge. Not only must project leaders cope with poor communication among managers, designers, and customers, but also they are strongly dependent on a complex web of external suppliers, complicated procurement systems, and lengthy, detailed contracts with subcontractors and other collaborators. No wonder system projects often encounter many problems in organizational and project structure. The next section summarizes the key issues that need attention when an organization undertakes a system project.

Key Issues in Managing System Projects

Defining, planning, and managing a system project is a complex managerial and organizational undertaking. Those who are accustomed to managing assembly projects must realize that a system project is not a repetitive duplication of an assembly. Rather, a system project requires a new set of skills and a different level of attention:

- You need to build a system approach and system thinking skills. This means seeing the system as a whole and not only as a collection of parts and subsystems. It also means taking a top-down view, which starts with a vision of the entire system goal and how it will serve the user and customer. System thinking can be developed only with time and maturity.

- Building systems requires a combination of the skills and disciplines of many people and the ability to integrate these skills in a coherent way. Often, people from different disciplines don't think alike and don't speak the same professional language. They have different views of the world, and each wants a certain piece of the pie. You must learn to make decisions at the interface of disciplines and subsystems, and often you must sacrifice local optimization of one or more parts to maximize total system optimization.

- Realizing and understanding the customer need for a system is complex, and it takes time. It involves the understanding and articulation of many perspectives and stakeholders' interests. The final need might change and evolve during project execution.

- Making the business case for a system is also tricky. It means understanding how the need can be addressed by a system that is technologically, economically, and organizationally feasible and can be realized in a reasonable amount of time. It all must make sense, both for the customer and for the performing organization. To take advantage of a business opportunity there must always be a match between the "needs and the seeds," namely, the ability of the organization to address this need.[20] For systems, this task is even more complex and requires extensive research and detailed economic and technical analysis.

- Translating the business case into system requirements is just as complex. System requirements are typically outlined in a voluminous document that is built over a long period with the involvement of stakeholders, managers, customers, potential users, experts, and subcontractors.

- *Systems engineering* is a technical and managerial discipline and process that translates system requirements into a system concept and system parameters, which are documented in a set of baseline specifications. The systems engineering process progressively decomposes the system requirements and system concept to the lowest possible level. The system concept is divided into components and subsystems, and the specifications for each entity are determined. Systems engineers are responsible for conducting trade-off studies, which lead to the final specifications. Systems engineers deal with interface control, risk management, verification management, and performance and testing management. They also define the approach for system integration and for the validation of each integration stage.[21] A crucial aspect of systems engineering is *system architecture.* There are very few good system architects around, and rarely are these skills taught in school.[22]

- One of the major problems and difficulties in system projects is *system integration,* a process whereby all subsystems are put together, assembled, and connected to form the total system. Even when all subsystems function perfectly and each one fully meets specifications, when they are all put together they rarely work as a system the first time. Mutual effects, space limitations, interference, and other unexpected factors often cause the system prototype to fail at first. Ignoring this reality may cause delays and surprises to project managers. The right approach is to allocate ample time in the plan for system integration. In complex systems such as aircraft, it may be months before the first system starts showing signs of functionality. The integration period must be part of the project plan, and the time for integration should be allocated up front.

- Another typical problem in system projects is configuration control and configuration management. Requirements and specifications often change during system building and design. You must maintain complete and systematic control of every change made and its impact on the other parts. Each item at the lowest level is called a *configuration item,* and each requires its own specifications, design reviews, testing, acceptance reviews, and operation and maintenance manuals. A configuration item is sometimes also an LRU (line replaceable unit) that can be replaced with a spare unit when needed.

- System projects are typically characterized by a high degree of user involvement. User involvement helps shape the right system and articulates how the user will operate it. User involvement is difficult at times, particularly when the user is also the customer and tries to dictate things to the system designer. Yet the value of user involvement surpasses the difficulty, and the earlier the customer is involved, the better the chance that the system will fulfill its needs.

- Building a system project requires the combined effort of many organizations, functional groups, and subcontractors. To organize the effort you must set up a central project (or program) office, which assigns roles and is responsible for subcontracting. This office is also responsible for defining the system requirements and for systems engineering, system architecture, and configuration management. It may also be responsible for the system integration (although this function may be subcontracted to another system integrator). The central project office is then responsible for system validation and for the delivery of the system to the final customer.

To illustrate the complexities of system projects, let's look now at the Harmony software project, which was performed by a large telecommunications corporation that we studied. We present it here as a showcase of how to handle a system project correctly.

The Harmony Project: A System Project Showcase

When a major U.S. telecommunications network provider found itself losing business every time its infrastructure went down, it initiated the Harmony project. The company serves thousands of business customers, which are billed for requested features and the bandwidth they use. Typically when service went down, the company restored it after an extended manual search and problem identification process, which sometimes took hours if not days. The process also suffered from communication difficulties among the support staff members who are responsible for the network's functioning and availability.

The project's goal was to optimize the network operations and reduce downtime, resulting in a better customer experience and maximum network utilization. The project required the design, development, and deployment of a new rule-based, software-driven infrastructure that would allow internal and external users to identify network failures and problems. Users could then dynamically program the system according to their recovery needs through a simple-to-use Web-based interface system.

Such a system had never been built; however, because it would replace an existing manual system, its novelty level was that of a platform. The company therefore correctly initiated a lengthy process of requirements preparation. This involved extensive market research and input from hundreds of its customers, which provided insights and information about their specific needs. The requirements freeze was scheduled for the end of the second quarter, but because managers were also concerned with creating product familiarity, they decided to share their early prototypes with customers as soon as they became available.

The company already had bits and pieces of the technology, but most of it was relatively new and had never been combined on one product. That made Harmony a high-tech project. To deal with this level of technological uncertainty, managers adopted a flexible style, allowing changes to be introduced late into the project and freezing the design during the third quarter of the project life cycle. Prototypes were used during development, together with customer involvement, to sort out design problems and rewrite technical specifications throughout most of the project's lifetime.

To achieve the interaction and knowledge needed in this highly uncertain environment, management selected highly skilled technical people and empowered them to make their own technical decisions while maintaining frequent and intensive communication channels. Finally, the team of this high-tech project mobilized the help of an external technical peer review group. The members of this group were not part of the formal executive review board or the day-to-day team. They were experts in enterprise architecture and other functional areas, and they served as consultants on a quarterly basis, providing valuable feedback on design and architecture decisions made by the core team.

The product consisted of a large collection of modules (sometimes called "engines" in computer software terminology). Among many others, they included a routing module, a normalization module, an event subscription module, a rule wizard, a scheduler module, a task engine, a notification engine, and a collaboration-on-demand module. To coordinate and integrate all these modules, the project required the collaboration of many functional groups such as enterprise architecture, systems engineering, software development, software testing, production support, and customer support.

This complexity placed the project at the system level, and to manage it managers established a formal and somewhat bureaucratic process of planning, monitoring, and decision making that supported requirements management, architecture building, development, integration, and testing. The team created an elaborate documentation and communication structure, but a certain level of informal interaction was also encouraged between team members and even customers. Additionally, top managers, understanding the importance of the project, provided full support when asked to help. The chief technical officer championed the project and made sure that all management decisions were made on a timely basis to allow the team to go forward as soon as it was ready to move.

Finally, the importance of the project to the company made it a fast/competitive project. Although missing the deadline would not be catastrophic, it would harm the bottom line. That point was stressed by top management and created a sense of urgency among the team members. They therefore tried to follow the structured process and keep tight control on costs and time.

In summary, the Harmony project adopted the right approach to its NTCP platform, high-tech, system, fast/competitive project. Figure 6-3 demonstrates that in this case the actual style and the required style were indeed in harmony (as the name of the project implied).

Chapter 7 further explores fast/competitive projects, together with the other levels of project pace, the final dimension of our diamond model.

Key Points and Action Items

- Project complexity depends on product complexity. In most situations there are six levels of product complexity and three levels of project complexity: assembly, system, and array. Each project requires a unique organization, bureaucracy, and focus.

FIGURE 6-3

The Harmony project

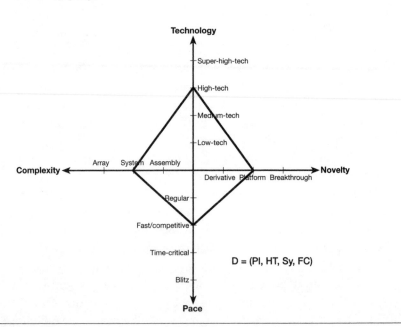

$D = (Pl, HT, Sy, FC)$

- An assembly project is usually performed within a single functional unit by a small team working in one location, with extensive informal communication among members.

- System projects require a central project (or program) office that coordinates the efforts of subgroups and subcontractors, with an increased level of formality and bureaucracy.

- Array projects deal with a dispersed collection of systems that function together to achieve a common purpose, sometimes called a system of systems. Such projects are spread over a wide geographical area and typically consist of a variety of system subprojects. Array projects are typically structured under an umbrella organization that deals mainly with financial, logistical, and legal issues.

- Moving from assembly to system projects is a major change. It requires extensive administrative and integration skills. Managers of system projects must have a system view and must manage the interfaces between disciplines.

- When moving into the array level, managers must learn to back off of technical matters and develop instead a broader view of the industry and its players. They must learn to deal with legal, environmental, and political issues, which usually are not addressed by managers at lower levels of project complexity.

- Organizations need to build their project managers' skills according to the hierarchy of systems and train people to build a system view over time.

❖ 7 ❖

PACE

I N THE COMPETITIVE WORLD, good ideas must get to market as soon as possible, and companies must keep introducing new products quickly and fix the flaws of old ones as soon as they find them. The accelerating pace of technological development, the shortened project life cycle, and the diversification of markets around the world continuously increase the demands on project teams to find better ways of speeding up project execution.

Accordingly, pace, the fourth dimension of the NTCP model (and the final base of the diamond), involves the urgency and criticality of meeting a project's time goals. Each project is time constrained, but this constraint may differ from project to project. Time constraints may come from market needs, competitive pressures, and management strategies, and from environmental, natural, or enemy threats that prompt immediate action. The time available to complete a project has a substantial effect on how a project is managed. The same goal but with different time frames may require different project structures, processes, and management attention. In this chapter we explore the impact of project pace on project management and discuss what managers can do to successfully run projects having different pace levels.

Several important recent studies have addressed the increased pace of projects and product introduction. For example, Kathleen Eisenhardt and Shona Brown have introduced the concept of time-paced strategies, where companies must pace their projects according to an expected evolutionary rhythm.[1] Marco Iansiti has studied product development in Internet time, when time competition becomes the driving force of modern industries.[2]

As we discuss later in this chapter, a project's pace usually falls into one of four types: regular, fast/competitive, time-critical, and blitz. The following story of the Mars Climate Orbiter program illustrates a time-critical case and shows how constraints in this category may cause sacrifices in other dimensions, leading to project failure. This case also demonstrates, once more, the importance that project managers must place on all four dimensions of the diamond.

The Mars Climate Orbiter Program

Mars Climate Orbiter (MCO) was one of two missions initiated by NASA in 1993 to build on previous successes in Mars exploration. (The second mission was Mars Polar Lander, or MPL.) MCO was expected to collect weather data from the red planet as well as assist in data transmission to and from the MPL. With a thirty-seven-month schedule and a financial cap of about $184 million, the project's scope included development of the spacecraft and its scientific payloads, and building and operating the ground operations system. But because of Mars's position with respect to Earth, the most critical element of this project's characteristics was pace. Based on its narrow window of opportunity to launch, MCO was clearly a time-critical project. Missing the time window meant program failure.

The development project was completed on time to meet the exact launch date. After traveling nine months in space, the orbiter reached the vicinity of Mars in September 1999; but as soon as it began its insertion maneuver, contact with the orbiter was lost and was never recovered. The failure was later attributed to a technical error made by engineers in failing to use metric units in the MCO's ground software.[3] Our analysis, however, suggests that the failure was not technical but managerial. By focusing on meeting the critical deadline, the team sacrificed the project's unique risks on other dimensions.

By its nature, the MCO was a mission that neither NASA nor anyone else had done. That would categorize it as a breakthrough project. MCO was also a system project. In addition to its own complexity as a system, MCO had to work together with MPL when it arrived on Mars. A mixture of existing and new technology was used. However, some of the technologies were used for the first time. That placed the project at the high-tech level.

To manage a breakthrough, high-tech, system, time-critical program would require a long period of requirements definition involving extensive interaction with customers, along with careful and systematic integration of all subsystems and stakeholders' interests. It also required numerous design cycles, extensive testing and technical reviews, and late design freeze; and it needed a continuous focus on time goals, with high priority given to meeting every milestone and no tolerance for delays due to bureaucracy or other reasons.

A careful look at the management of the MCO project shows that the cost constraints imposed by NASA's "better, faster, cheaper" (BFC) attitude forced MCO managers to employ a less than optimal project management style. Managers were almost forced to see the program as another generation in an existing product family (platform) and as a product that involved well-known technologies (medium-tech). For example, the navigation software system was the most novel and uncertain part of all the systems, in both its use and its technical maturity; yet it received no more testing or reviews than any other subsystem. In addition, interaction with customers was sometimes defined as "confusing."[4] Furthermore, there was not enough testing, reviews, or communication—all things that high-tech projects demand in abundance. Inheriting subsystems (such as navigation) from previous programs eventually became a contributing factor to MCO's failure. MCO was treated as "just like MGS," a previous space navigation program. Thus some of the testing, verification, and validation were limited, and design was frozen relatively early.

Second, budget and time constraints caused the project managers to exercise only limited control of subsystem integration and less than needed end-to-end verification and validation through program reviews. In retrospect, although much of the project was treated as a system, certain subsystems having high levels of uncertainty were managed as assembly projects. Just as a chain is only as strong as its weakest link, treating any part of a system as an assembly means treating the entire system as an assembly.

Yet MCO was indeed managed as a time-critical project. Realizing the criticality of the launch window, project procedures were shortened and nonbureaucratic, and top management remained highly involved and constantly supportive. However, the team members sometimes had to work one hundred hours per week just to stay on schedule. Noel Hinners, vice president for flight systems, stated, "We were so busy doing the work that had to get done, we did not have the luxury of just sitting back on a weekend or when you got home at night and thinking about what went on."[5] Ironically, however, with all its constraints, the MCO team maintained high spirits with an unmatched drive to be successful.

Figure 7-1 shows the optimal versus the actual project management style. In retrospect, treating the project as a safer program than it actually was led the team to sacrifice some of the critical activities of testing and integration. It allowed a component to be used that was not fully tested. This can be attributed to the pressures and challenges of the BFC era at NASA, which resulted in cuts that later played a key role in MCO's failure. Designing to capability, not cost, might have revealed that this project could not have been done under the specified budget and pressured mentality of BFC.

FIGURE 7-1

Mars Climate Orbiter project

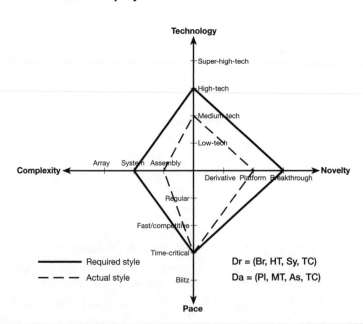

The Four Levels of Project Pace

The classification presented here is based on degrees of urgency at the time of project initiation.[6] We associate such urgency with how critical the time of delivery is or simply how much time is available. Table 7-1 shows the four levels of urgency, or pace.

Regular Projects

Projects we refer to as *regular* pace typically are carried out to achieve long-term or infrastructure goals, but with no real time pressure. They may include construction of public buildings, road building, organizational improvements such as reengineering, and technology build-up efforts. Although regular pace projects are planned for completion on a certain date, missing the deadline may be tolerated, because time is not critical to immediate organizational success. Unless completion time is specifically made a priority, such projects are managed casually and may often be delayed or even pushed aside by more pressing assignments.

A good example of this type of project is the Sydney Opera House, which is described in chapter 2. With no real pressure and no changes in city politics, the building was completed after sixteen years of stops and starts instead of the original six-year schedule. The lesson is clear: with no external, competitive, or enforced pressure, regular projects may take much longer than planned.

TABLE 7-1

Four levels of project pace

	Regular	Fast/Competitive	Time-Critical	Blitz
Definitions	Time not critical to organizational success	Project completion on time is important for company's competitive advantage and/or the organization's leadership position	Meeting time goal is critical for project success; any delay means project failure	Crisis projects; utmost urgency; project should be completed as soon as possible
Examples	Public works, some government initiatives, some internal projects	Business-related projects; new product introduction, new plant construction in response to market growth	Projects with a definite deadline or a window of opportunity; space launch restricted by a time window; Y2K	War; fast response to natural disasters; fast response to business-related surprises

Fast/Competitive Projects

These are the most common projects carried out by industrial and for-profit organizations, but they also can be found in public or government organizations when priority is given to a timely completion of the project. Fast/competitive projects are typically initiated to address a market opportunity, create a strategic positioning, or form a new business line. The time of project completion is directly associated with competitiveness, leadership positions, or organizational sustainability. Although missing the deadline may not be fatal, it might hurt profits, competitive advantage, or organizational strength. The point is that these projects are influenced by market or internal pressure to get them done as soon as possible.

Fast/competitive projects must be managed with a strategic mind-set. Project managers should focus on meeting schedules but also on achieving profit goals and addressing customer and market needs. Managing time to market should be one of the main concerns. Eli Goldratt asserted in his book *Critical Chain* that time is a critical resource and that the critical path is the project's constraint.[7] The theory of constraints suggests subordinating the system to the time constraint by creating a central project time buffer (rather than individual buffers for each activity), adding buffers to each activity that feeds the critical path. Top management must support and closely monitor these projects at each major milestone, but at the same time be alert if something goes wrong in between.

Time-Critical Projects

These projects are focused on a specific completion date that cannot be changed. The Mars Climate Orbiter example (recounted earlier in this chapter) was such a project. For a time-critical project, failing to meet the time goal means project failure. Such projects are initiated to meet a window of opportunity that cannot be missed.

As we have seen, some space projects are time-critical because they require a specific alignment of the planets. Other well-known examples include a Y2K project, where meeting the millennium date was critical to success, and completion of an Olympic village before the start of the games. A similar situation can occur in a business context, where a product may be rendered obsolete if it reaches the market after a certain date—for example, New Year's Day.

In these projects, time is the most critical constraint; all others, such as budget, facilities, and so on, are made secondary to enable on-time completion. Contingency plans must be prepared to deal with situations that might delay completion. To overcome project uncertainties and unexpected problems, you must develop alternative solutions in parallel, and the fastest solution usually wins. Project reviews are focused on the project's preparations for meeting the completion date and the risk of missing it; time plans are updated and carefully monitored on an ongoing basis to make sure no time is lost.

Blitz Projects

Blitz projects are the most urgent projects. They are typically initiated in response to a crisis or as a result of an unexpected event. Examples are wartime events, natural disasters (such as earthquake rescue efforts), or industrial crises, when an organization must leapfrog a surprising move by competitors. A famous example was the effort to save the *Apollo 13* crew after the craft's fuel tank exploded, when only a few hours were left before oxygen and power would run out. Ron Howard's Academy Award-winning movie, *Apollo 13,* starring Tom Hanks, illustrates well the crisis environment, the structure, and the relationships in a blitz project.

To succeed, such projects must be managed differently from other types. First, because most blitz projects are responding to crisis, typically there is no time for detailed planning. Although contingency plans may be useful, in many cases the situation is unexpected and managers must start acting before there is a detailed plan and improvise as they proceed. Work is performed almost around the clock, with nonstop interaction and continuous decision making. There is usually no time for detailed documentation or report writing, and all regular bureaucracy is eliminated.

Project managers of blitz projects must be given absolute autonomy. Project organization must involve a pure project structure, with all team members reporting directly to the leader. Finally, in blitz projects top management must be present at all times to support, monitor, and make the necessary decisions. Without a full commitment of all parties, blitz projects cannot succeed.

The difference between time-critical and blitz projects is that in time-critical projects, the target date or window of opportunity is well known in advance. Managers have ample time to plan and prepare the project to meet this target. Blitz projects, in contrast, emerge from a crisis, when unexpected events prompt the need for immediate action. Sometimes, however, a time-critical project may turn into a blitz when the project is running out of time. This situation happened in one of the Y2K projects we studied.

How a Time-Critical Project Turned into a Blitz: The Y2K Case

In the spring of 1998, a small manufacturing company considered acquiring one of its archrivals. Before the possible merger, the two Y2K project managers met to discuss each other's projects. They reviewed all the possibilities that the two companies might face when and if they merged. Each company had its own enterprise resource planning (ERP) system, and both were in the process of upgrading their systems to be Y2K compliant.

In December 1998, the merger was completed, and the two companies became one. The new company had only one year to prepare for Y2K. A decision had to be made: should it continue upgrading the two ERP systems, or switch to one system? Based on the project managers' recommendations, the company's president decided to use an ERP system produced by a major supplier under the condition that it could support the company's manufacturing environment.

However, a few weeks later, new problems started to surface. After reviewing all alternatives, managers decided that the company should abandon the current ERP project, implement the existing production resources management system (PRMS) in the acquired division, and upgrade the system to be Y2K compliant.

The new decision represented a U-turn for the company. To deal with the risk, small focus groups were formed to identify any problems that would prevent the company from pursuing that approach. However, most of the programmers who had been working with the ERP system provider had left the company, and after a few months one of the two project managers also left.

That situation turned the Y2K project into a blitz project (see figure 7-2). A war room was set up for the team, and 24/7 shifts became the norm. This effort became the highest priority in the company. The project drew people from other projects, putting extra pressure on the rest of the workers, who had to take on the responsibilities of those who were drafted by the Y2K team.

The company planned to go live for the first time on October 1, 1999, to enable final testing and training before the critical date. Yet October slowly faded away and the system was still not ready. Less than two months were left to make it happen. The team grew

FIGURE 7-2

The Y2K project

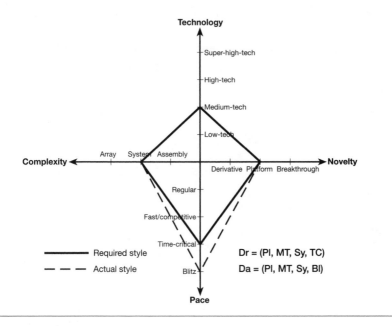

by the week. It seemed that the whole company was working on this project. You could feel the tension in the air as you entered the war room.

Supported by top management, the team recommended starting live testing during the last weekend before New Year's Day. Saturday passed, however, and the system still had not gone live. Sunday, the team worked as the hours disappeared. Everyone was exhausted. Finally, after 8:00 p.m., testing began, and it continued on Monday while the rest of the company was locked out of the system. A few bugs were found and fixed in the next few days.

On January 1, 2000, the core team members came in to make sure that the system was running correctly. It appeared that all the hard work for the past year had paid off. The system worked flawlessly. To show his appreciation, the company's president invited the entire team for dinner, where he announced he was doubling their yearly bonuses.

The Impact of Pace on Project Management

Table 7-2 lists the characteristics of project management at various pace levels. Although the focus of fast/competitive projects is on getting to market as soon as possible, the focus in time-critical projects is specifically centered on the window of opportunity. In contrast, blitz projects

TABLE 7-2

Characteristics of project pace levels

		LEVEL OF PROJECT PACE		
Characteristic	*Regular*	*Fast/Competitive*	*Time-Critical*	*Blitz*
Focus	No particular focus	Strategically focused on time to market	Centered on a specific window of opportunity	Swift solution of the crisis
Possible risk	No particular risk due to time of completion	Risk of being late to market and letting competitors take part of the business	Risk of project failure if target date not met	Risk of slow response to crisis, which may significantly increase the damage
Organization	No unique structure	Mostly matrix teams; strong coordination of subcontractors	Pure project is desirable; often co-location or skunk works	Immediate and special task force; team has great autonomy
Personnel	People not assigned to more urgent jobs	Qualified for the job	Specifically picked	Immediately available; taken out and released from other assignments
Procedures and processes	No specific attention	Structured procedures; new concepts and methods for shortening development cycle[a]	Shortened, simple; tight schedule control; parallel and redundant processes to guarantee meeting the deadline	No bureaucracy, no documentation; work goes on around the clock; can benefit from prepared contingency plans but must be ready to improvise
Top management involvement	Management by exception	Go-ahead approvals at major project phases and gates[b]	Highly involved; engaged in tight monitoring of time	Available at all times; constantly providing support, resources, and needed decisions

a. Smith and Reinertsen provide concepts and methods for compressing the critical fuzzy front end of the development process, thus shortening the development cycle and getting new products to the market faster. P. G. Smith and D. G. Reinertsen, *Developing Products in Half the Time: New Rules, New Tools,* 2nd ed. (New York: Wiley, 1997).

b. *Stage-Gate* is a term first used by R. G. Cooper, *Winning at New Products,* 3rd ed. (Cambridge, MA: Perseus Publishing, 2001).

must focus on solving the crisis swiftly. The risk of underestimating project pace varies, starting at no risk at the regular level and rising to the loss of market share in fast/competitive projects. In a blitz project, failure to respond immediately can result in a significant increase in damage or even loss of lives.

As discussed next, the major difference lies in the organizational structure employed, the people engaged, and the procedures and processes applied. Appendix 7 discusses the impact of pace on traditional project management according to the major PMBoK knowledge areas.

The Impact on the Organization

Because fast/competitive is the most common pace for industrial projects, this kind of project usually employs a typical matrix organization, with tight control on project subteams and subcontractors. The real change can be seen in time-critical projects, where regular matrices are often insufficient to guarantee that the projects will meet the target date. In these projects you may be better off by employing a pure project organization where all team members report directly to the project manager. Often, you also gather team members in one location (co-location) and use a skunk works structure, where members of the team are specifically picked and isolated from other activities of the organization. Similarly, in blitz projects, there is no alternative except a pure project organization.

Team Autonomy

Blitz project teams are more time-focused than in any other project type. Having to deal with a crisis situation, team members are taken from other assignments and are released from any other commitment. They form an immediate task force, with total autonomy to make and carry out decisions on the spot. Such projects do not follow any procedures or bureaucracy; they do not write extensive documents or reports, and they typically work around the clock to resolve the crisis.

Although blitz projects cannot follow typical organizational project procedures, they can benefit from prepared contingency plans that are written in anticipation of a possible crisis. Such plans tell teams what to do and how to mobilize resources, rather than start from scratch when the crisis arrives. Although this approach is common in military operations planning, organizations can benefit from the same mind-set. If you are prepared for crisis, the solution is much easier.

However, many situations cannot be predicted and contingency plans may not be available for every scenario. The solution then is improvisation. You must be ready to act even without a plan. You must start working immediately and build your plan as you proceed. Efficiency will be sacrificed, but in crisis situations a swift solution is more important than saving organizational resources.

Top Management Involvement

Top management involvement varies from the typical executive go-ahead decisions at the completion of major project phases in fast/competitive projects, to guaranteeing timely completion of time-critical projects, to ongoing involvement and support for teams in blitz projects.

This chapter completes part 2, the detailed description of the diamond model. But to make things work in real organizations, you must look at your projects in their actual context and apply the right approach to each situation. Part 3 deals with the practical implications of our model in various contexts. Chapter 8 begins with the business and innovation context.

Key Points and Action Items

- Project pace is determined by how much time is available to complete the project. There are four levels of pace: regular, fast/competitive, time-critical, and blitz.

- In regular projects, time is not critical to immediate organizational success.

- Fast/competitive projects are the most common projects carried out by industrial and for-profit organizations. Such projects are under time pressure to get a product to market or to address a critical organizational need. They are managed strategically, with focus on the competitive nature of the time of completion.

- Time-critical projects are focused on a predefined, specific completion date that cannot be changed. Failing to meet the time goal means project failure. In time-critical projects, time is the single most critical constraint; all other constraints are made secondary to enable on-time completion.

- Blitz projects are the most urgent. They are responding to a crisis or an unexpected event. Project managers in blitz projects must be given absolute autonomy, and project organization should be a pure project structure, with all team members reporting directly to the leader. Top management must be present at all times to support, monitor, and make the necessary decisions.

- The major difference among projects due to pace is in the organizational structure, the participants, and the procedures and processes.

- Top management support is critical in all except regular projects. Managers must adjust the organizational procedures to the time criticality of the project. In fast/competitive projects, they should provide timely go-ahead decisions at the completion of major project phases. They should guarantee precise, timely completion of time-critical projects, and they should provide intensive involvement and ongoing presence at project sites in blitz projects.

Part Three

PUTTING THE DIAMOND APPROACH TO WORK

◆ 8 ◆

MANAGING PROJECTS FOR BUSINESS INNOVATION

I N THE EARLY 2000s, after twenty-five years in the computer business, Apple Computer decided to take advantage of a new trend: young people downloading music from the Internet.[1] Using its experience in designing exciting products and integrating them with easy-to-run software, the company made a strategic decision to launch several innovative projects, such as the iPod personal music player, iTunes software, and iTunes Music Store. Together, these products created a successful new business for the company.

Building a business based on an innovation, as Apple did with the iPod, can be one of the reasons companies initiate projects. But not every project is about creating a new business or innovation. Companies also initiate projects to expand an existing business, extend the life of a mature product, build new infrastructure, or fix a problem that hinders the organization's ability to grow. In other words, projects may address diverse business goals, and those goals have different effects on the projects undertaken to achieve them.

This chapter examines how an organization's business and innovation context affects its project management. Within this realm we first deal with project selection and resource allocation; we then move to the often unresolved question of the relationship between project management and successful innovation. Specifically, we discuss how to select the right project for the right type of innovation, how to deal with the innovator's dilemma, and how to address the product's customers' adoption cycle.

How Companies Select Projects and Allocate Resources

Because most organizations manage more than one project, they cannot avoid dealing with the problems of project portfolio management. Unfortunately, portfolio management is one of the most controversial and problematic activities in almost every organization. We define *portfolio management* as the actions and decisions a company takes to select or reject projects to include in its collection of ongoing projects, and to allocate the resources among projects in the most effective way.[2]

Project selection, then, is the first problem managers need to address.[3] The situation illustrated in the following example—a company with which we worked—will likely sound familiar to many executives and project managers.

The Case of the Media Corporation

The executives of the IT group of a large media corporation face a similar dilemma each year: how to select which projects to begin and how to allocate their limited resources to those projects that have been approved. The group serves various businesses that deal with external customers, but it also serves the company's internal needs. The IT group consists of unique experts in various disciplines; some are dedicated to specific business units, and others are part of a common pool of experts that serves the entire organization.

Not all projects are of the same nature. Some are large infrastructure projects, some are improvements of existing products, others are initiatives to create new products, and still others are maintenance projects to keep the lights on. Project proposals come from different units and businesses, each of which tries to justify the importance of its project.

When faced every year with dozens of project proposals, the managers of the group get together for long sessions of assessment and debate. They use common criteria, such as impact on the business, expected return, and risk. Projects are quickly divided into four groups: "must fund," "probably fund," "probably not fund," and "not fund." Then the real debate begins: whether to fund projects in the two "probable" groups.

Every year, however, managers are left with a feeling that perhaps not all worthy projects have been approved.

When projects are finally selected, the next question comes up: how to allocate the critical resources (mostly experts' time) from the common pool. This dilemma keeps arising throughout the year, with no clear solution.

What guidelines would make these managers feel more comfortable in their decisions? The media corporation executives need a framework that will help them assess the benefits and risks of projects and set priorities to make the best decisions for the company's business goals.

Step 1: Divide Projects Based on Business Goals and Customer Groups

When assigning priorities to projects, the first consideration is business goals. The simplest and perhaps the most effective way is to categorize projects along two dimensions: strategic versus operational projects, and internal versus external projects.[4]

Strategic projects are prime efforts made to create or sustain strategic positions in markets or businesses. These projects are initiated to maintain or enhance the company's competitive position, change the basis of competition, create new markets, or create new product lines. In sum, these projects are intended to create new muscles for the organization and are typically initiated with a long-term perspective in mind. Examples are new and innovative products or major new models in existing product lines. Strategic projects can also include internal efforts to build new infrastructure.

Operational projects relate to existing businesses. Don't let the name fool you; they are part of the *projects* in the organization, and not the *operations* mentioned in chapter 1. Operational projects are initiated to help the organization keep doing what it is doing. Such projects are initiated to improve and extend the lives of existing products, get more out of previous initiatives, improve existing production lines, or maintain projects that simply keep the lights on.

External projects are those made for outside customers. They are usually customers with whom the company has a contract, or customers who will buy the product in the free market.

Internal projects are those made for internal customers: people and groups within the organization that will be the users and beneficiaries of the project result. They might be internal departments, other units, staff functions, and so on.

Combining the two dimensions creates a 2×2 matrix, as shown in table 8-1.

Step 2: Allocate Resources Among the Cells

The next step is to allocate the company's (or business unit's) resources to each group of projects based on the company's strategic goals and policy. The policy may depend on the expected benefits and value from each group, the timing of the decision, the environment, industry trends, and the company's competitive position and life-cycle stage. It will also greatly depend on the company's strategic plans. For example, if the company is growing, it will allocate a higher portion to the strategic–external cell; if it is consolidating and reducing costs, perhaps the internal–operational part will get a bigger share. If managers first allocate resources to groups, each project competes only with other projects in the same group. The selection is now much easier, because apples and oranges do not compete.

Step 3: Identify Your Operational and Strategic Diamonds

Using the NTCP dimensions demonstrates the difference between operational and strategic projects. Operational projects are almost always derivatives, whereas strategic projects are either platforms or breakthroughs. The technological uncertainty of operational projects is typically no higher than medium-tech, whereas strategic projects can span the entire spectrum of technological uncertainty. However, operational projects can be urgent, requiring a blitz attitude; in contrast, strategic projects, because of their greater novelty, are rarely done during a crisis, and thus they normally do not reach the level of blitz.

TABLE 8-1

The goal-customer matrix

Customer type	Operational projects	Strategic projects
External	Extending life of an existing product; product improvement	New product introduction
Internal	Improve an existing internal process; maintain an internal process; solve a particular problem; gain access to a specific capability or technology	A new internal infrastructure project such as ERP; a major internal utility or capital project; a research project

FIGURE 8-1

Typical differences between operational and strategic projects

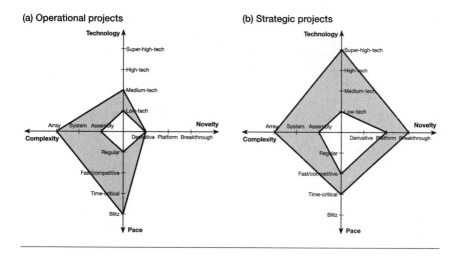

(a) Operational projects

(b) Strategic projects

Figure 8-1 shows the typical distinctions between operational and strategic projects. Whether a project is external or internal does not affect these distinctions. The larger diamond of strategic projects represents greater opportunity as well as higher risk, as we discuss next.

Step 4: Use the Diamond Model to Select Individual Projects

As discussed in chapter 3, the size of the diamond represents risk *and* opportunity, and as we have seen in chapters 4 through 7, each of its dimensions represents a different kind of risk and a different kind of opportunity. When making the final selection of individual projects, you can use the NTCP dimensions to assess specific risks and benefits.

However, the major dimension for such assessment is novelty. Greater novelty means higher market risk and greater potential benefits. Complexity is associated with the level of investment and thus potential gain or loss. But increased complexity is also associated with difficulties in co-ordination and proper integration, as somecases in previous chapters have shown. Technology provides an opportunity for better performance than in the past and gives you the ability to do new things; but it also bears the risk of technical failure. And pace provides the opportunity to gain a time-based advantage, as well as the risk of delays. Table 8-2 summarizes the specific risks and benefits for each dimension of the NCTP model.

TABLE 8-2

Potential risks and opportunities

Diamond dimension	Potential benefit and opportunity	Potential risk or difficulty
Novelty	Innovative ideas; new markets; new customers	Misassessing customer needs; missing market opportunities
Complexity	Scope of business based on size	Substantial losses; coordination and integration difficulties
Technology	Improved performance; new uses of technology	Technical failures; lack of technical skills
Pace	Timing advantage	Risk of delays; risk of errors due to speed

The final step in project selection is to make a cost-benefit analysis of projects within each group. The risks and benefits identified in each project are translated into expected monetary values to help you make a rational decision within each cell. A typical assessment matrix is shown in figure 8-3, where those projects in the high benefit/low risk group are approved immediately, and those in the low benefit/high risk area are rejected immediately. In this way, you are left with fewer projects for a more refined assessment based on critical resources, policy, or specific internal needs.

Once the right projects have been selected, you need to choose the right approach for managing each project. Within this context, we turn next to the management of innovation.

FIGURE 8-2

Risk and benefit assessment matrix

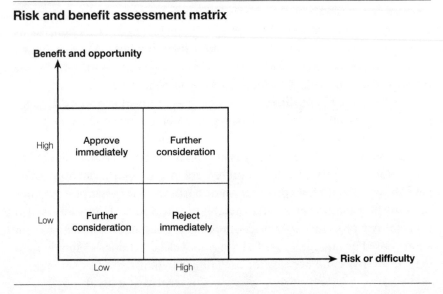

Toward a Disciplined Project Management Approach to Innovation

Competitive markets force companies to keep creating innovation-driven growth businesses.[5] Yet having the best and most innovative idea is not enough. Modern businesses must learn how to run projects that will carry those innovations from idea to profitable commercialization. In this section we deal with one of the most difficult and perhaps least understood questions about the management of innovation. Although the innovation literature is rich and informative, rarely has anything been written about the relationship between innovation and project management. Yet any successful innovation depends on a sound project. Our goal is to show how management can apply a disciplined approach to innovation.

There are various types of innovations, and they require various project management styles. Adopting the right approach may substantially increase the chances that an innovation will succeed. The following story, based on a case study from our research, demonstrates how a company adopted the correct approach to an innovative project presenting extensive risks and potentially high benefits.

The Market Watch Project

When managers at ISO Insurance Corporation were looking to expand their business, they identified an old service that was based on outdated techniques and limited in scope and performance. They defined a new software package, to be called Market Watch, that would produce a new index for forecasting changes in future premium levels and would serve the entire insurance industry. The index would help customers anticipate trends in the insurance market and accurately determine product prices. It would also help individual company players plan their own business strategies and anticipate volatile insurance pricing cycles.

The Market Watch project was managed in an effective and efficient way; it was completed on time and has created substantial value for the company and its customers. A retrospective analysis of project activities suggests that management had a clear vision of the business model and clearly identified the product's competitive advantage. It was also fully aware of the best timing for product introduction as well as the associated risks and benefits.

Although the company had a previous, much simpler product, it concluded that the new system would be treated as a breakthrough product, because customers and suppliers had never used a similar large-scale monitoring approach. The system involved integrating several components: an existing database, a cumulative flow of industry data, an analysis module that combined past and present data, and an output report that was shared with member companies. However, in terms of technology, the project was designed to be less risky; most of the development tools were already available, and only a few software modules needed some development work (see figure 8-3).

The major risk, therefore, involved the product's novelty. To cope with this novelty, the team used a new approach to product development, coining it "the development highway." It was defined as a new business process that forced the creation of partnerships and accountability by IT, marketing, product development, and relevant business functions responsible for the project. The project's core multidisciplinary team was required to proceed through a series of tollgates, which were structured as status review sessions. These sessions were conducted with a senior management steering committee as well as a group of technical experts and potential customers.

FIGURE 8-3

Market Watch project

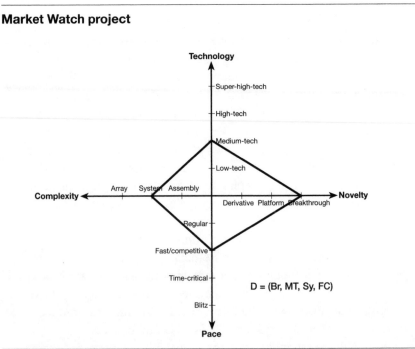

$$D = (Br, MT, Sy, FC)$$

Because this product was the first of its kind, the company hesitated to set the final requirements up front. Rather, it treated its customers as market research consultants. Managers assumed that it would be better to get an initial, immature version of the product into customer hands and then use their feedback to drive subsequent development. In this way the product gradually evolved to its full potential, while generating revenue as it progressed.

In retrospect, the company used the right approach. Developing early prototypes and testing them with customers as soon as possible was one of the keys to success. Similarly, a "keep it simple" approach and continuous monitoring by management and technical experts were also critical. The project would not have been finished in a timely fashion if the company had not employed its "development highway" process. As the company's CEO summarized the experience, "We would have never had all our ducks in a row if we didn't adhere to this new structure."

The Different Types of Innovation

The innovation research literature is perhaps more developed than the project management literature. The first landmark study, by Burns and Stalker in 1961, suggested what became a classical distinction between incremental (evolutionary) and radical (revolutionary) innovation, and between organic and mechanistic organizations.[6] Later studies have mentioned the idea of system innovation or have suggested further distinctions, such as architectural versus modular, and sustaining versus disruptive, innovation.[7]

Almost all writers agree that different types of innovation require different organizational practices and processes.[8] But in a somewhat paradoxical way, the question of how to actually adapt the organization's work to different types of innovation remained unresolved. Perhaps the answer may be easier now that we have a disciplined model for distinguishing among projects. The rules established in chapters 4 through 7 can now serve us as we look at various types of innovation. The idea is that most innovation types can simply be mapped into the dimensions of the NTCP model, making it clearer how to manage them in the most effective and efficient way.

From Innovation to Project Types

The most commonly mentioned distinction between incremental and radical innovation does not typically specify where the change is. It might be a radical or incremental change in the market (or product use), in the technology (aimed at a similar use), or both.[9] Similarly, a modular change in a product suggests that the product's basic structure (or architecture) remains unchanged but some modules are replaced by new ones, whereas an architectural change requires a new design of the entire system structure.[10] Each of these changes requires its own type of project with its own levels of novelty, technology, complexity, and pace.

The extent of market change can be addressed by projects of various novelty levels. Incremental market innovation is either a derivative or a platform project, and radical innovation is a breakthrough project. Similarly, an incremental change in technology is addressed by a low-tech or medium-tech project, and a radical change by a high-tech or super-high-tech project (see figure 8-4).

Less straightforward is the distinction made by Henderson and Clark between modular and architectural innovations.[11] Studying the photo-

FIGURE 8-4

Innovation categories and project types

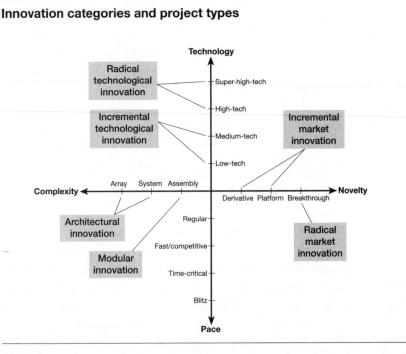

lithographic industry, they observed that companies succeed better with modular change when they use the preceding generation's modules to create a new product in a similar structure to the old one. They have difficulty, however, in coping with architectural innovation when a new order of modules is needed in a new architecture. If we apply the diamond model, we can see that the difficulties of architectural innovation are those of projects whose levels of complexity are of the system and array types (see figure 8-4). A modular change is a change in assemblies, whereas an architectural change requires the system approach (as we explained in detail in chapter 6).

A Project Management Perspective on the Innovator's Dilemma

Clayton Christensen has offered a rigorous theory of *disruptive* and *sustaining* innovation, showing that good companies may still fail when faced with the *innovator's dilemma.*[12] According to this theory, sustaining technologies (which can be incremental or radical) improve product performance along the dimensions that customers have learned to expect and demand. Disruptive technologies, in contrast, may initially offer lower performance than existing sustaining technologies, but their performance improves at a higher rate than customers expect. Because these technologies are underperforming, they are often ignored by major corporations that see no immediate match with their existing high-volume markets. With time, however, these technologies outperform sustaining technologies in performance and price, causing small, young entrants to take over business from the big players.

Among Christensen's cases are Digital Equipment Corporation's failure to acknowledge the disruption of desktop computers into its minicomputer business; Sears, which failed to join the trend of discount retailing and home centers; and Western Union, which turned down Alexander Graham Bell's offer to acquire the patents to telephony. According to Christensen, most companies with a well-established practice of listening to their customers are rarely able to build a case for investing in disruptive technologies until it is too late. That is the innovator's dilemma.

A classic failure to address the innovator's dilemma was Motorola's slow move from analog to digital technology in cell phones. As the Gartner Group reported, Motorola, the world leader in cellular phone technology, lost that position in the late 1990s when the new technology was still young and underperforming. Its choice to invest heavily in better analog phones opened an opportunity for European and Asian companies to beat the leader at its own game.[13]

Our model provides a project management perspective to the innovator's dilemma. Figure 8-5 illustrates the disruptive model of project management. As Christensen wrote, disruptive technology should be framed as a marketing challenge and not a technological one. Thus, the relevant dimension to explain the dilemma is novelty and not technology. Companies that listen to their customers according to the sustaining path will typically create new products based on a platform project model. By nature, such projects are initiated after extensive market studies, which determine the expectations customers have for the next generation of products.

Disruptive progress should be addressed, however, by a different project type. As the theory suggests, existing customers will never tell companies to offer products based on disruptive technologies. They either do not know these technologies exist, or they regard them as inferior. The right approach is the breakthrough novelty model. As described in chapter 4, breakthrough projects never rely on marketing studies; they are defined by managerial intuition and refined by rapid customer feedback from early prototypes. Furthermore, customers need to be educated about the value and use of the new disruptive product before they can fully appreciate its benefit.

FIGURE 8-5

The innovator's dilemma and project management

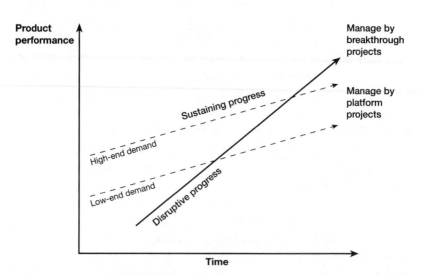

Source: Adapted from Clayton M. Christensen, *The Innovator's Dilemma* (Boston: Harvard Business School Press, 1997).

Big companies must make an effort to learn the difference between platform and breakthrough projects. They should realize that in addition to their large investments in sustaining technologies, they need a few breakthrough initiatives, which should be kept separate from the major sustaining efforts. These initiatives specialize in managing projects in a different way: less certainty in goal definition, no availability of market data, and no detailed business plans as a condition for project approval. Potentially, some of these initiatives will bear fruit and may help corporations ride the disruptive trend instead of leaving the field to agile newcomers.

The following case demonstrates, once again, that a leading company can fail in exploiting a disruptive technology that may be growing, unnoticed by management, in its own backyard.

The Invention of Flash Memory

Flash memory was one of the fastest-growing digital storage technologies in the early 2000s.[14] It enabled the retention of large batches of information on a small memory device when the power was turned off. It is a common myth that flash memory was invented by Intel in 1988 and followed up by Samsung and Toshiba in 1989. The truth is that flash memory was first invented at Toshiba in the early 1980s by a young engineer named Fujio Masuoka. Toshiba's executives, however, did not pursue this technology, failing to appreciate its disruptive nature.

What inspired Masuoka was one of the biggest challenges facing the industry in the 1970s: finding a way to retain memory so that data didn't vanish every time the power was turned off. Masuoka's insight was that information needed to be stored in big batches for a very short time rather than being stored in single bits for long periods. This was breakthrough thinking in the industry. Although the solution was much simpler and more compact in design than previous storage techniques, it required extensive further development to make the technology commercially available.

Masuoka introduced the first flash memory in 1984 at the annual International Electronics Developers meeting in San Jose, California. His managers were surprised when a number of U.S. companies, including Intel, asked for samples.

Appreciating the potential, Intel immediately put more than three hundred engineers to work on flash memory. Meanwhile, at Toshiba, Masuoka was given five people on a part-time basis to help him pursue his ideas, while the team's major effort was focused on the company's cash cow DRAM products. Although Masuoka's group was first in the market with a flash memory product (to be used in cars), it was not long before Intel dominated the market. Flash memory became Intel's number 2 product line after microprocessors.

Once again, understanding the uniqueness of breakthrough projects and the need to separate them from the major sustaining effort was the key to Intel's success and Toshiba's failure.

Product Innovation and Customers' Adoption Cycle

Geoffrey Moore, in his book *Crossing the Chasm,* has suggested a practical approach to the introduction of innovations in the market.[15] His framework is based on Everett Rogers's segmentation of customers based on their patterns of product adoption.[16] Rogers's adoption cycle is composed of five phases; in each one, customers have different characteristics and behave in different ways:

- **Innovators.** The customers of the first phase are usually called the *innovators,* or "techies." They persue novel products aggressively, sometimes seeking them even before a formal marketing program has been launched. This is a small but important group, because companies can learn a lot from these few innovators in any market segment.

- **Early adopters.** The customers of the scond phase are the *early adopters,* or visionaries. Like innovators, they buy new products early in their life cycle. Unlike the innovators, however, early adopters are not techies but rather are people who appreciate the benefits of the new product and the potential impact on their daily lives. Early adopters do not rely on well-established references and therefore are key to opening new market segments.

- **Early majority.** The third phase of customers are the *early majority,* who represent the biggest leap. These customers can relate to technology but ultimately are driven by a strong sense of practicality. They typically wait and see how other people are making out before making a buying decision. The market share of the early majority is estimated to be one-third of the entire market segment.

- **Late majority.** The *late majority* are the customers who come after the early majority and share similar concerns. In contrast to the early majority, they don't feel comfortable with their ability to use technology. As a result they wait until the new product has become a standard, produced by well-known companies that can provide the required service and support. The market share of the late majority is comparable to the share of the early majority. Together, these two groups make up about two-thirds of the market segment.

- **Laggards.** The last type of customers are called the *laggards;* they don't want anything to do with new, sophisticated products. They buy them only when they are forced to or when the product is part of another product. Laggards are generally regarded as a nonissue when a target audience is pursued.

Moore discussed the gaps and barriers that companies must cross to move from one group of customers to the next. The major gap is between the early adopters and the early majority, which Moore calls "the chasm." When companies are successful in crossing the chasm, they are on the road from a marginal to a mainstream product and to extensive growth and product profitablity (see figure 8-6).

Crossing the Chasm and Project Management

Moore's work uses the term "high-tech" products. In our context, however, they should be seen as new-to-the-world, or breakthrough, products. Although new-to-the-world products can be based on new technology, they can also involve a new idea based on a well-known technology. Rogers and Moore's adoption cycle is thus based on the newness of products to customers and can be addressed along the novelty dimension rather than the technology dimension. Other dimensions, however, also may be relevant (see figure 8-6).

New-to-the-world products are created by breakthrough projects. They can be adopted only by innovators and early adopters. In these innovative efforts, companies need to convince nonuser customers that there is a real opportunity to significantly improve the way they are doing business or managing their daily lives.

The most serious challenge, however, lies in crossing the chasm and capturing the early majority market. From a project management perspective,

FIGURE 8-6

The evolution of project types along the product life cycle

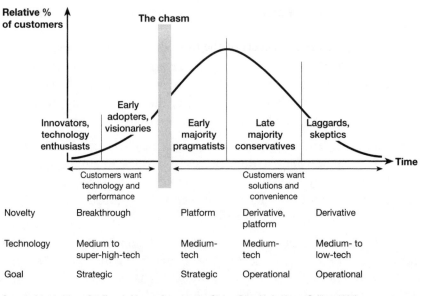

Source: Adapted from Geoffrey A. Moore, *Crossing the Chasm* (New York: HarperCollins, 1991).

this requires a change in novelty level from breakthrough to platform. Products aimed at the early majority must overcome problems associated with the first generation and must prove to be practical and economically viable to large groups of customers. To reduce production costs and support adaptation of the product to specific niches, teams should design the basic platform to allow further improvements and modifications for the late majority market, as well as easy upgrades in future incremental projects.

But crossing the chasm and moving from one customer group to the other not only affects project novelty levels but may also affect the three other dimensions of project management. Management, therefore, not only must understand the impact on customers and markets but also must know how to adopt the most suitable project management approach for each phase of the adoption cycle. This is demonstrated in the following example, which describes the evolution of the microwave oven.

The microwave oven, which has significantly changed our home habits, was not a planned innovation but a fortunate coincidence.[17] Its history is described in the following story, which was prepared by Brian Sauser.

The History of the Microwave Oven

During World War II, Raytheon Company became the major supplier of magnetron vacuum tubes, which were used by Britain in its shortwave and microwave radars for early detection of enemy aircraft. Raytheon's top expert of the tube was Dr. Percy Spencer.[18] In 1946 he became by accident the first inventor of the microwave oven. One day he was standing near a tube when he discovered that a chocolate bar in his pocket had melted due to the unknown food-heating property of microwave power. He immediately filed a patent, which marked the birth of the microwave oven (figure 8-7).

The evolution of this innovation can be seen as an ongoing, changing pattern of different project management styles described by different diamonds (see figure 8-8). For each step, the solid lines describe the current diamond, and the dotted lines represent (for comparison) the preceding step.

FIGURE 8-7

Original microwave oven patent

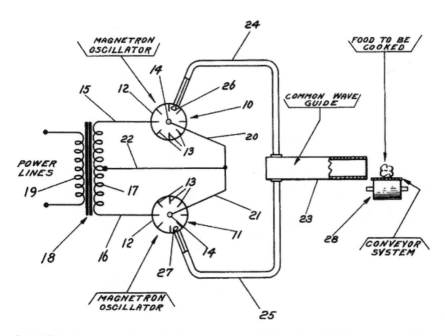

Source: Original microwave oven patent by Dr. Percy L. Spencer, US Patent No. 02495429, filed Jan. 24, 1950.

FIGURE 8-8

Evolution of the microwave oven

Step 1: The discovery—1946
D = (Br, SHT, As, Re)

During testing of the magnetron, after discovering that a candy bar had melted in his pocket, Dr. Percy Spencer confirmed his discovery by placing popcorn kernels near the tube and watching them pop. He quickly designed a metal box with an opening into which he fed microwave power to confirm that microwaves could cook food faster than conventional ovens.

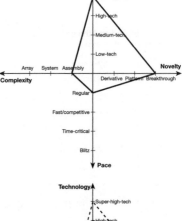

Step 2: The first oven—1946 to 1947
D = (Br, HT, Sy, Re)

Spencer realized the great potential for using microwave energy in the commercial cooking market. He put together a team of engineers at Raytheon to develop and refine his discovery for practical use. The team quickly fabricated what would be the first microwave oven, and Raytheon filed a patent proposing the microwave's use for cooking. In 1947, Raytheon produced for the first commercial microwave oven, standing 5 1/2 feet tall, weighing over 750 lbs., and costing $5,000. Raytheon believed that the most potential for their invention was in the commercial restaurant industry and introduced their first oven in a Boston restaurant for testing.

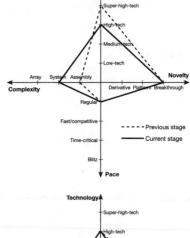

Step 3: The next generation—1947
D = (Pl, HT, Sy, FC)

Consumers were highly resistant to the first microwave oven units, and initial sales were disappointing. Further improvements and refinements produced a more reliable and lightweight oven that was less expensive.

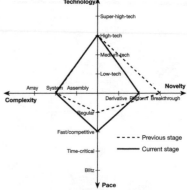

FIGURE 8-8 (continued)

Evolution of the microwave oven

Step 4: Commercial success—1948 to 1952
D = (Pl, HT, As, FC)

As the restaurant food industry discovered the oven, demand exploded and the microwave oven became a necessity in this commercial market. It also spawned new uses and versatility for the oven in the commercial market, such as drying cork, ceramics, paper, flowers, and more.

Step 5: Consumer breakthrough—1952
D = (Br, HT, As, FC)

During the period 1952–1955 Tappan Industries introduced the first home model at a cost of $1,295. Even with its commercial success in the restaurant industry, the microwave oven was now moving into a different market, where customers were not previously exposed to the new device. That moved the project back to the breakthrough level.

Step 6: Consumer acceptance—1965
Crossing the chasm
D = (Pl, MT, As, FC)

In 1965, Raytheon acquired Amana Refrigerator, and two years later introduced the first countertop oven. It was a 100-volt microwave oven that cost less than $500 and was small, safer than its predecessors, and more reliable.

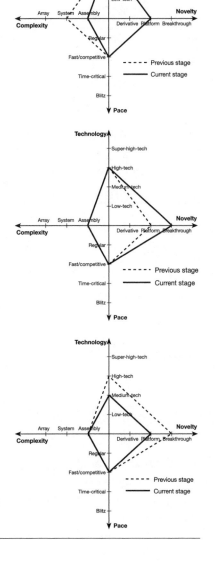

FIGURE 8-8 *(continued)*

Evolution of the microwave oven

Step 7: Consumer success—1975
D = (De, MT, As, FC)

By 1975, sales of microwave ovens, for the first time, exceeded those of gas ranges, and in 1976, the microwave oven became a commonly owned kitchen appliance, reaching nearly 60% of U.S. households. This step required a major shift in project work. It was no longer an exotic product. Mass production and low cost became increasingly important, and efficient manufacturing was the key to continued product success.

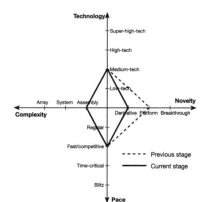

Step 8: Today—the rest is history
D = (De, LT, As, FC)

Once considered a luxury, the microwave oven has become a practical necessity. An expanding market has demanded ovens to suit every taste, size, shape, and kitchen. At this stage product development is no more than a derivative, low-tech, assembly, and fast/competitive project.

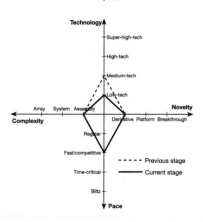

Source: Facts of the history of the microwave oven were acquired from C. J. Gallawa, *The Complete Microwave Oven Service Handbook* (New York: Prentice Hall, 1989).

The major change occurred between 1965 and 1975, when this innovation crossed the chasm and became an affordable home appliance. The projects that built the product changed from breakthrough to platform and later to derivative. With prices falling and performance improving, the once unimaginable device became a commodity. Understanding this pattern may be critical to succeeding with any new innovation.

Now that we have explored the business and innovation contexts of project management, we turn in chapter 9 to the internal perspective of projects and examine how the adaptive approach can be applied to projects in any organization.

Key Points and Action Items

- Companies initiate projects for various reasons. Some projects create new businesses and markets; others deal with existing businesses or the organizational infrastructure. To select projects, you can divide prospective projects into those that entail strategic versus operational business goals, and into those that will serve external or internal customers. Company resources are allocated to each group according to the firm's strategy and current policy.

- All project proposals are then mapped into separate cells in a simple 2×2 matrix, and the selection and competition is limited to projects in the same group. You select projects within each group based on the criteria of benefits and opportunities versus risk and difficulty.

- The innovation literature distinguishes among types of innovation but has not offered ideas on how to actually manage those innovations. The NTCP model provides guidelines for managing different innovation types in different ways.

- Innovation can be radical or incremental in either the market or the technology. The management of these innovations can be distinguished through the novelty and technology dimensions of the NTCP model. Modular or architectural innovation can be distinguished through the complexity dimension.

- The innovator's dilemma presents a risk for companies: to follow customer demand based on sustaining progress may cause you to miss the opportunities presented by fast, disruptive change. The project management solution to the innovator's dilemma is to learn the distinction between breakthrough and platform projects. While investing in sustaining large businesses, which are handled by platform or derivative projects, companies must initiate a few breakthrough projects that are managed separately according to different rules, thereby addressing the potential opportunities of disruptive change.

- Rogers and Moore distinguished between five groups of customers according to their patterns of new product adoption: innovators, early adopters, early majority, late majority, and laggards. The greatest opportunity to capture a market is by learning how to cross the chasm between the early adopters and the early majority. Crossing the chasm requires a drastic change in project management styles from breakthrough to platform projects. As innovations mature, they require a change in project management. The project diamond becomes smaller and less risky when a product moves from introduction to maturity.

❖ 9 ❖

MANAGING PROJECTS WITHIN THE EXISTING ORGANIZATION

H OW CAN ORGANIZATIONS integrate the adaptive and flexible approach into their traditional, well-established project management practices? Fortunately, this is not very difficult. As we show here, once managers understand and accept the adaptive concept, they will find it relatively easy to add several new steps and activities to the conventional practices and integrate the lessons of this book into corporate project planning and execution. For many practitioners, it may not feel completely new. In their struggle to keep their projects in good shape, many project managers are implicitly using similar ideas, although not always in a formal way that is offered by the discipline. With this chapter we hope to help organizations and managers explicitly formalize the adaptive approach in a rigorous way.

We begin by outlining the steps and activities that managers need to add to their current practices, and later we discuss the impact of the adaptive approach on project planning, managing project uncertainty, risk management, and how to improve project efficiencies through common building blocks and selective outsourcing.

Building on Classic Project Phases and Activities

The classic linear model of project progress includes four phases: definition, planning, execution, and termination.[1] Because one size does not fit all, it would be impossible to describe all variations that project phases can take. We therefore use the most basic description of phases as a template to illustrate the additions and changes teams need to make in the traditional approach to lead their project in a more adaptive and flexible way.

Most literature describes these phases as sequential, but in reality, no project's phases are performed in a purely linear process. In the real world, project activities reiterate between phases, and often you need to go back to a previous phase to repeat or correct an earlier activity or decision. In its simplest form, this reality is illustrated in figure 9-1.

The adaptive approach requires adding a few new activities to the main activities typically performed in each step, as well as modifying others. Table 9-1 lists typical activities, both traditional and new. The new activities are shown in boldface. We describe these activities in more detail in the sections that follow. Note, however, that in addition to the new activities, the adaptive approach affects almost all project activities and decisions, as you will see later.

Identify Your Project's Type

At this point in the book, you should easily be able to identify your project type. Project novelty is derivative, platform, or breakthrough, based on the newness of the product to its users and customers and the certainty with which the requirements can be determined. It is low-tech, medium-tech, high-tech, or super-high-tech, based on how much new technology is needed to create or manufacture the product. It is an assembly, system, or array project, based on the hierarchy of systems and subsystems of the project's product and the complexity of the organization needed to build it. And its pace is regular, fast/competitive, time-critical, or blitz, based on the time available to complete the project.

In addition to the NTCP dimensions, you may need to classify the project on other relevant dimensions. For example, you can identify a project as strategic if it deals with new business, or as operational if it

FIGURE 9-1

Classical project phases modified to an adaptive iterative approach

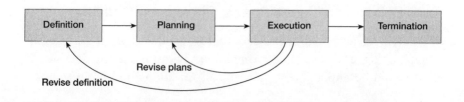

TABLE 9-1

Typical project activities across project phases

Phase	Activity	Details
Definition	Market definition	Market/customer identification
		Customer need
	Business objective	Define the expected business objective that will be achieved when the project is completed
	Product definition	Product description
		Product requirements
	Project definition	Statement of work (scope)
		Approximate duration
		Approximate budget
		Project manager and team
	Identifying project type	**Categorize a project based on strategic or operational business goal, internal or external user, novelty, technology, complexity, pace, and other relevant dimensions**
	Success and failure criteria	**Define management's expectation on five or more relevant success dimensions, and define what can go wrong**
Planning	**Impact of project type on project management**	**Decide how each project category will affect project organization, processes, plans, activities, and team**
	Requirements management plan	**Estimate uncertainty in initial requirements**
		Market data collection
		Number of market prototypes
		Timing of requirements freeze
	Product creation plan	Initial technical specifications
		Initial product design
		Number of design cycles
		Timing of design freeze
		Product testing plan
	WBS	Break scope into detailed work packages and activities
	Communication	Reporting structure and meeting schedule
		Means and technology of communication—local, global
	Organization	Project team structure
		Organizational responsibility matrix (who does what)
	Project process plan	Major phases, gates, and milestones
	Schedule	Detailed network and timing of activities
	Budget	Detailed cost of project based on cost of WBS items
	Risk management	**Risk identification and mitigation plan based on project type**
	Integration plan	Timing and duration of integration activities
	Procurement	Subcontracting and vendor management plan
	Quality	Quality management plan
	Human resources	Team development and training
		Team motivation activities
	Project monitoring plan	Project reviews, plans, and decisions needed at gates
Execution	Product requirements	**Refine product requirements**
		Freeze product requirements
	Product building	Product design
		Prototype building and testing
		Additional design cycles (redesign, rebuild, retest)
		Freeze product specifications and design
		Product building
		Product testing
	Project monitoring	Progress and status of budget, time, and activities performed
	Project replanning	**Update plans and make changes**
Termination	Customer preparedness	Documentation
		Training materials and means
		Simulation of product use
	Commercialization	Product introduction plan
		Product assimilation
		Product distribution
	Project wrap-up	Project summary report
		Lessons learned report
		Next generation planning

deals with existing business; you also can classify it as external or internal according to the expected user, customer, or buyer. And often, as we've mentioned, companies use a categorization that is specific to their environment or industry.[2]

Define Project Success and Failure Criteria

Similarly, managers and project teams determine how to evaluate the project's success based on several dimensions: efficiency (time and budget goals), impact on the customer, impact on the team, business success results, and preparation for the future. In addition to these five general dimensions, you could define dimensions specific to your project, such as approval by regulatory agencies.

The specific expectations for each dimension will depend on the specific project type. For example, the expected business results will be greatly affected by the product's novelty. These results can be defined in general terms of market share or profit, or in a detailed plan of future sales. The greater the novelty, the less detailed and less specific the plan can be.

Planning for success also involves preparing for the possibility of failure. You therefore need to assess what can go wrong with the project and include it in your plan along with the success criteria. The possibility of failure (or what can go wrong) will serve as a basis for the detailed risk management plan, which we discuss later in the chapter.

Determine the Impact of Project Type on Your Project Management Style

After you have classified the project and determined how to evaluate the project's success, the most significant next step is to determine the impact of each specific project type on project management. Table 9-2 shows a simple way to assess this factor. Figure 9-2 shows the major changes in project management along the dimensions of the NTCP diamond. In what follows, we describe in more detail the activities and processes that characterize the adaptive approach beyond the traditional project management steps.

Managing Your Project's Uncertainties

As we've stressed throughout this book, the adaptive approach to project management differs from the conventional model in its basic assumptions. Instead of seeing a project as a linear, predictable process of sequential

TABLE 9-2

The impact of project type on project management

Project dimension	Project type	Managerial decisions and main concerns	Specific cases
Business goal	Strategic, operational	Level of top management involvement; resource allocation; organizational structure	Strategic projects often require a separate organization (i.e., the skunk works concept)
Customer	Internal, external	Customer involvement; degree of formality; type of contract	No formal contract is signed for internal projects
Market	Consumer, industrial, public/ government	Customer involvement; methods for collecting customer requirements and needs; type of contract	Often difficult to collect and understand consumer needs
Novelty	Derivative, platform, breakthrough	Duration of definition phase; number of requirements iterations; timing of requirements freeze; need for product prototypes for market testing; marketing methods; risk management	Breakthrough projects require fast prototyping before requirements freeze and innovative approaches for introducing the product to the market; they may also require an organization separate from the company's mainstream activities
Technology	Low-tech, medium-tech, high-tech, super-high-tech	Number of design cycles; time of design freeze; extent of risk management; number and type of prototypes; type of contract; technical skills of project manager and team members	In high- and super-high-tech projects consider switching from cost-plus contracts to fixed-price contracts after design freeze; super-high-tech projects must have small-scale prototypes
Complexity	Assembly, system, array	Level of formality; type of reporting and communication; extent of systems engineering and integration; use of subcontractors; organizational structure; co-location vs. decentralization; risk management	System projects require systems engineering and long periods of integration
Pace	Regular, fast/competitive, time-critical, blitz	Autonomy of project teams; frequency of monitoring and control; contingency plans; improvisation	In time-critical projects, use proven technologies whenever possible and focus on the specific date; blitz projects require full autonomy of team for immediate decisions and considerable amount of improvisation

steps that can be determined with a high level of certainty at project initiation, the adaptive approach perceives a project as an unpredictable, nonlinear, and iterative process. Many things are still unknown during project launch; initial assumptions are highly uncertain, and many early decisions will most likely change as the project progresses.

FIGURE 9-2

The impact of the NTCP dimensions on project management

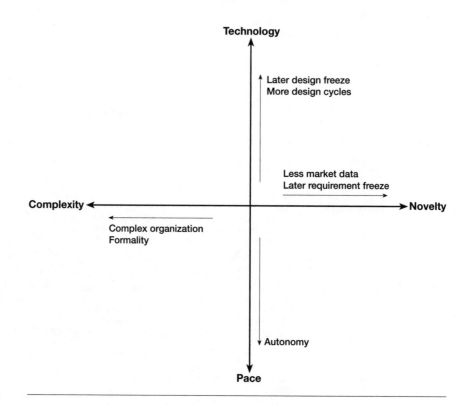

Adaptive project management focuses on resolving project uncertainties and making the necessary changes as the project progresses. Accepting this reality is one of the most important lessons executives and managers need to learn in their quest for better project management. In this section we deal with the management of project uncertainties: how to distinguish among them, how to define them up front, and, perhaps more importantly, how to control and reduce them during project execution. The premise is that it is the responsibility of the project manager to control project uncertainties throughout the project until they are reduced to zero.

Market and Technological Uncertainty

Alex Laufer conceptualized a project as a process whose goal is to reduce uncertainty.[3] He discussed two types of uncertainty: "what" uncertainty and "how" uncertainty. In our context these uncertainties correspond to the uncertainty of product requirements, which depend on market uncertainty (or novelty), and the uncertainty of the technical specifications and the final design, which depend on technological uncertainty. Although projects may face additional types of uncertainty, these are the two most common uncertainties in many projects.

Freeze Requirements and Design at the Right Moment

In an ideal world, you would expect to resolve the "what" uncertainty first—namely, by first determining what your product and market are all about—and then resolve the "how" uncertainty, namely, how to build your product. In reality, however, no project can completely freeze the final requirements and then start working on product design.

To some degree all projects make changes in product requirements after the work has begun. The greatest number of changes occur in those projects that have the highest novelty to begin with. So in the real world you resolve these uncertainties simultaneously, until the final requirements are frozen and the design completed (see figure 9-3). Note that the axes in figure 9-3 are drawn outward in the same directions as the novelty and technology axes in the NTCP model. And because uncertainties decrease during project execution, the arrow representing the project's progress moves downward toward zero uncertainty on both dimensions.

FIGURE 9-3

Reducing requirements and design uncertainty

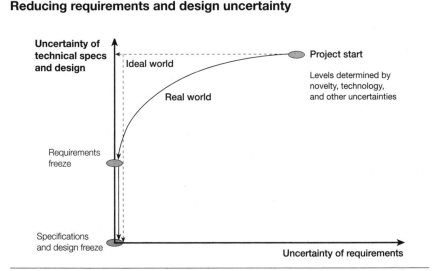

Define Requirements and Design Cycles

Once you have grasped the idea that project managers need to manage their projects' uncertainties, you need to see how it is done in practice. As mentioned, novelty or market uncertainty determine how well you can define your product requirements up front. The greater the novelty, the fuzzier the initial requirements. You can reduce this uncertainty by obtaining data from markets and customers, by testing the product's prototype on real customers, or both. You may often need several iterations (cycles) of this process until final requirements can be frozen. As described in chapter 4, the number of cycles and the time to requirements freeze increase with the initial market uncertainty (or novelty).

Similarly, the initial technological uncertainty determines how well you can define the product's technical specifications and design. You can reduce this uncertainty by conducting several design, build, and test cycles (design cycles). You update the specifications and modify the design after each cycle until the final design is frozen. As described in chapter 5, the number of design cycles and the time to design freeze increase with the level of technological uncertainty.

This dual iterative process, which is illustrated in figure 9-4, continues for both uncertainties until the final decisions about the product and its design are made. Since correctly defining this process is one of the most important elements in the adaptive approach, it must be included in project planning, as we discuss later. It is also important to note that once the requirements and technical specifications have been frozen, unless no major surprises occur, the project can continue from that moment on according to the traditional approach (figure 9-4). From there you should attempt to complete the product in the most efficient way by focusing the project on its updated triple constraint.

Typically, once the requirements and design are frozen, you don't expect any changes. Circumstances, however, may require that in rare cases you will need to introduce changes in these parameters even after the freezing point. However, this should be seen as an exception, rather than the norm. Normally, you should resist any temptation to make changes after the freeze, even if they improve the end result. The rule should be that changes are allowed only if preventing them means project failure. Such situations might involve identifying a safety problem, a serious error, or an external event that could endanger the project's success. Using a rigid attitude and a bureaucratic approval process, modifications or improvements should not be permitted at this time; otherwise your project may keep dragging on indefinitely.

FIGURE 9-4

Iterative process of requirements and design freeze

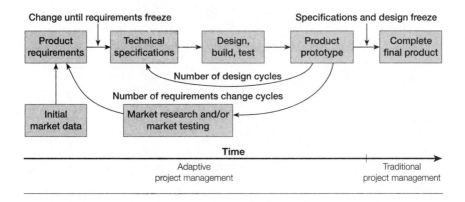

At each major milestone or after each cycle, the requirements and design uncertainties are reassessed, and, if needed, the project plan is updated to reflect the residual uncertainties along the two dimensions. The process of learning customer needs and acquiring the required technological capabilities gradually turns projects with high uncertainties into projects with lower uncertainty levels.

Although you classify the project at project initiation, with time its reduced levels of uncertainty may become similar to the uncertainty of projects having lower initial levels. Here again, the diamond's N and T dimensions can serve as a reference. For example, the technological uncertainty of a super-high-tech project becomes equivalent to the uncertainty of a high-tech project once the formerly nonexistent technologies have been developed and selected.

Use Prototypes, Small Pilot Projects, and Contingencies

A common way to deal with project uncertainties is to build fast and sometimes small-scale prototypes. A prototype is an initial version of the project's product, typically having reduced features and performance. The goal of making a prototype is to test your preliminary assumptions and obtain information that will help later when you define and build the final full-scale product. Prototypes let you do things quickly and test them as you go, rather than spend months writing requirements and specifications (which will change anyway). You can use prototypes to identify and fix bugs early rather than carry the problems to the full-scale product, where getting rid of them is difficult and costly.

You may also need to try a pilot program before making the commitment to the main effort. A small-scale pilot project can be seen as a "whole project prototype," and it serves the same objectives. A pilot program lets you define the full-scale project in terms of objectives, requirements, and your ability to make a more accurate estimate of the resources and the time needed for the full project. Josh Weston, former CEO of ADP Corporation, uses the phrase "Pilot before you pile it" to express the value of pilot programs. According to Weston, it is often better to "overspend" up front on piloting with quick, small implementations to save later resources and avoid mistakes and misunderstanding.[4]

Prototypes and pilots are helpful when projects face high levels of uncertainty, but they are not needed in more certain situations. It all depends on the project type. For example, low-tech construction projects can be designed and built based on blueprints and engineering designs. In contrast, super-high-tech projects may require that you build multiple prototypes before you select the final technologies and finalize the end product. The specific levels of project technology and novelty determine how much prototyping and piloting is needed. The use of computers and software enables companies to reduce the number of actual prototypes by creating virtual prototypes and evaluating alternatives before they build an actual model. Nevertheless, a real prototype is often needed before final requirements are frozen.

Finally, because projects are uncertain and risky endeavors, it is often difficult to predict up front the exact level of resources and time you will need to complete a project. You should therefore allocate a contingent resource reserve in your budget and schedule, to be used in case all planned resources are consumed before the project is completed or when unexpected difficulties are encountered.[5] The exact level of these contingencies depends, again, on a project's initial level of uncertainty. In the next section, we indicate the typical contingency for different levels of uncertainty.

Integrate Uncertainty into Management Activities

Managing project uncertainties is one of the most important and critical factors for successful completion. A careful assessment of project uncertainty at the outset and a deliberate selection of the activities needed will ensure that project uncertainties are kept under control until the final result is achieved. Using the novelty and technology dimensions of the NTCP model in a combined way, we can define four levels of initial project uncertainty: low (level 1), medium (level 2), high (level 3), and super-high (level 4). Table 9-3 shows the levels of project uncertainty for different levels of novelty and technology. The level of project uncertainty (U) is determined as the maximal value between novelty (N) and technology (T), and expressed by the relationship

$$U = \text{Max } (N, T)$$

As we have discussed, uncertainty affects the number of iterations required during project execution and the number of prototypes needed before requirements and design can be frozen. Table 9-3 also shows the impact of initial project uncertainty on planning and its relevant variables, such as the number of iterations, the number of prototypes, and the typical contingency reserve, that are needed for each level of uncertainty. As you will see shortly, these as well as other activities of the adaptive approach have a significant impact on project planning.

Managing Your Project Risk

Because each project is unique and is being done for the first time, it involves a certain degree of risk. Please note that although risk and uncertainty are related, they are not the same thing. Uncertainty is the unknown, whereas risk is what can go wrong. Clearly, a great deal of project risk depends on uncertainty, but there are other factors contributing to a project's risk, among them complexity, time pressure, shortage of resources, and inadequate skills.

The project management literature has devoted a great deal of writing to project risk and risk management.[6] The diamond model provides a help-

TABLE 9-3

Combined project uncertainty and its impact

Uncertainty level	Quantitative level	Novelty	Technology	Number of iterations	Number of prototypes	Time and budget reserve levels
Low	1	Derivative	Low-Tech	Few (1–2)	None	5%
Medium	2	Platform	Medium-Tech	Several (2–3)	Few (1–2)	5%–10%
High	3	Breakthrough	High-Tech	Many (3–4)	Many (3–4)	10%–25%
Super-High	4	—	Super-High-Tech	Multiple (n + 3)	Multiple (n + 3)	25%–50%

n = the number of cycles and prototypes needed until the final technologies are selected

ful framework for assessing and determining project risk as a function of various dimensions. In what follows we offer a brief overview of project risk management and explain how it is affected by project type. We first review the common definitions and practices and then apply the diamond model for risk management.

What Is Project Risk?

Project risk is typically defined as an undesired event or condition that, if it occurs, has a negative effect on a project objective. A risk has a cause and, if the worst occurs, a consequence.[7] *Risk management* is defined as the systematic process of planning for, identifying, analyzing, responding to, and monitoring project risk. It involves processes, tools, and techniques that help project managers maximize the probability and consequences of positive events and minimize the probability and consequences of negative events.

According to the project management literature, risk management comprises five steps:

1. **Risk identification.** Prepare a project risk list.

2. **Qualitative risk analysis.** Create a prioritized list of risks. Typically, you classify risks as high, moderate, or low, or you assess the cost impact of the risk if it happens.

3. **Quantitative risk analysis.** Analyze the project's likelihood of achieving its objectives or the probabilities that the risks on the list will happen. Then calculate the expected cost of each risk by multiplying the expected cost by its probability of occurrence.

4. **Risk response planning.** Detail the ways you will mitigate the negative effects of project risks and their cost. Compare these costs to the expected cost of each risk and decide whether you will include each response in your project plan.

5. **Risk monitoring and control.** Develop work around plans. As you progress, take corrective actions and update the risk response plan.

Qualitative risk analysis assesses the importance of the identified risks and develops prioritized lists of risks for further analysis to determine how to reduce their potential impact. Sometimes experts from functional units are called upon to help in assessing the risks and their potential impact. Risk response planning focuses on the high-risk items evaluated in the risk analysis and assigns people to take responsibility for each risk response.

The traditional approach to risk management assigns a certain risk level (low, medium, or high) to a project *as a whole*, depending on the probable impact on the project goals (time, budget, and scope), without identifying the cause of the probable impact. Project teams usually identify project risks by using their own knowledge of and by consulting others. However, it has often been claimed that risk management techniques are mostly heuristic and do not provide a clear framework for identifying the levels of risk.[8]

Using the Diamond Model for Risk Management

The diamond model enables us now to offer a rigorous and quantitative approach to the assessment of project risk. It allows you to break the risk into separable and quantitative components rather than rely on simple heuristic and subjective assessments. Thus the diamond can help you isolate risk sources with greater resolution and focus your attention on the riskier dimensions to improve the chances of project success.

The novelty dimension corresponds to the risk associated with misunderstanding customers' needs and requirements. The technology dimension is related to implementation risks, especially the availability of the needed technologies to produce the end product. The complexity dimension refers to the risk associated with coordination of many components and the mutual effects among them. The pace dimension represents the risk involved in failing to meet your time goals or failing to resolve all potential problems because of the time constraint.

Let's look at a combined diamond model of project risk. As with uncertainty, the ascending levels on each dimension correspond to higher levels of risk; therefore, the larger the diamond, the greater the risk. Within the diamond, you can identify areas of lower or higher levels of risk based on project type in each dimension. For example, high-tech or array projects involve high risk because of technological uncertainty and complexity; similarly, breakthrough projects involve high risk because of market uncertainty. Figure 9-5 suggests areas of low, medium, high, and super-high levels of risk.[9]

We can also quantify the risk levels by simply assigning numerical values of risk to each project type on each dimension on a scale of 1 to 4.

With this representation, project planners can focus first on the highest level of risk and pay increased attention to mitigate it. For example, figure 9-5 shows the project profile of the Segway case, which we discussed in chapter 4. The diamond representation of this project is D = (Br, HT, Sy, FC), and its risk levels, R = (3, 3, 2, 2). We can see that this project penetrates the high-risk area along two dimensions: novelty and technology. Therefore, more management attention should be directed to these risk sources, and less to the complexity and pace dimensions.

FIGURE 9-5

Risk assessment

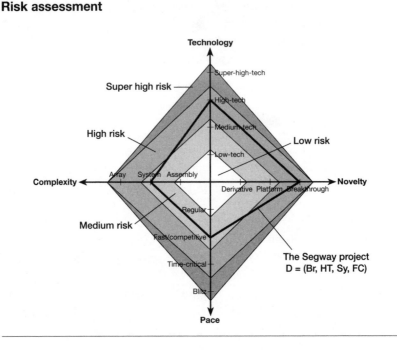

Once you have identified the risk levels on each dimension you can determine in more detail what can go wrong, its probability, and the cost or consequences. This analysis will guide you in making mitigation decisions for each undesirable event, as is common in the discipline.

But assessing the level of risk on each dimension may not be enough. It would be helpful to have a combined measure of project risk as a function of all dimensions. You could use this tool to assess overall project risk when you compare risk and benefits across projects in the organization or when you assign leaders to specific projects.

We therefore offer a simple formula as an example of how to determine this measure. It is based on the levels of the risk according to the diamond model, but with different weights for each dimension. The suggested formula is as follows:

$$R = a \times N + b \times T + c \times C + d \times P$$

The weights (a, b, c, d) are dependent on the specific context, industry, or organization. A typical value for these weights might be (0.2, 0.15, 0.5, 0.15), because the risk of novelty may be higher than that of technology or pace, and complexity is typically associated with expenses, whose implications may be greater in case of failure than all the other risks. Using this example, the combined risk of the Segway project is

$$R = (0.2 \times 3 + 0.15 \times 3 + 0.5 \times 2 + 0.15 \times 2) = 2.35$$

Based on this formula the combined risk measure of the Apollo mission (discussed in chapter 5) is 3.15, and that of the Walkman product (discussed in chapter 3) is 1.7.

Note that when using this formula, you may want to use different weights based on your particular situation and industry. Finally, in order to assess the cost of the project's risk, you need to multiply the risk level times the investment the company makes in the project. If I represents the investment level, the formula for the cost involved in a certain risk is

$$C_R = R \times I$$

Using an Adaptive Approach in Your Project Planning

Project planning typically includes preparing several plans, such as a work breakdown structure (WBS), schedule, budget, risk management plan, and so on. The classic approach is based on the belief that project teams should prepare detailed plans at project initiation and then stick to the plans as much as possible. As we mentioned in chapter 1, this "management as planned" concept focuses on the famous triple constraint. This mind-set is represented by the old saying, "Plan your work, and work your plan."

But real projects cannot always follow that belief. In the real world, you seldom find a project that sticks to its initial plan. Even in the most stable environments, such as construction or oil, projects undergo changes and the end result is never exactly as envisioned. Needless to say, in more dynamic environments, such as high technology or biotechnology, projects and their products are substantially different from what managers envision up front.

How many times have you seen a project team work hard during project initiation to prepare a detailed scheduling plan that spans the entire period of project execution? Such plans include every detail as accurately as possible and schedule each activity with an exact date for completion. Quite often on paper, these plans fill the walls of entire rooms, and to the outsider they look like an endless web of details. Unfortunately, this situation is too common, perhaps even imposed by customers of large projects who believe that detailed plans guarantee that things will go well.

Yet soon after the project has started, these plans become outdated. Things don't turn out the way planners expected them to, and to stay accurate, the plan must be updated almost every month. Real-world teams do not bother updating the plan on a monthly basis. Often, such "mega" plans remain monuments to the team's initial hard work while things move on without them. (You may often find such initial plans displayed on the walls to impress visitors who have no clue what is really going on.)

The adaptive, flexible approach presented in this book views projects as dynamic, unstable, and hard-to-predict processes. It assumes that changes *will* take place during project execution—changes in the environment, the business, the markets, technologies, and people. According to this approach, project plans must be adapted to changes that could not have been predicted at the outset. Thus, a project plan is not a fixed document that is prepared once for the entire project. Rather, project plans are dynamic, living entities that evolve as the project progresses and change when new information is revealed.

The solution is simple. Rather than "plan your work, and work your plan," you should follow a process more like "plan some of your work, work that plan, and then replan the next piece of your work, and so on." Rather than prepare detailed plans at the outset, you should plan only for those things that you are highly certain will not change. The idea is to replace the "management as planned" concept with "management as planned and replanned." You should see a project as a continuous process of action and reflection, followed by more action.

With this approach, you may not need to create a full-scale project plan at the outset. Instead, a short-term, less detailed plan often is all you need to launch a project. Imagine, for example, that you decide to do a small pilot project to test some unknown ideas. Obviously, there is no need to plan everything in advance. Once you work this short-term plan, you will know what you need to do next. Thus, the project can be subdivided into a sequence of short-term stages until the final product is completed. The results achieved in each stage will help you better define and plan the next stage. A structured way of doing this is called the "rolling wave of planning," as you will see next.

Implement the Rolling Wave of Planning

In *Simultaneous Management,* Alex Laufer has suggested using three hierarchical plans rather than one.[10] Each of the three plans has its own time horizon and its own degree of detail, and each serves a unique managerial level.

According to Laufer's definition, plans should "stand the test of time." Because you cannot predict with great accuracy every detail of the work years in advance, you should plan only those things that you know will not change. And you should continuously gather information that will prepare you for the next step of planning. Figure 9-6 shows the three levels of the rolling wave of project plans. The width of the shapes represents the amount of detail in the plans at each level and the length of their time horizon.

The plan shown at the top in figure 9-6 is the *master* plan—the highest-level plan. It spans the entire project life cycle and contains very little detail. It outlines only the major milestones, such as completion of major phases, important delivery dates, or the customer payments schedule. This plan allows top management to see the big picture. If things go well, the master plan will not change, and hopefully the project will end at the predicted time. But if things go wrong, you may need to update even the master plan.

The second plan is the *middle-level* plan. Its time horizon is usually four to six months. It is more detailed than the master plan, and it includes "medium-level" events that happen between major milestones, such as testing prototypes, issuing major purchase orders, and so on. This plan is directed to middle-level managers who oversee the project's effort together with other projects in the same department or business. A new version of this plan is built every few months to prepare for the next middle-level period of the project.

FIGURE 9-6

The "Rolling Wave" planning concept

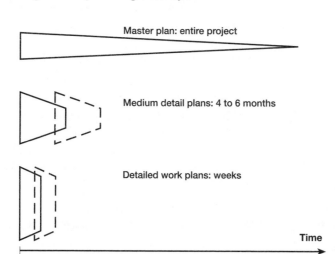

Master plan: entire project

Medium detail plans: 4 to 6 months

Detailed work plans: weeks

Time

The third plan is the *detailed work* plan. Its time horizon is only a few weeks, and it is used by the project team and individual members. This is the plan that outlines every activity that every person will do in the next few weeks, and it is prepared each month for the next short-term period.

Adapt Your Planning to Your Project Type

Traditional project management assumes that all project plans look pretty much the same. In reality, project plans differ, and different project types require different planning and different kinds of plans. Combining the rolling wave approach with the concepts of this book can help project teams adapt their planning to the project type and circumstances.

Each of the NTCP dimensions affects project planning in its own way. The specific project types are discussed in chapters 4 through 7. Here is a brief reminder of how project type affects project plans. For example, the complexity dimension may determine the number of planning levels and the degree of detail required. An assembly project typically requires only one or two levels of planning, whereas system and array projects typically require all three levels (or even more). In addition, with higher-complexity projects you need to put more effort into carefully organizing the teams and subcontractors; you must use much more documentation and software for configuration management, integration, system interfaces, and so on, and you must employ extensive means for monitoring the project to make sure things stay on track.

Pace, in contrast, affects the plan in those activities and decisions that have to do with timely completion of the project. Fast/competitive projects need extensive managerial focus on time to market, because delaying project launch may cause you to lose sales to faster competitors. Time-critical projects may need even tighter focus on time. In some cases these projects may have plenty of time before their deadline, but they cannot afford to miss it. For these projects, you should thus include in your plans frequent reviews with top management to make sure the deadline is met. Blitz projects seldom have the time to prepare detailed and accurate project plans. Contingency plans must be prepared in advance for every possible and imaginable situation, but as we know, crises typically do not behave according to plans. In these projects, traditional planning is replaced with improvisation, together with minimal planning conducted on the fly while crisis resolution activities are under way.

To complete the cycle we now return to the dimensions of novelty and technology, which have the main impact on project planning. As mentioned, uncertainty affects the number of iterations required during project execution, the possible planning horizons for the various project plans, the degree of detail in each plan, and the number of prototypes needed before requirements and design can be frozen.

If your project has a high degree of novelty, your master plan must cover repeated prototyping and must aim to set requirements freeze late, but also it must leave open many activities for the medium- and lower-level work plans as more information about the market is collected and assessed. Similarly, with a high level of technology, you have limited information about the final specifications and design, so only a rough master plan can be prepared for top management. Using this master plan, you create a more detailed plan for the lower level, and you focus this planning on the activities needed to close the uncertainty gap, such as building technology demonstrations and functional prototypes. As the project progresses, you collect more data. This reduces the level of uncertainty and lets you create updated, more detailed plans for the next steps of engineering, design, and implementation.

We turn now to another important aspect of project management— managing projects in the most efficient way.

Improving the Efficiency of Your Projects

Most modern organizations can improve their efficiency in some way. Although each project is unique and to some extent the first of its kind, not all project activities are new. Some activities are simpler than others, are repeated within the project, have been done in previous projects, or are similar across projects in the organization. Often you may find that different projects need the same building blocks to complete the work. This gives you an opportunity to increase organizational efficiency by standardizing activities within and across projects and by outsourcing some activities.

Thus, organizations can improve efficiency and reduce costs by sometimes examining their entire project activity as part of the operations of the organization. The following sections apply an adaptive approach to the work packages within and across projects. We provide a model for dealing with efficiency across projects and then continue with a discussion of the dilemma of outsourcing.

Use an Adaptive Approach
to Project Building Blocks and Work Packages

So far we've proposed a model for classifying projects as a whole and adapting your management style to the specific nature of the projects. But most projects are complex entities, incorporating many activities that are or-chestrated together to achieve a common goal. As we know, project activities are commonly broken down into *work packages,* which are built hierarchi-cally in a document called a work breakdown structure (WBS). At the lowest level in the WBS, a work package provides a detailed definition of the work needed to complete a task. The work package defines the resources re-quired and the budget available for the task, the detailed plan and milestones for accomplishing it, and a method for reporting progress to management.

Yet not all project activities are the same. They may differ in difficulty, uncertainty, and risk, and they should not be treated in the same way. It makes sense, therefore, to apply the adaptive approach not only at the project level but also at the level of work packages.

The output of each activity can vary. Some activities produce tangible pieces of hardware, whereas others create intangible results, such as infor-mation or decisions in the form of documents, software, or drawings; in addition, some require only basic skills, whereas others involve creativity and ingenuity. The following section provides a simple model to help you identify the specific characteristics of each work package, adopt the right method for each package, and identify its risk level.

The Two Dimensions of Work Package Management

We use two dimensions to distinguish among work packages: the type of outcome, and the type of work that is needed to complete the package.[11] Outcomes may be tangible or intangible, and work can be classified as in-ventive, engineering, or craft.

Tangible outcomes of work packages are physical artifacts (hardware). These artifacts are the essence of the product and distinguish it from other products (its value). Any piece of equipment, such as a computer key-board or a car's transmission unit, is a tangible product. Tangible prod-ucts must be physically assembled and reproduced. Product and process design must therefore be integrated to create a manufacturing process for that piece of hardware and must be subjected to quality control, assembly operations, and cost of production control.

Intangible outcomes, in contrast, are not artifacts (physical objects), although they may be embedded in a physical product. Intangible prod-ucts essentially produce information, which can then be stored on phys-ical media such as CD-ROMs, flash memory, or paper. Software code, manuals, books, newspapers, blueprints, and even movies are intangible products. Reproducing them in high quantities is easy, instant, and inex-pensive, and it does not require dedicated production lines.

Inventive work requires imagination and artistic efforts. Because such activities have not been done before, they are exploratory in nature and require new ideas. Any artwork is inventive in some way, and so are activities that need design, architecture, or new ideas. In fact, many companies use design departments or design firms to mold their product's shape and external features. And some companies employ system architects to come up with new system configurations that have not been done before.

Engineering work involves applying science and engineering principles to solve technical problems and finalize product specifications and engineering design. It differs from inventive work in that it involves well-proven methods, calculations, equations, and simulations to come up with the final product.

Craft work involves repetitive efforts and activities that have been done previously. Although craft work requires time and other resources, its outcome is predictable, and its duration can be accurately anticipated; thus, it is subject to the classic learning curve—that is, learning by repetition. Examples of craft include machine shop work, a paint job, making a piece of furniture, or assembling a printed board.

Two examples illustrate the difference between the three types of work. A new building needs an architect for the inventive and creative work, an engineer for the engineering part (which creates the exact structure specifications and blueprints), and the craft of a builder to put things in place. Similarly, a new car requires the creativity of designers, the engineering of engineers, and the craft work of production and assembly people.

The work package classifications we've just listed create a framework of six cells. Each cell requires its own methods and management style, and each cell represents a different level of risk, as shown in table 9-4.

Improving Efficiency Through Common Low-Risk Work Packages

So how can an organization improve efficiency by using the work package classifications? In an individual project, you may be able to save time and cost by identifying a few standard or repetitive building blocks and duplicating their manufacturing, particularly for the craft and engineering blocks. But the best reward may come when an organization is doing multiple projects. Any organization should look for ways to standardize some of its project work by identifying common themes across its projects. It should look for work packages that are similar, repetitive over time, and use the same skills and resources. The following example shows how one construction company has used these concepts to streamline its project operations.

TABLE 9-4

Classification of work packages

Work outcome	WORK PACKAGE CLASSIFICATION		
	Inventive	*Engineering*	*Craft*
Tangible	Designing the shape and architecture of hardware; requires creative and artistic ability; result often new to the world and not seen before; requires building several prototypes and testing them with customers; high risk of failure to appeal to customer taste	Engineering design of hardware products; involves applying established scientific and engineering principles, rules, algorithms, and methods to solve a specific problem; often requires several iterations of engineering, design, and testing; moderate risk of engineering errors or failure to meet required specifications	Produces well-known types of hardware; involves repetitive tasks; needs the ability to make good estimates of work duration and other resources; may need costly but predictable process building resources; low risk; easy to make into standard building blocks across projects
Intangible	Creating a new algorithm that did not exist before; building software based on new principles; high risk that new ideas may not work or solve the problem; needs extensive testing in different situations; hard to predict all possible failures; an example is the artistic work of movie creation	Writing software code based on existing principles and algorithms; moderate risk of inability to achieve full requirements and creating unexpected bugs; needs extensive testing and software debugging	Writing routine plans or procedures; no new ideas are required; minimal risk to produce routine text

The Quadrant Model

Quadrant is a subsidiary of *Fortune* 500 Weyerhaeuser Company.[12] Quadrant is a project-driven homebuilding company, building more than one thousand homes per year. Using ideas taken from lean manufacturing and just-in-time, the company developed a unique model that made it the number 1 homebuilder in its geographical area, generating an industry-leading profit margin.[13] How did it do it?

Although projects are typically viewed as unique kinds of operations for which special techniques are applicable, the company realized that there are substantial overlaps between projects, and a great part of the activity can be seen as routine operations. The company also realized that customers who purchased Quadrant homes wanted as much space as they could get, more choices in features, and a good value that combined space and choices.

Based on these preferences, the company reconceptualized its design strategy to create homes with maximum space, converted its business model from make-to-stock to make-to-order to give its customers a greater range of choices, and looked for new ways to drive down cost and waste and reduce flow time.

To achieve these goals, the company now groups its design work into several standard elements:

- Group projects by design footprints. Group the design into major elements, reduce excessive numbers of options, and create more opportunity for standardization.

- Make designs that are applicable to multiple building sites.

- Allow options for room arrangements. Create prepour foundations, but leave optional rearrangements for different lifestyles.

- Use common elements across designs in standard components such as window options, roofs, and columns.

Similarly, the implementation process uses a simple scheduling method called "stringline," which shows up-to-date progress for multiple houses and multiple subcontractors, rather than the standard single-project Gantt chart. Here, too, activities are grouped by type and by day per project. Each day's project activity is well known from day one and is performed according to a standard process for that day. For example, on the first day of construction the builders deliver lumber and install first-floor joists; on the second day they conduct under-floor inspection, frame the garage walls, and so on. Finally, when there are delays at a certain site, crews are divided by specialty (such as floors, wall, or roofs) and are sent as reinforcements to complete unfinished tasks.

This process has increased project efficiency dramatically. Between 1996 and 2003, the average home construction time was reduced from 135 to 54 days, with almost no variance. The square foot cost, which had been $60, has been reduced to $30, increasing the company's net margin per home from 2 percent to 6 percent.

The Outsourcing Dilemma

As competition grows and markets become global, companies increasingly are farming out the manufacturing *and* design of new products. One of the most difficult issues faced by business organizations is deciding which activities to keep in house and which to outsource to gain a cost advantage. This is a change from the 1980s and 1990s, when companies insisted that all important R&D remain in-house. Now, almost all major corporations are buying complete designs from Asian developers, tweaking them to their own specifications, and slapping on their own brand names.[14]

Cutting R&D costs is tempting, but it has its risks. The major risk is the danger of fostering new competitors. If you teach your partners abroad how to design your next product, they may be able to do it themselves next time. Another danger is to share intellectual property and newly developed technology secrets. Finally, there is the risk of losing your company's unique brand by admitting that someone else is building your branded products. In this case, what, then, is still unique about your brand? The critical question is, therefore, what must remain in house and what can be farmed out?

What Not to Outsource

Many companies are creating global networks of partners to help them build a greater share of their products through *original design manufacturers* (ODMs). ODMs can do the packaging design, materials acquisition, and, of course, low-cost manufacturing. Some routine jobs can easily be shared with partners. Those may include transforming prototypes into workable designs, upgrading mature products, testing, conducting quality assurance, writing manuals, and qualifying vendor parts. However, what should remain inside is the core knowledge that provides the competitive advantage and is unique to the company's strength: propriety architecture, key specifications, intimate contract details, and management of the international R&D teams.

Now we can use our work package categorization, together with the diamond model, to distinguish between those project types (or project parts) that can be easily outsourced, those that should stay inside, and those that should be outsourced selectively. Figure 9-7a shows the three areas for distinct work packages and 9-7b for entire projects within the NTCP model.

- **Outsource.** You can easily outsource those activities that are routine, are less critical, are based on previous ideas, have lower complexity, and are based primarily on existing technology. At the work package level, they involve all the craft activities and perhaps most engineering activities. At the entire project level, as represented by the inner part of the diamond, we include derivative and assembly projects, low- and medium-tech projects, and regular and fast/competitive projects.

- **Do not outsource.** You should not outsource those activities that involve the latest strategic initiative and new market ideas; those

FIGURE 9-7

(a) Outsourcing work packages; (b) outsourcing entire projects

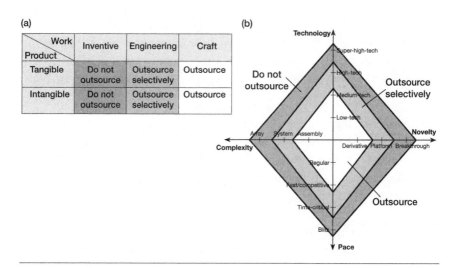

that involve higher complexity, which require careful integration of subsystems; and projects that involve the newest technologies. The inventive work packages should most likely stay inside for the entire project; this is represented by the outer part of the diamond— the breakthrough, super-high-tech, and array projects.

- **Outsource selectively.** This category includes work that may involve unique skills. For work packages, it includes the engineering activities. For the entire project, many high-tech projects include activities that involve less advanced and more familiar technologies. Therefore, you should examine carefully which parts can be outsourced without hurting your competitive advantage. In this category you should also include your platform, system, and time-critical projects.

In this chapter, we have summarized the internal organizational implications of our adaptive model and have offered practical guidelines for using them during project planning and execution. Chapter 10 takes us into the external environment. It explores different markets and customer contexts in various industrial environments.

Key Points and Action Items

- Once you understand and accept the adaptive concepts, it is relatively easy to add a few new activities to your own well-established practices and integrate the lessons of this book into project planning and execution.

- Most literature describes project execution as a sequential, linear process, but no project performs all its phases in a purely linear way. Project activities reiterate between phases, and often you need to go back to a previous phase to repeat or correct an earlier activity or decision.

- You must learn how to control and manage your project's uncertainties. There are two major types: the what and the how uncertainties. These correspond to the uncertainty of requirements and the uncertainty of technical specifications and design, which are measured by project novelty and technology. No project can freeze the final requirements and then start working on designing the product. These uncertainties are resolved simultaneously, until the final requirements are frozen and the design completed.

- You can reduce your project's uncertainties by using an iterative process of updating requirements until you are sure you fully understand customer needs and revising product design until you reach the optimal design that satisfies these needs. The number of iterations depends on the initial levels of uncertainty. In addition, in highly uncertain projects you need to build small-scale prototypes and initiate pilot projects to resolve the unknowns before you embark on the full-scale effort.

- You should manage your project risk by implementing a systematic process of planning for, identifying, analyzing, responding to, and monitoring project risk. Use the diamond model to isolate the sources of risk and to focus attention on the riskier dimensions.

- Rather than "plan your work, and work your plan," you should "plan some of your work, work that plan, and then replan the next piece of your work, and so on." Plan only for those things that you are highly certain will not change. Instead of one plan, projects should use multiple levels of plans with different time horizons and different degrees of detail. The short-term plans should be written periodically, based on the results and experience of the previous period.

- To improve your organizational efficiency you should look for standard and repetitive building blocks in your projects. Any building block or work package can be distinguished by task outcome and the type of work that needs to be done to achieve it. Task outcomes may be tangible or intangible, and work can be classified as inventive, engineering, or craft.

- Use the diamond model to distinguish between project activities that can be outsourced and those that should stay inside for competitive reasons.

◆ 10 ◆

HOW MARKETS AND INDUSTRIES
AFFECT PROJECT MANAGEMENT

T HROUGHOUT THIS BOOK we've claimed that project success depends on adapting project management style to the project's goal, task, and environment. In this chapter we examine the external environmental context of projects and show how the context-free nature of the diamond model can help identify differences among projects in different environments. The environmental context might involve specific markets, industries, geographical regions, or even countries, with their unique cultures.

This chapter is devoted to two of the main environmental contexts of projects: the market (or the customer of the project's product) and the industry (or the technical discipline in which the project operates). Specifically, we examine three markets (or groups of customers): consumers, industrial or business, and public or government. Later we briefly discuss the differences in project management in major industries, such as construction, devices and systems, pharmaceuticals, software, and processes.

How Markets and Customers Influence
Project Management

Different customers and markets behave and think differently. Thus, knowing the customer is one of the most important issues any project manager must face. Project teams must know how their customers think; what their major problems are; and how they make decisions, finance the project, and communicate. Project teams should also understand how their customer organizations function, and know the people who represent their customers.

Table 10-1 shows project classifications based on the following three customer groups: consumers (business to consumer, or B2C), industrial or business organizations (business to business, or B2B), and government (business to government, or B2G). Figure 10-1 uses the diamond model to identify the typical spectrum of projects that are characteristic of each customer group, and the discussion that follows compares the specific project management approaches for each group.

FIGURE 10-1

Possible project types for various markets

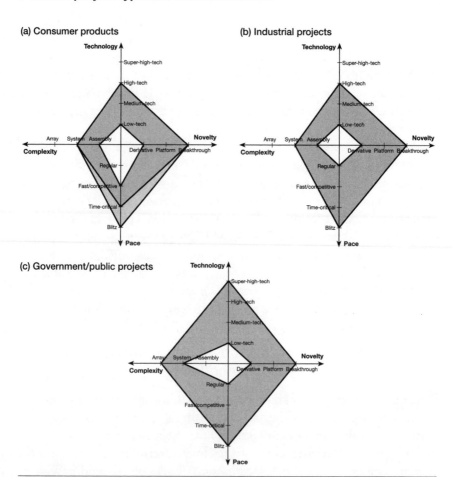

TABLE 10-1

Characteristics of projects for various customers

	CUSTOMER TYPE		
Characteristic	*Consumer (B2C)*	*Industrial/Business (B2B)*	*Government/Public (B2G)*
Examples of products	MP3 player, PC, cars	AS/400, B777, ERP systems	Hubble telescope, FCS, Army communication
Value to customer	Impact on quality of life	Impact on business	Impact on public goals and needs
Producer's objective	High volume, market share	Industry leadership, preferred provider	Long-term relationship
Project focus	High focus on time, cost, and quality	High focus on time and cost	High focus on performance
Importance of time	Time to market is a competitive advantage	Time to delivery is critical to customer	Time sometimes sacrificed for other concerns
Product definition	Defined by marketing; based on perceived customer needs, market research, and projections	Continuous customer involvement	Defined by or with customer
Project scope: work, goals, deliverables	Defined by producer	Defined by producer with customer	Defined by or with customer
Contractual obligations	No contract, internal commitment	Either external contract or internal commitment	Contracted project, obligations to customer
Reviews	Internal reviews	Internal or external reviews	Customer reviews
Customer involvement	No direct involvement; customer opinion through focus groups or market trials	Sometimes direct customer involvement	Intense customer involvement; often a full-time customer representative on the team
Financing	Internally financed	Internally financed, or contracted by customer	Financed by customer according to contract
Marketing	Mass marketing, advertisement; brand management; distribution channels	Industry image creation	Competition for bids; focused on major decision makers
Preparation for production	Mass production preparedness, outsourcing	Mass production, or tailored to customer	Limited production; integration by main contractor
Reliability	High reliability required	Reliability may be traded off for timely delivery	Reliability focused on safety
Risk issues	Safety, health, environmental	Time delays	Public or political concerns; safety
Product support	Service availability	Training, documentation, on-call support	Training, documentation, on-call support

Projects for the Consumer Market (B2C)

Consumers are private individuals who purchase products for their personal use. The objective of businesses that address consumers' needs is typically to achieve high sales volume and large production runs and to gain market share. For their part, consumers determine a product's value by how well it serves and improves their quality of life in areas such as health, entertainment, transportation, work at home, and food.

Producers need to focus on product quality and cost and must get the product to market as early as possible. The producer is the one who determines the product's definition, requirements, and scope, with customer input obtained through focus groups or market surveys. Typically, producers have no direct connections with consumers, and obviously no contract is signed before the project starts. Thus, the project must be initiated, funded, and reviewed internally. Marketing must be focused on the mass market, advertising, brand management, and efficient distribution channels. Producers of consumer products must pay special attention to reliability, safety, and availability of service.[1]

Figure 10-1a shows the four-dimensional spectrum for classifying consumer projects. Consumer projects are never as complex as arrays because of the latter's huge cost and physical nature. Similarly, they are seldom initiated before the required basic technologies are developed, and therefore are rarely super-high-tech projects. Yet they can easily cover all levels of novelty, including breakthrough, and all levels of pace, including blitz (in those cases when a competitor invades the company's own niche or has completely changed the basis of competition, as shown in the light gray area in figure 10-1a). For example, when Dell discovered that it had missed a generation of laptops in the late 1990s, it quickly assembled a crash program to fill the gap. That was a blitz project initiated to save as much as possible of the company's territory.

Projects for Business Customers (B2B)

Products made for business or industrial customers are very different from those made for consumers. Typical examples are computer servers, subsystems such as central air-conditioning systems, or company information systems such as ERP. These projects provide business customers the means and tools to run and improve their businesses. Producers must therefore think about their clients' businesses. The producer's goal, however, is often centered on creating industry leadership and remaining the preferred provider, with a long-term relationship and repeated sales. Project focus is typically on cost, time, and maintainability, with the aim to support efficient operation of the customer's product without interruptions and downtime.

Producers define the product and review the project either by themselves or jointly with the customer. It is common for them to finance the project or to enter into a contractual agreement with the customer, who pays for the development and is strongly involved in the project process. Customers, however, are sensitive mostly to the issues of delivery time and cost. Any delay will have an impact on their own business. For that reason they may tolerate reliability problems as long as the product is delivered on time. Finally, business-related projects are often delivered to customers together with training and extensive maintenance and support documentation.[2]

Figure 10-1b shows the classification space for business-related projects. Such projects may cover most of the four-dimensional spectrum of possible projects. However, in terms of complexity there are typically no array projects; their outcomes are usually subsystems or OEM products that may be parts of bigger projects, or stand-alone systems required by another business for its operations.

As with consumer projects, industrial projects are not initiated before the required basic technologies are in existence. Thus, these projects seldom reach the super-high-tech level of technological uncertainty. The role of developing completely new technologies is typically left for projects made for the governmental customers or public organizations such as universities. As for novelty or pace, you can find business-related projects covering the entire spectrum, from derivative to breakthrough and from regular to blitz.

The following case demonstrates a project for an industrial customer. The producer understood well the nature of the relationship with its customer, but it failed to address the complexity dimension of the project. (Company names are withheld to protect confidentiality.)

An Industrial Blitz Project: The Wire Coating Project

In the early 2000s one of the major U.S. suppliers of plastic found itself in trouble. It had just lost one of its top ten customers to its biggest rival. The company's customer was concerned about the performance of the resin with which it made insulated plastic wire covers. It seemed that the casing would occasionally crack when it was wound onto large storage reels, especially in cold weather. This was a core product for the plastics company, and a cash cow for the business. After three failures of the resin, the customer began to switch to the competitor's product. This was the worst possible scenario: the company lost substantial market share and millions of dollars, and it had to react quickly before things got worse.

A capable team was assembled to respond. As is common in industrial projects, the team worked closely with the customer's people. At first, managers thought that the product was failing because of improper customer processing conditions. But after a team was sent to the customer site to identify the difficulty, it became clear that the problem was worse than they had thought. The team realized it needed to change the company's product or lose the business completely. Top management reassured the customer, however, that the company would get it right.

When the project was officially kicked off, the team was given six months to reinvent the product. The new resin had to have equal or better performance than the next best material on the market, at a very competitive price. The project enjoyed overwhelming involvement and support from senior management.

After six weeks, management reviewed the project plan and decided to add more contingencies to the system. They approved the use of additional people only if they could join the effort without training. The immediate plan needed to focus on the shortest time to market. The idea was to first reclaim lost volume and then to redesign the product to meet additional regulatory requirements that would be imposed if the resin differed significantly from the current formula. A new constraint was therefore put into place: to avoid lengthy regulatory testing and approval, the new product needed to have comparable properties and similar building blocks to the old one.

Although the product was developed on time, manufacturing it proved to be a challenge. The laboratory attained the target properties using smaller-scale equipment and even identified the critical manufacturing parameters. However, the product required new raw materials as well as new health, engineering, and safety practices in manufacturing. Several trials were conducted and proved insufficient. That led management to enhance the visibility and criticality of the project throughout the organization. Mobilizing external manufacturing resources finally yielded a solution.

The result was only half successful. Although a satisfactory new resin was developed, its time line was too tight to allow building an entirely new product and the accompanying production facilities. Unfortunately, the opportunity for conducting customer trials before the holiday season had passed. The customer could test and validate the new product only after the beginning of the next year, and this prevented the company from achieving its expected business goals for that year.

In retrospect, our analysis suggests that the company treated the business customer correctly, with continuous involvement and frequent reporting. However, other factors were missing. The project was run as a platform, high-tech, subsystem (assembly), blitz project. The technology needed for this project was known outside the company but was unknown to the team before the work was undertaken. Yet, in addition to the blitz pace, the dominating factor facing the business situation was complexity. Considering the required changes in the production process, the project had difficulty integrating the solution into manufacturing. Thus, it needed to be treated as a system project, rather than an assembly. The difference between the actual classification and the required one is demonstrated in figure 10-2.

FIGURE 10-2

Wire and cable coating project

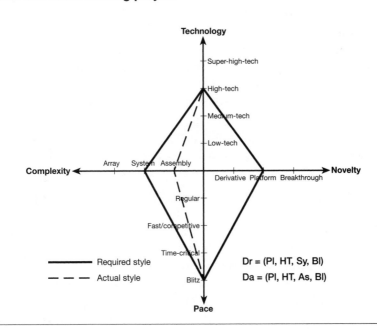

—— Required style	Dr = (Pl, HT, Sy, Bl)	
– – – Actual style	Da = (Pl, HT, As, Bl)	

Government and Public Projects (B2G)

Unlike business-focused customers, the governmental customer isn't motivated by profit. Rather, it buys or orders systems that have an impact on public needs: security, health, transportation, and education.[3] Those who work on a government project must understand the difference; they should know what is critical to the customer and what can be compromised. Government suppliers should seek to create a long-term relationship, which will result in subsequent contracts for manufacturing, maintenance, and support, and repeated orders for next generations.

The government usually chooses suppliers through competitive bids and processes of proposal evaluation. Moreover, marketing to the government is different from marketing to businesses or consumers. Suppliers need to stay on the radar screen of the decision makers and get to know the players well. Although all government contractors have marketing departments, much of the marketing is done by top managers, who build relationships with the decision makers.

The government customer is first and foremost focused on performance. Often, government representatives will declare that time and cost are important (usually because of budget constraints). Compared with business or consumer customers, however, government customers have fewer financial pressures, and they want the best for their users (particularly for defense systems). Time can thus sometimes be sacrificed for better performance. That is perhaps why many government programs suffer schedule delays.

The customer of government projects is closely involved with the producer. The process typically starts with defining customer needs and product requirements and then moves on to a detailed contractual relationship, and later intense customer reviews of the ongoing project.

In large programs, the customer often places an on-site representative to work with the project team. At first this may seem a burden to the team, but it is actually a blessing in the long run. First, the representative's job is to make sure that the team stays on course and addresses the exact needs of the customer in real time. Ultimately, the producer is served by gaining reassurance that it is targeting the exact customer expectations. Second, the customer representative solves problems and answers questions on the spot. When in doubt, the rep can clarify the priorities of the customer and determine what can be compromised if needed.

Third, customer representatives often become project advocates when they meet with their managers back home. They may convince their managers that the team is doing a good job and increase the client's confidence in the contractor. Finally, having a customer representative on the team adds, free of charge, another intelligent worker to the team for solving problems, producing ideas, and even doing some of the project work when needed. A good customer representative with the right attitude and relationship can be a real asset to the project.

Government projects are not usually made for mass production (except for military systems such as aircraft or armored vehicles). On the other hand, such projects are focused tightly on safety, because in many cases the risk to users might involve human life. Other risks in government projects concern political and public issues such as image, good citizenship, and quality of life. And as with industrial projects, government projects are delivered together with a great deal of documentation, support, and training.[4]

Public projects can be initiated not only by national authorities but also by local authorities such as municipalities, or even by nonprofit organizations. Such projects, although sometimes very large (buildings, transportation systems, water supply systems, etc.), typically do not reach the super-high-tech level of technology or the breakthrough level of novelty. They are administered like similar projects, with the main concern being citizens' standard of living and safety. Nevertheless, in many cases public projects may be plagued by local politics and the interests of powerful local groups.[5]

Because public customers typically do not deal with small efforts, their projects can span all levels of the classification dimensions, except perhaps the assembly level of complexity (see figure 10-1c). On the other hand, government is often best positioned to push the frontiers of science and technology and in some cases also those of novelty and newness of use. Thus, government projects extend, more than any other sector, into the super-high-tech and breakthrough territory. Obviously, space programs are of this nature. By exploring the boundaries of the universe and by attempting to conduct the most far-reaching scientific missions, these projects are the most risky and the most difficult to run.[6]

Sometimes, however, public projects need to be addressed as blitz projects. They may be launched in response to an emergency, such as a terror attack or a natural disaster that may cause the loss of hundreds or thousands of lives. As you saw in the Katrina case mentioned in chapter 3, the most important factor for success in such emergency projects is to make contingency plans in advance, to act swiftly when the disaster occurs, and to improvise when there is no information and no detailed plans for the situation at hand. Cost and efficiency are not a factor in a case of emergency.

The Industry Context

One of the major contextual factors affecting project management is the specific industry in which the project is being run. It is no secret that different industries have different ways of managing projects. Although you can find specific books and studies on project management in particular industries, the differences in project management among industries have rarely been identified, studied, collected, or reported.[7] Yet understanding these differences is of great interest for practitioners, students, educators, and researchers. The difference can be found in, among other things, processes, tools, techniques, standards, applications, and, of course, the technical disciplines and the specific technologies.

It would be impossible to cover all industries in one chapter or go into depth within any particular industry. Therefore, we outline here only the major differences among projects in the most common industries. As we will see, almost no industry spans the entire spectrum of projects covered by the NTCP model. This gives us some hope, because no one can be expected to understand and excel in all kinds of projects. But for the educator and student, seeing the big picture may be a good starting point to further focus on projects in a specific industrial environment.

The Major Industries

From a long list of industries, we have chosen five major ones as a representative sample of the spectrum:

- **Construction:** Buildings, roads, bridges, utilities, and so on

- **Equipment and devices:** Tangible hardware products, perhaps containing embedded software for private or industrial use— appliances, automobiles, machinery, and so on

- **Pharmaceuticals and health care:** Drugs, medicines, and medical products

- **Software:** Applications, corporate planning systems, service management systems

- **Processes:** Production lines for products such as chemicals, oil refineries, and plastics

This list represents a variety of industries with differing project management attributes. We recognize, however, that other industries can also be discussed at the next level of analysis. They might include automobiles, finance, movies, insurance, education, consulting, and many others.

Differences in Project Management by Industry

Table 10-2 shows representative types of projects according to the five main industries that we have chosen. Figure 10-3 shows the possible spectrum of project types in each industry according to the NTCP model.

As shown in figure 10-3a, construction projects are confined to the two lowest levels of technology and novelty. Only in rare cases do we find breakthrough construction projects, such as building the first subway system (more than one hundred years ago) or using an extremely innovative architectural design such as in the Guggenheim Museum in Bilbao, Spain. However, construction projects can be complex and sometimes urgent. Building a new city such as Brasilia, which was built in less than five years during the late 1950s as the capital city of Brazil, was an array project, as was the construction of the English Channel tunnel, described in chapter 6. In emergency situations such as in wartime, there might be a need for blitz construction projects. Construction projects are typically designed by architects and structural design specialists. They have strong regulatory and political constraints, and their design is frozen before construction starts, after the engineering blueprints have been approved and the contract signed.

Projects to build equipment and devices are the most common type—the development of things such as a new cell phone, washing machine, stereo system, or personal computer. These projects usually combine hardware and software development. Every appliance, communication device, and even car has an embedded computer that controls the device. Devices can be simple, small, and not very innovative (a derivative assembly), or they can be large, complex, and technologically challenging. As shown in figure 10-3b, they can cover the spectrum of classification in our NTCP model. In most cases such projects involve developing the product as well as creating the manufacturing lines and facilities to produce it in quantity.

As shown in table 10-2, the major factor in pharmaceutical and health care projects is the need to get the approval of regulation authorities (such as the Food and Drug Administration). As figure 10-3c shows, the two dominating dimensions of the diamond model in this industry are novelty and technology. Drug development projects are always innovative and risky to some extent. Even if a generic drug (a generic version of a drug whose patent has expired) is developed, there are still safety risks involved and an official approval is required. A drug is usually comparable to a subsystem in its level of complexity, but when the production facilities are part of the project, the complexity can rise to the system level.

Because of the life span of drug development projects (the process takes, on average, twelve to fifteen years), they usually proceed at a regular pace.

TABLE 10-2

Characteristics of projects in various industries

Characteristic	Construction	Equipment and devices	Pharmaceutical and health care	Software	Process
Typical products	Buildings, roads, etc.	Combination of hardware and software; tangible products	Drugs, medical devices	Applications and services	Process to produce materials: oil, chemical substances
Focus	Functional and architectural aesthetics	Cost, product performance, and product features	Impact on public health, longevity, and quality of life	Functionality, cost, upgrade compatibility	Volume, cost, continuity, efficiency
Product definition	Defined by customer or contractor	Defined by producer and/or customer	Defined by company	Defined by producer and/or customer	Defined by customer or producer
Regulations, standards, approval	Construction and municipal regulations and approval	Specific to industry: defense, automobile, etc.	Strongly affected by regulatory requirements and extensive approval process for products	Almost no regulations; some standards and maturity models	Environmental regulations conformity and approval
Processes	Structured process; built to blueprint; design by design firms; execution by contractors	Designed and developed by same contractor; top-down design of systems; building of subsystems first, followed by system integration	Implementation of research or extensive screening for successful solution; extensive testing process with numerous approval stages	System analysis and development; extensive debugging, testing, and verification needed; release by versions and upgrades	Pilot process design, building, and testing; full-scale process design and construction
Preparation for production	None	Simultaneous product and process development	Mass manufacturing process	No manufacturing needed	One-of-a-kind project
Risk issues	Work delays because of labor disputes or political constraints; unexpected acts of God	Safety	Human life and side effects risk	Extensive time delays	Hazardous materials, toxics, waste, environment
Product support	Warranty	Warranty, maintenance, and service	None for drugs; some for medical devices	Service and help desk	Maintenance

INDUSTRY

FIGURE 10-3

Possible project types for various industries

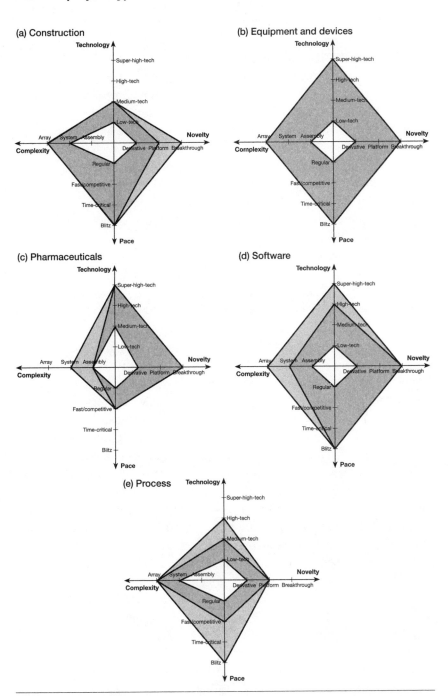

In rare cases, however, the development of a generic drug can be fast/competitive, especially when several companies are competing in a limited-protection time frame (six months, according to the current regulations). Development of medical devices is much simpler and faster than for drugs, but even these products require government approval and their development and testing may take several years.

Most software projects are unique in the sense that there is no hardware developed as an integral part of the project. Although service or business software systems (such as ERP or office automation) require hardware infrastructure for their operation, this infrastructure is built on standard hardware purchased from other vendors and is integrated with the developed software package. One of the major concerns in software development is the need for extensive testing and verification of the code. This process may often take as long as the writing of the code itself, and in some companies it involves different teams from the developers. This requires extensive coordination and the creation of a common language in the company.

Many software projects are innovative and new to the market, but they almost always rely on existing technologies developed elsewhere. In rare cases, when a completely new generation of software is developed (for example, one employing an unproven algorithm), the project can turn into a super-high-tech effort. Software projects are often system projects; but when they are deployed in different geographical sites and integrated to serve as a combined network, they reach the complexity level of an array. A typical example of such a program was the replacement of all operating software packages in the main switches of AT&T's international telephone network, which covers the entire United States. Figure 10-3d displays the classification space of software projects, with the lightly shaded areas representing these rare cases of super-high-tech or array projects.

Process projects are usually confined to a narrow classification space. Process projects are rarely assembly or high-tech projects. Because of their large scale, these projects often involve building a pilot production line before a full-scale facility is assembled. In most cases process projects are either regular or fast/competitive in pace. However, there may be exceptions that drive these projects into blitz speed. When a major production line is destroyed by fire, accident, or a similar cause, it can result in great damage to the environment, as happened in the case of the Chernobyl nuclear plant in the Ukraine. In these cases immediate emergency efforts must be taken to limit the damage.

Now that we have explored the external contexts of projects in terms of business, markets, and industries, our final chapter summarizes the ideas behind our models and provides a top-down list of action items for implementing the adaptive approach throughout the organization. It also offers some thoughts about the future evolution of project management.

Key Points and Action Items

- Different customers and markets behave and think differently. Knowing the customer is one of the most important issues any project manager must face. This chapter differentiates projects based on three customer groups: consumers (B2C), industrial or business organizations (B2B), and government (B2G).

- Consumers are private individuals who purchase products for their personal use. The value proposition to the consumer is improvement of the quality of life. Producers need to focus on product quality and cost, and they must get the product to market as early as possible to beat the competition.

- B2B projects provide business customers the means and tools to run and improve their businesses. A producer must think about its client's business, and the project's focus is typically on cost, time, and maintainability, to ensure efficient operation of the client's business. Products are therefore supplied with a great many support items, such as documentation and training, and producers' goals often center on creating industry leadership and long-term relationships with customers.

- Governments buy systems that have an impact on public needs and security. Government projects may involve political and public issues such as image, good citizenship, security, and quality of life. Government customers (particularly for defense systems) may have fewer time pressures, and they want the best for their users. Time may be sacrificed for better performance. Government projects require a great deal of documentation, support, and training, and producers need to build long-term relationships with customers.

- Another major contextual factor affecting project management is the specific industry in which the project is being run. Different industries have different ways of managing projects. This chapter summarizes the major differences that exist among projects and project management practices for some of the most common industries: construction, equipment and devices, pharmaceuticals and health care, software, and processes.

◆ 11 ◆

REINVENTING PROJECT MANAGEMENT FOR YOUR ORGANIZATION

A S THE ORGANIZATIONAL ENVIRONMENT becomes progressively more project intensive, it is time to unleash the power and energy embedded in projects. The troubling low rate of project success makes it imperative that organizations pay more attention to their project activity and to the potential and competitive advantage that projects can bring. Unfortunately, as we have shown in this book, projects have been kept too long in the dark, often ignored by top executives, while project managers were left to struggle on their own. The discipline of project management has not been very helpful. Focused on time, budget, and performance goals as the rigid drivers of success, it has missed a key point: that projects are always put in place for business reasons.

As we have argued, improving project management presents a great opportunity. After all, how long can organizations milk their operations in an effort to be more efficient? Soon organizations will reach the limitations of efficiency, and further improvements will be only marginal. In a time when every organization must keep changing, the only way it can change is through projects. No new strategy, investment plan, idea, innovation, or business can progress or succeed without projects.

The time has come to learn a set of new rules, which will show executives and teams that there is a better way than the old approach. Our adaptive project management approach, with its symbol, the diamond, offers a new road map and a new language that managers and teams can use to plan, communicate, and make decisions about projects and about the best way to run them.

In this final chapter we review the main lessons we've presented and then outline action items that executives can undertake to put into practice the ideas presented here and turn their organizations' project management into a tangible competitive asset. We conclude with a few thoughts about the future evolution of project management.

Main Lessons

- Project management is not about delivering a project on time, on budget, and within requirements. Instead, project management is about serving a customer need and creating business results to support the company's short- and long-term objectives.

- Project management is not a linear, predictable process. At project initiation, most modern projects involve uncertainties and many unknowns. Often, it is difficult to predict exactly how a project will end. Project planning, therefore, is not a one-time activity, done once and for all at the project's start. Rather, you must plan and manage projects in an adaptable, flexible, and iterative way, adjusting to changes made along the way, according to the project's progress and the dynamic changes in the environment.

- Project planning should involve early identification of what is expected from the project in terms of your company's needs and those of your customers. Instead of setting time, budget, and requirements goals as the major drivers of project success, you need to decide how the project will be judged when completed. This judgment can typically be based on five dimensions: efficiency; impact on the customer; impact on the team; business success; and preparation for the future. Each dimension might consist of several relevant measures. If needed, you should identify other specific dimensions and metrics that are relevant to your industry, business, or project. You should also identify your failure criteria—namely, what can go wrong—and take the steps that will protect you if it happens.

- Project management is not a universal activity with one set of rules and processes for all projects. Rather, it is situational and contextual, and one size does not fit all. To succeed in projects you must use an adaptive project management approach, adapting your project management style to the environment, the goal, and the project task.

- To help managers identify potential risks and benefits and select the right management style for each project, this book uses the diamond model and the diamond analysis tool, which classify a project based on its novelty, technology, complexity, and pace. Each dimension includes three or four project types and affects project management in its own way.

- Novelty represents the uncertainty of the goal and the uncertainty in the market. This dimension measures how new the project's product is to markets, customers, and users, and thus how clearly you can define the project requirements up front. Novelty includes three project types: derivative, platform, and breakthrough. It affects the accuracy of market data and the effort, time, and number of iterations (including prototypes) it takes to finalize and freeze the product's requirements.

- Technology represents the task uncertainty in terms of the technology used—that is, how much new technology is required to complete the project. The technology dimension includes four project types: low-tech, medium-tech, high-tech, and super-high-tech. Technology affects the length of time and number of iterations it will take to get the design right and freeze it, and the degree of intensity of the technical activities—such as design, testing, and prototyping—as well as the technical skills required by the project manager and team.

- Complexity is based on the complexity of the product and the task. This dimension includes three types: assembly, system, and array. Complexity affects the kind of project organization you need and the level of bureaucracy and formality required for managing it.

- Pace represents the urgency of the project—how much time there is to complete the job. Pace includes four types: regular, fast/competitive, time-critical, and blitz. This dimension affects your planning and reviews, the autonomy of the project team, and the involvement of top management, particularly in the most urgent projects.

- To select a portfolio of projects, you can classify projects based on their business goals, whether they deal with existing or new businesses, and whether they are directed to internal or external customers. This distinction creates four groups of project proposals.

You should allocate project resources to each group based on the organization's policy and strategy. Only then should you select individual projects within the groups based on specific criteria for each group.

- Innovation should be managed according to its type. The diamond model enables you to select the right management approach for each type of innovation.

- Applying the adaptive approach to a project need not be difficult. First, you treat project execution as an iterative, and not a linear, process. This means you may need to go back to project definition and project planning based on the project's initial uncertainties and later findings during execution. Second, during project execution you need to add a few new steps and action items to the conventional procedure of managing a project, and you adjust these procedures to the specific project type. During the planning phase, you should determine your expected success and failure criteria: the expectations of and the agreement between executives and teams about how to judge success and what can go wrong. At this stage you should also assess the impact of your project type on your project management approach, identifying the actions you need to take that are specific to the adaptive approach and to the project type.

- For projects having high uncertainty, you may need to conduct small pilot efforts to help reduce uncertainties before a full-scale commitment is made. Similarly, projects need to identify in-between milestones in a modular way, where prototypes enable teams to make corrections in requirements, technical specifications, and design until they are frozen.

- Project plans may include three levels. First, you create a master plan that lists major milestones throughout the project and serves to report to and communicate with top management. Second, you create a series of middle-level plans with a time horizon of a few months. You will update these plans periodically and use them to report to and communicate with middle-level management. Third, you write highly detailed work plans, which will be updated every month and will outline each activity of the project team members.

- Projects can help improve operational efficiency in organizations and reduce cost. You should analyze project building blocks and work packages based on their outcome (tangible or intangible) and the work needed to create this outcome (inventive, engineering, or craft). These will determine the difficulty and risk involved in each block. You should then identify common building blocks across projects in the organization and create systems that will efficiently build these blocks. Similar assessments can be made about outsourcing entire projects, or parts of projects, based on the diamond model or the work package analysis.

Now let's look in detail at the specific initiatives that CEOs and top management can take to implement the ideas in this book.

Implement New Policies

- Treat project management as the next core of your competitive assets. Raise the awareness of managers at all levels about the potential of their projects. Make it clear that project management is not the business only of project managers. It should be the business of everyone at every managerial level: marketing, sales, advertising, manufacturing, engineering, quality, and so on. All have a part in project success. Create a career path for project managers (see more on that later in this chapter), and appoint an executive to become a chief projects officer.

- Treat your projects as investments, not costs. Your investment in projects is perhaps the best investment you can make for your organization, often more important than capital investments.

- Get the best people to lead projects. Avoid the temptation (and the norm) to put your best people in charge of operations. Remember that it is easier to manage operations than complex, uncertain projects. Future operations will be profitable only if the projects that created them were selected correctly and done well.

- Treat process building as a project. The models in this book are applicable not only to new product development or construction but also to process building or building process-based services.

- Implement a mechanism to identify failure before it is too late. Use short planning and execution intervals and milestones, and not just dates.

- Implement a policy that encourages project managers to overspend on the up-front planning plus prototyping that will enable quick, small implementations to resolve early unknowns in bigger programs.

Create an Organizational Framework and Handbook for Project Management

Because every organization is unique in its environment, businesses, people, and technology, the models suggested in this book may fit most organizations but not all, and not fully. An organization should first decide what its needs are in managing its project portfolio and individual projects. Your needs might include portfolio management, resource allocation, skill development, project organization, project locations, or other specific needs.

After defining your specific needs, you must identify the most valuable models for classifying your projects. For instance, technological uncertainty may not be a viable dimension for a construction company, because all its projects use the same level of technology. However, other related dimensions may apply, such as complexity and pace. Similarly, a company in the pharmaceutical industry may need to distinguish projects according to levels of risk and the clinical testing required for each project type.

The next step is to develop a handbook of project management that outlines the relevant models and dimensions for classifying your projects. Your handbook also should outline the related managerial implications for each project type.

A major part of this book defines the project management processes for various project types. The process for small projects is not the same as for large projects, and low-tech projects will differ from high-tech projects. For example, your handbook might outline the life cycle and typical phases of various types of projects in the company, including the major milestones and approval gates. It should describe the decisions to be made at each gate, along with the required documentation. The handbook also should include specific tools, templates, and documents for planning, reporting, monitoring, and coordinating projects, as well as selected software applications.

Create a Policy for Portfolio Management and Project Selection

After you have established your unique way to distinguish among projects, you should set a policy for project portfolio management—that is, for selecting projects and allocating resources to them. To do this, you divide the collection of project proposals into major groups. Possible groups might differentiate between those that extend an existing business or create a new business, and those that serve internal versus external customers.

By dividing projects into major groups, executives can allocate the company's resources based on strategy, market position, and strategic goals. Once these resources have been allocated, all project suggestions are compared to the other proposals in their group based on a unique set of criteria developed for that group.

Develop a Project Management Training Program

Based on your specific project management needs, you need to create a unique set of training packages for project managers at various levels and for various project types. Clearly, project managers for smaller projects will be younger and less experienced, and they will require fundamental training, whereas project managers who control projects of higher complexity, and particularly of higher uncertainty, require more advanced training delivered by more experienced people. You may also find it helpful to build an internal certification program, with accreditation levels that reflect several stages of project management maturity.

Internal training should teach general knowledge about project management theory as well as practice and experience from the larger world. Additionally, the program should present your own models and processes and should include the study of internal lessons and project case studies of previous programs (including failures) to carry the lessons over from generation to generation.

Develop Career Paths for Project Managers and Criteria for Their Selection

Training alone is not enough. If a company wants to make project management a core competitive asset, it should invest in project management in the long term and in the careers of its project managers. First, you need to develop clear guidelines and criteria for the selection of project managers. Project managers should not be selected based only on their technical competence (as is often the case). A clear set of criteria should be established based on, among other things, leadership skills, communication skills, organizing ability, self-confidence and drive, and the ability to see the big picture.

You would also do well to establish a clear career path in project management. Project management should not be a one-time assignment, but rather a profession, one whose expertise is treated as a company asset. People should be noted for their ability to climb the project management ladder up to an executive level (chief projects officer and CEO).

The process of growing project managers should be monitored and managed. Young project managers should be given mentors and coaches to guide them through their early stages, and mature project managers should participate in the training program as instructors and advisers.

Create a Learning Environment Around Projects

Every project effort creates a unique learning opportunity. Things change rapidly, decisions are constantly made, and mistakes are made. Lessons can be learned every week and at every milestone, and clearly at project completion. But few organizations have the habit of recording, documenting, and sharing project lessons throughout the company. For example, whenever a project is terminated, there are valuable lessons that must be learned. Yet managers (perhaps because of human nature) often tend to avoid discussing or dwelling on any failures; they would rather move on.

Company executives and CEOs should instill a learning culture around projects. It should become a habit to summarize lessons learned in each opportunity or major event and to document a completed project (whether a success or failure) with a summary report describing the lessons learned. This report should be prepared after all team members have shared their thoughts during a long session of discussion about what went right or wrong and why, and then it should be distributed to the rest of the company, perhaps on its Intranet. In this way the company will retain its organizational memory and will be able to avoid repeated failures of the same kind.

In addition, you should select several key projects as showcases and build an internal library of case studies based on them. These case studies, which should use a common format, will serve as learning tools for your in-house training and educational programs. Each case should involve a full case history, a learning case, and an executive summary containing a short list of the major lessons.

A Note About the Role of Educators and Scholars

Project management education is typically focused on doing things in the traditional way. Most current educational programs teach students the basic tools of planning, scheduling, risk management, procurement, and the like. Ironically, however, most leading business schools don't offer project management in their curricula, and the academic educational needs in this field are addressed mostly by engineering or technology management schools.

As this book has shown, however, project management is applicable not only in technical environments. If, as we predict, the demand for better project management will keep growing, so will the need for education. This creates an opportunity for major business schools. First, project management courses should be added to current curricula. Second, the educational arena in management should be expanded, and academic programs should be developed in the new directions of adaptive and strategic approaches. Third, a similar role can be played by the consulting and training industry in project management.

Furthermore, we believe that the current state of project management also provides a great opportunity for the research community. If project management catches the attention of leading scholars in organization theory and management science, both worlds will benefit. Researchers will find a rich, understudied field, with very little theory, where they can apply their experience and methods, develop new frameworks, and find new grounds. This will create a constant stream of new ideas and new knowledge in a long ignored field.

Final Thoughts: What's Next in Project Management?

We began this book by discussing some of the shortcomings of today's project management discipline—namely, that the conventional discipline focuses too much on the delivery of projects on time, within budget, and to specifications, and the existing project management body of knowledge assumes that one size fits all. It is based on a rigid, linear, predictable model for planning and managing projects. In this book we have tried to build a practical, research-based approach that is flexible and adaptive, one that will enable companies to deal with the dynamics of change and uncertainty in modern projects in a literate and systematic way.

So what's next? It seems that project management will remain and even grow further as a central activity in most organizations. We hope that the ideas presented here will stimulate further development. More theories and frameworks will certainly be developed in the future, and they will give us a deeper and better understanding of the project phenomenon. Such theories and frameworks will influence future education, research, and project management in practice. We predict that in the coming years, project management will evolve to become a more strategic activity.[1] Project managers and teams will learn how to better focus their attention on business results, rather than only on "getting the job done," and they will deal more vigorously and rigorously with the expected effect of their project both on the customer and on the company's bottom line.

APPENDIX 1

OUR RESEARCH STEPS

THIS BOOK IS BASED on fifteen years of studies in project management, starting in the early 1990s. During this period we collected data on more than six hundred projects in the United States and Israel. Our research took place in several phases and its models evolved gradually in a long, iterative, and seldom smooth process of going back and forth between data and theory. Some of the models were apparent from the start; others emerged as more data was collected and tested.

Similarly, the specific project types kept evolving until the final picture was well defined and unchanged by additional data. Some projects exhibited additional (out of the model) characteristics; we mention them, therefore, as additional insights throughout the book.

The steps and phases of our study were as follows:

- We started with a conceptual phase, suggesting a possible effect of technology on project management styles (Shenhar, 1991, 1993). The work distinguished among four groups of projects associated with differing levels of technological uncertainty. In 1992 we used this concept to analyze the management of the space shuttle development project and to discuss its implications on the *Challenger* accident (Shenhar, 1992). Shortly thereafter we added the notion of project complexity based on a hierarchy of systems and subsystems

---

A bibliography of sources for this appendix appears at the end of the appendix.

(e.g., Shenhar, Dvir, and Shulman, 1995). During the first phase of data collection we documented twenty-six case projects on which we applied a multiple case study approach, focusing on the dynamics within single settings (Yin, 1984; Eisenhardt, 1989). The data analysis confirmed our hypothesis that major differences exist between projects and project management styles based on differing levels of technological uncertainty and system complexity (Shenhar, 1998).

- The next step involved collecting quantitative data on 127 projects in 76 companies in Israel in the commercial, defense, and nonprofit sectors. The projects we studied ranged in budget from $40,000 to $2.5 billion, and in duration from three months to twelve years. We used this data to build a typological theory of project management (Shenhar and Dvir, 1996) and to extend the classic concept of contingency theory to the project management arena (Shenhar, 2001). During this period we started exploring the issue of project success dimensions. Based on a previous study on success measures of strategic business units (Dvir and Shenhar, 1992), we tried to extend the concept of the Balanced Scorecard to projects. The data showed that you can assess project success by using at least four different success measures (Shenhar, Dvir, and Levy, 1997; Shenhar, Dvir, Levy, and Maltz, 2001).

- The focus of the third phase was to extend the well-known concept of project success factors to distinguish between types of projects. We also continued our investigation into the differences among projects and success measures. For this phase we collected data on 110 defense development projects. The data was both qualitative and quantitative, and for each project we interviewed three to eight stakeholders within and outside the project. Several findings characterized this step. First, we were able to show that there are different success factors for different types of projects (Tishler, Dvir, Shenhar, and Lipovetsky, 1996). We also tested which dimensions have the most impact on project classification, showing that the complexity dimension proved to be one of the major determinants (Dvir, Lipovetsky, Shenhar, and Tishler, 1998). Finally we tested the relative importance of project success measures. We found "benefit to the customer" to be the most important factor (Lipovetsky, Tishler, Dvir, and Shenhar, 1997).

- We then started an ongoing effort to collect additional case data on projects in the United States. This work produced more than two hundred eighty detailed case studies in a wide range of industries.

Our work with several major corporations and government agencies provided additional insights and enabled the assessment of the implementation of these frameworks. At this stage we added the pace dimension to our model (Shenhar, Dvir, Lechler, and Poli, 2002).

• It was not until we started planning this book that we realized that three dimensions are not sufficient to deal with the newness of products in the market. We therefore adopted Steven Wheelwright and Kim Clark's classification (1992), which we named *novelty*. The data proved indeed that it is a separate dimension and at least as important for project classification as the other three, thus completing the diamond model.

References

Dvir, Dov, and Aaron J. Shenhar. "Measuring the Success of Technology-Based Strategic Business Units." *Engineering Management Journal* 4, no. 4 (1992): 33–38.

Dvir, Dov, Eli Segev, and Aaron J. Shenhar. "Technology's Varying Impact on the Success of Strategic Business Units within the Miles and Snow Typology," *Strategic Management Journal* 14 (1993): 155–162.

Dvir, Dov, Stan Lipovetsky, Aaron J. Shenhar, and Asher Tishler. "In Search of Project Classification: A Non-Universal Approach to Project Success Factors." *Research Policy* 27 (1998): 915–935.

Dvir, Dov, Aaron J. Shenhar, and Shlomo Alkaher. "From a Single Discipline Product to a Multidisciplinary System: Adapting the Right Style to the Right Project." *System Engineering* 6, no. 3 (2003): 123–134.

Eisenhardt, Kathleen M. "Building Theories from Case Study Research." *Academy of Management Review* 14 (1989): 532–550.

Lipovetsky, Stan, Asher Tishler, Dov Dvir, and Aaron J. Shenhar. "The Relative Importance of Project Success Dimensions." *R&D Management* 27, no. 1 (1997): 97–106.

Raz, Tzvi, Aaron J. Shenhar, and Dov Dvir. "Risk Management, Project Success, and Technological Uncertainty." *R&D Management* 32, no. 2 (2002): 101–109.

Shenhar, Aaron J. "Project Management Style and Technological Uncertainty: From Low- to High-Tech." *Project Management Journal* 22, no. 4 (1991): 11–17.

Shenhar, Aaron J. "Project Management Style and the Space Shuttle Program: A Retrospective Look." *Project Management Journal* 23, no. 1 (1992): 32–37.

Shenhar, Aaron J. "From Low- to High-Tech Project Management." *R&D Management* 23, no. 3 (1993): 199–214.

Shenhar, Aaron J., Dov Dvir, and Yechiel Shulman. "A Two Dimensional Taxonomy of Products and Innovations." *Journal of Engineering and Technology Management* 12 (1995): 175–200.

Shenhar, Aaron J., and Alexander Laufer. "Integrating Product and Project Management: A New Synergistic Approach." *Engineering Management Journal* 7, no. 3 (1995): 11–15.

Shenhar Aaron J., and Dov Dvir. "Toward a Typological Theory of Project Management." *Research Policy* 25 (1996): 607–632.

Shenhar, Aaron J., Dov Dvir, and Ofer Levy. "Mapping the Dimensions of Project Success." *Project Management Journal* 28, no. 2 (1997): 5–13.

Shenhar, Aaron J. "From Theory to Practice: Toward a Typology of Project Management Styles." *IEEE Transactions on Engineering Management* 41, no. 1 (1998): 33–48.

Shenhar, Aaron J. "One Size Does Not Fit All Projects: Exploring Classical Contingency Domains." *Management Science* 47, no. 3 (2001): 394–414.

Shenhar, Aaron J., Dov Dvir, Ofer Levy, and Alan Maltz. "Project Success: A Multidimensional, Strategic Concept." *Long Range Planning* 34 (2001): 699–725.

Shenhar, Aaron J., Dov Dvir, Thomas Lechler, and Michael Poli. "One Size Does Not Fit All: True for Projects, True for Frameworks." Paper presented at the PMI Research Conference, Seattle, 2002.

Tishler, Asher, Dov Dvir, Aaron J. Shenhar, and Stan Lipovetsky. "Identifying Critical Success Factors in Defense Development Projects: A Multivariate Analysis." *Technological Forecasting and Social Change* 51, no. 2 (1996): 151–171.

Wheelwright, Steven C., and Kim B. Clark. *Revolutionizing Product Development: Quantum Leaps in Speed, Efficiency and Quality.* New York: The Free Press, 1992.

Yin, Robert K. *Case Study Research: Design and Methods.* Beverly Hills, CA: Sage Publishing, 1984.

PROJECT SUCCESS ASSESSMENT QUESTIONNAIRE

PLEASE RESPOND to each of the following statements about your project. Indicate the degree to which you *agree* or *disagree* with the statement by marking one response for each item.

S_1 Project Efficiency	Strongly Disagree	Disagree	Agree	Strongly Agree	N/A
S_{11} The project was completed on time or earlier.	☐	☐	☐	☐	☐
S_{12} The project was completed within or below budget.	☐	☐	☐	☐	☐
S_{13} The project had only minor changes.	☐	☐	☐	☐	☐
S_{14} Other efficiency measures were achieved.	☐	☐	☐	☐	☐
S_2 Impact on the Customer/User					
S_{21} The product improved the customer's performance.	☐	☐	☐	☐	☐
S_{22} The customer was satisfied.	☐	☐	☐	☐	☐
S_{23} The product met the customer's requirements.	☐	☐	☐	☐	☐
S_{24} The customer is using the product.	☐	☐	☐	☐	☐
S_{25} The customer will come back for future work.	☐	☐	☐	☐	☐

	Strongly Disagree	Disagree	Agree	Strongly Agree	N/A

S_3 Impact on the Team

S_{31} The project team was highly satisfied and motivated.	☐	☐	☐	☐	☐
S_{32} The team was highly loyal to the project.	☐	☐	☐	☐	☐
S_{33} The project team had high morale and energy.	☐	☐	☐	☐	☐
S_{34} The team felt that working on this project was fun.	☐	☐	☐	☐	☐
S_{35} Team members experienced personal growth.	☐	☐	☐	☐	☐
S_{36} Team members wanted to stay in the organization	☐	☐	☐	☐	☐

S_4 Business and Direct Organizational Success

S_{41} The project was an economic business success.	☐	☐	☐	☐	☐
S_{42} The project increased the organization's profitability.	☐	☐	☐	☐	☐
S_{43} The project has a positive return on investment.	☐	☐	☐	☐	☐
S_{44} The project increased the organization's market share.	☐	☐	☐	☐	☐
S_{45} The project contributed to shareholders' value.	☐	☐	☐	☐	☐
S_{46} The project contributed to the organization's direct performance.	☐	☐	☐	☐	☐

S_5 Preparing for the Future

S_{51} The project outcome will contribute to future projects.	☐	☐	☐	☐	☐
S_{52} The project will lead to additional new products.	☐	☐	☐	☐	☐
S_{53} The project will help create new markets.	☐	☐	☐	☐	☐
S_{54} The project created new technologies for future use.	☐	☐	☐	☐	☐
S_{55} The project contributed to new business processes.	☐	☐	☐	☐	☐
S_{56} The project developed better managerial capabilities.	☐	☐	☐	☐	☐

S_6 Additional success dimensions relevant to this project. Write in and assess success.

S_{61}	☐	☐	☐	☐	☐
S_{62}	☐	☐	☐	☐	☐

S_7 Overall Success

S_{71} Overall the project was a great success.	☐	☐	☐	☐	☐

BUILDING THE CONTINGENCY APPROACH TO PROJECT MANAGEMENT

TO UNDERSTAND the fundamental ways that organizations can classify their projects, we could look at the classic contingency theory of innovation. This theory asserts that different conditions might require different organizational settings, and that the effectiveness of the organization is contingent on the amount of fit between structural and environmental variables.[1]

But how would classic contingency arguments hold in the dynamic, temporary, and changing world of projects? Unlike companies, projects are temporary organizations. They are time limited, often are part of a larger organization, and perform mostly new tasks that have not been done before.

Yet ironically, the classic theory has not had a significant impact on contemporary project management.[2] Although various ideas were mentioned in the past, no standard, empirically based model has so far been adopted.[3] In search of major distinctions among projects, however, several observations can be made.[4] First, the fundamental nature of projects as tasks that have never been done leads us naturally to look at project uncertainty as a major dimension for sorting projects.[5] Second, some projects may be more complex than others, and thus, the complexity of the task and of the organization is another clear candidate for distinction.[6] Notably, the combination of uncertainty and complexity also has often been mentioned as a basis for distinction.[7] Finally, since every project has a time limit, we can also look at the time constraint as a basis for project differentiation.[8]

The Basic Theoretical Framework: The UCP Model

Our research has identified three initial dimensions to distinguish among project tasks: uncertainty, complexity, and pace. Together, we called them the UCP model, and they form a context-free theoretical framework for selecting the proper management style (see figure 1).[9] Let's look at these dimensions in more detail and try to see in what way they can affect project management.

- **Uncertainty.** Uncertainty means how much we don't know at project initiation. Different projects present, at the outset, different levels of uncertainty. Project uncertainties may be external or internal, depending on the environment or the specific task and the ability to perform it. For example, sending the first humans to the moon was a highly uncertain task. It represented an enormous mission and technical uncertainties. In contrast, the construction of a new home represents much less uncertainty, either in task or means, and the ability to predict the outcome is much better. Correctly assessing and defining project uncertainty at the outset

FIGURE 1

The UCP model

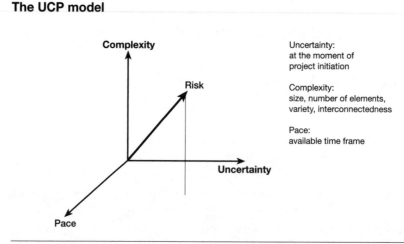

Uncertainty:
at the moment of
project initiation

Complexity:
size, number of elements,
variety, interconnectedness

Pace:
available time frame

is therefore a major factor in project management. It clearly has an impact on the plans, the resources, the completeness of requirements, the time needed, and much more.

- **Complexity.** Complexity depends on product and task complexity—in particular, product structure and functionality as well as the number and variety of elements, subtasks, and the interconnections among them. Complexity is not the same thing as uncertainty. Some projects may be low in uncertainty but high in complexity. Developing a new neighborhood with hundreds of buildings may be a highly complex project but quite certain in terms of means and the ability to perform it. Product and task complexity may have an impact on the complexity of the project organization and on the processes and the tools used to plan and monitor the project.

- **Pace.** The third dimension involves the urgency and criticality of time goals. Pace depends on the available time given for project completion and the degree of urgency. When *Apollo 13* was in danger of not returning, the project of saving its astronauts became a crisis project. In contrast, when the Sydney Opera House was built, time did not really play a major role for its political decision makers. The same goal with a different pace may require different project structures, different management attention, and different rates of decision making.

PROJECT CLASSIFICATION QUESTIONNAIRE

Project Number _____ Project Name _____

1XX Industry		
	☐ 01 Pharmaceuticals	☐ 11 Advertising
	☐ 02 Consumer Electronics	☐ 12 Entertainment
	☐ 03 Telecommunications	☐ 13 Health Care
	☐ 04 Information Technology	☐ 14 Insurance
	☐ 05 Financial Services	☐ 15 Construction
	☐ 06 Automobile	☐ 16 Travel
	☐ 07 Defense	☐ 17 Consulting
	☐ 08 Energy	☐ 18 E-Commerce
	☐ 09 Software	☐ 19 Other
	☐ 10 Manufacturing	_____

Product Description	A short description of the *product* produced by the *project:*
Project Description	A short description of the scope of the *work* in the *project:*

PROJECT TYPE

20X Product Novelty	1 Derivative (Improvement)	☐
	2 Platform (A new generation in an existing product line)	☐
	3 Breakthrough (A new-to-the-world product)	☐

30X	**Technological Uncertainty**	1 A Type Low-tech (No new technology)	☐
		2 B Type Medium-tech (Some new technology)	☐
		3 C Type High-tech (All or mostly new but existing technologies)	☐
		4 D Type Super-high-tech (Project will use nonexistent technologies at project initiation)	☐
40X	**Complexity (System Scope)**	1 Assembly (A subsystem—performing a single function)	☐
		2 System (A collection of subsystems—performing multiple functions)	☐
		3 Array (System of systems—a widely dispersed collection of systems serving a common mission)	☐
50X	**Pace**	1 Regular (Delays not critical)	☐
		2 Fast/competitive (Time to market is a competitive advantage)	☐
		3 Time-critical (Completion time is critical to success, window of opportunity)	☐
		4 Blitz (Crisis project)	☐
60X	**Business Goal**	1 Operational (Extension of existing business)	☐
		2 Strategic (Creating a new business)	☐
70X	**Customer**	1 External (External contract or consumers)	☐
		2 Internal (Internal users or another department)	☐
80X	**Strategic Goal**	1 Extension (Improving, upgrading an existing product)	☐
		2 Strategic (Prime—creating strategic positions in businesses through new products or markets)	☐
		3 Problem solving (Acquire or develop a new technology or a new capability)	☐
		4 Maintenance (Routine maintenance, fixing regular problems)	☐
		5 Utility (Keep the lights on—acquiring and installing new equipment or software, implementing new methods or new processes, reorganization, reengineering)	☐
		6 Research and development (Study—exploring future ideas, no specific product in mind)	☐
	Project Start Date	*(Month/year)*	
	Project Duration	*(Months)*	
	Budget	*($)*	

PRINCIPLES AND DESIGN OF CLASSIFICATION SYSTEMS

C LASSIFICATION IS a way of making knowledge of the world more manageable. In fact, classification is so much a part of our lives that we are often unaware of its pervasiveness, and some writers suggest that the need to classify, label, and group things is an innate part of human nature.[10]

Arbitrary and intuitive classification systems that focus primarily on the classes have little value beyond a short-term, instrumental use for which they may be rapidly designed. A sound classification system is based on meticulous selection and definition of the classes and the attributes that distinguish them, ensuring that meaningful differences are recognized. You should express relationships between the classes in a way that enhances your understanding of the phenomenon, and ideally the classification possesses predictive ability. If this is achieved, and if it is designed also for a specific purpose with the needs of users in mind, then

This appendix is based on Lynn Crawford, Brian Hobbs, and Rodney J. Turner, *Project Categorization Research Report* (Newtown Square, PA: Project Management Institute, Research Department, 2004). We also thank Lynn Crawford for preparing additional notes on classification, which helped in shaping this appendix.

the classification system will have sound potential for sharing and creating new knowledge and contributing to development of theory.

Functions and Purposes of Classification

Classifications can be used to provide easier access to items, giving you a context or system through which to interpret an area or to define and establish its boundaries. The purpose of the classification determines which attributes are significant for identifying the difference between it and other entities.

A classification assists us in making sense of the world by providing ways of describing or representing entities that encourage "consistency of mental representations both within and across individuals."[11] Classification focuses on identification of similarities and differences between entities and assists us in storing and making use of past experience. Classification systems provide a standardized language, a navigation system, and a basis for comparability that is fundamental to rendering knowledge transferable, accessible, and usable.

Kwasnik maintains that classification schemes "not only reflect knowledge by being based on theory and displaying it in a useful way . . . but also classifications in themselves function as theories do and serve a similar role in inquiry: that is the role of explanation, parsimonious and elegant description and the generation of new knowledge."[12] Jacob provides an excellent example: "By grouping patients according to observable similarities, clinicians and diagnosticians can access knowledge based on previous experiences to predict the utility of alternative approaches to therapy and can apply that knowledge in the treatment of the individuals. In this manner, the apprehension of similarity brings knowledge."[13]

Principles of Classification

In practice, we often refer to "classification" of things into "categories," and we use the terms *classification* and *categorization* interchangeably.[14] But strict interpretation draws a distinction between classification as the "slotting of objects, events, or properties . . . into mutually exclusive classes within the hierarchical structure imposed by an arbitrary and predetermined ordering of reality," and categorization as a "process of dividing the world of experience into groups—or categories—whose members bear some perceived relation of similarity to each other."[15] This definition of categorization can be considered pragmatically more applicable to projects than that given for classification.

Classification systems have two main functions: definition and arrangement. *Definition* is the determination of classes of entities that share characteristic attributes, and *arrangement* involves a systematic ordering of classes that expresses conceptual relationships within the overall structure.[16]

The classification schemes presented in this book take the form of categories. Here, the phenomena being classified (projects) are grouped into classes according to shared characteristics along two or more dimensions. Each project shares the characteristic represented by each of the dimensions but does so at different levels. For example, the dimension "technology uncertainty level" (T) is divided into four levels: low-tech, medium-tech, high-tech, and super-high-tech. The relationship between the items is signified by their shared position on a grid or matrix. This matrix can be considered a form of facet analysis, in which the dimensions of the matrix are the facets of the project and each dimension or facet of the matrix has its own specific rules for further division.[17]

When we design a classification scheme, according to Bowker and Star we should take into account three parameters: comparability, visibility and control.[18] *Comparability* refers to the ability of the classification scheme to provide "comparability across sites to ensure that there is regularity in semantics and objects from one to the other, thus enhancing communication." *Visibility* is concerned with the problem that as long as knowledge remains invisible it cannot be classified. *Control* indicates that complexity needs to be harnessed in order to provide some form of understanding of the intricacies developed in the classification scheme. There is a tension between freedom and structure, but some form of control is required if we are to make sense of information.[19] If a classification system is highly detailed and complicated, it will not be used.

Characteristics of Classification Systems

Although classic classification theory requires the existence of common critical attributes, the concept of categories based on family resemblances where there may be unclear boundaries between categories is more appropriate to entities such as projects. To avoid excessive complexity, "all classification systems miss something or are unable to capture some aspect of the phenomena of interest."[20]

A classification scheme should be shaped by its purpose. In effect, the purpose guides the selection of categories and attributes that signify difference. Each classification system therefore tends to be specific and applicable only to a limited field, although it is not unusual for the same classification system to be used for different purposes.[21] For instance, you might use the same project classification system as the basis for allocation of resources, thereby ensuring alignment with your strategy, project monitoring, and control as well as management reporting on a portfolio of projects. It is also common for different classification schemes to be applied to the same body of knowledge or set of entities.

It is important to remember that a "class" is not an objective phenomenon waiting to be discovered. Rather, it is a construct that provides the most coherent meaning to users within the limit of their knowledge and is therefore "dependent upon human experience."[22]

Boundary issues arise from the drawing of demarcation lines between categories in a classification scheme. For instance, decisions need to be made concerning the level of detail (how many categories) that should be identified as well as what should be defined and what should remain invisible within the scheme. A further consideration is the degree of differentiation in a graded structure that signifies the boundary between classes.

Once a classification system is created, people are likely to socialize themselves to the attributes of the constituent categories and the system can be expected to influence behavior.[23] Work may change to conform to a classification scheme. A classification system is therefore not an objective or neutral framework but rather one that has potential to act on and influence interactions in its environment. An aspect of this is that organizational memory "is filtered through classification systems," and these systems influence what information is recorded and how it can be retrieved.[24]

The Design of Project Classification Systems

Our examination of the material on categorization outside the project management literature has identified two important points. First, categorization systems are driven by the purposes they serve and categorization can serve many needs. Second, the design and use of a categorization system in a professional or organizational context bring many interrelated issues into play. The project management literature has focused on a limited set of uses to which project categorization systems can be put.

Attributes Used to Sort Projects into Categories

An organization's system for categorizing projects can be seen as composed of attributes, labels, and definitions. By *attribute* we mean the underlying characteristic that is being used to categorize projects. A simple example is size. The *labels* are the names that the organization uses to identify the groups of projects. An example might be "large" and "small." In some instances, the label is self-explanatory, as are many of the categorizations by geographic location. In others, a *definition* must be given for the label to have meaning.

An examination of the many examples of systems of categories found in the literature and in organizations reveals many commonalities in the attributes being used, but there is significantly less commonality in the specific groupings, labels, and definitions. For example, many organizations group their projects by geographic location, but each system is specific to the locations covered by the organization. Size is another attribute commonly used to group projects into categories. However, what is a large project for one organization may be very small for another.[25] There are thus many commonalities at the level of the attributes being used to categorize projects, but the categories being used by organizations tend to be specific to the context.

Within a specific organizational context, a clear link exists between organizational purpose and the categories in use. Many examples can be found of the same purpose being pursued by different organizations using different attributes to categorize their projects. Similarly, there are many examples in which different organizations are using the same attributes for different purposes. For example, the common attribute of geographical region is used by many organizations for many purposes. Some use it to indicate which regional office will do the work, others use it to adapt to differences in regulatory frameworks, and still others use it to align their market penetration strategy. Similarly, many organizations group projects into categories in order to develop specific tools and methods for each category. It all depends on the relevant sources of variation among the organization's projects. For some organizations, the product type or the technology is the primary source of variation. For others, it is the geographical division, with international projects being managed differently from domestic projects. For still other organizations, the variation may be primarily by contract type or complexity or level of risk or size.

The relationship between the organizational purposes served by the systems and the attributes that are most relevant is context specific. Two organizations pursuing the same objective in different contexts will use different attributes to categorize their projects. This divorce between organizational purposes and attributes makes model building in this field more complex.

PROJECT NOVELTY AND TRADITIONAL PROJECT MANAGEMENT

N THIS APPENDIX we observe the impact of the various levels of novelty on the classic processes of project management. We use the nine common PMBoK knowledge areas. Table 1 shows how various levels of product novelty affect these areas. The higher your product's novelty, the less clear things are at the outset. Thus, the estimates are less accurate and the risk is higher, and you need more flexibility and creativity to bring the project to a successful completion.

TABLE 1

Product novelty and PMBoK knowledge areas

PMBoK knowledge area	LEVEL OF PROJECT NOVELTY		
	Derivative	*Platform*	*Breakthrough*
Integration	Simple integration based on previous experience; focus on derivative added value and on quick transfer to operations and sales	Extensive cross-functional and customer involvement; focus on integration of new elements and new capabilities in the new generation; extensive testing during integration period	Integration focused on core functions to prove product concept validity; incorporate customer feedback through fast prototyping and beta sites; integrate organizational functions to create market awareness
Scope	Focus mainly on work needed for incorporating value added to product	Define top-down work from scratch; tight scope control to ensure smooth product introduction	Flexible scope management to enable changes based on market feedback and testing
Time	Fast-tracking time management to ensure quick delivery to market	Plan enough time to maximize product's new capabilities and eliminate all product faults; but time to market is important for competitiveness	Allow for enough product versions before final product defined; be flexible in considering new ideas; avoid shortcuts; make contingency plans for possible difficulties
Cost	Design to cost and tight budget control; improved cost effectiveness	Detailed cost planning and careful control; allocate budget for thorough testing; beware of potential overruns due to unnecessary additions	Flexible cost control before final product definition; allocate resources for prototypes and market testing
Quality	Focus on continuous incremental product quality improvement	Extensive quality planning and quality assurance; continuous debugging throughout the project	Quality less critical due to product newness; some quality planning in later stages of project
Human resources	Efficiency-, cost-, and time-conscious people; no-nonsense people; rigid management style	Well-organized, cross-functional team members; people who can see the big picture; semirigid management style	Look for creative and innovative people in various functions; allow freedom to express and test new ideas; highly flexible management style
Communications	Short and quick communication channels; minimal level of formal communication	Extensive and multiple communication channels across all functional areas; formal communication and documentation complemented by some informal interaction	Extensive and frequent informal communication If possible, consider co-location; formal documentation of final decisions
Risk	Minimal risk; risk management is focused on product changes	Extensive risk management plan; identify potential risk areas early; create contingency plans and redundancies to protect from failures	High risk due to many unknowns; different design approaches coupled with contingency plans
Procurement	Use off-the-shelf items when possible; use multiple sources to guarantee lower cost and avoid delays in market introduction	Involve suppliers in definition and design of major components and subsystems; use multiple sources for other components	Use any available source, including trial versions, to guarantee substantial product advantage in first prototypes; secure supply sources for final version

EMPIRICAL RESULTS FOR PROJECT TECHNOLOGY

THE QUANTITATIVE PARTS of our studies strengthen the validity of the qualitative findings by measuring statistical differences in managerial variables among various project types and identifying contingency trends.[26] Table 2 contains information about the differing resources consumed by various project types. It includes the descriptive statistics

TABLE 2

Project resources for various levels of technological uncertainty

	TECHNOLOGICAL UNCERTAINTY				ANOVA		
Variables	LT Mean (S.D.)	MT Mean (S.D.)	HT Mean (S.D.)	SHT Mean (S.D.)	df	F	Correlation
Project budget scale level	3.03 (1.17)	3.11 (1.16)	3.51 (0.78)	3.70 (0.67)	3,123	2.04	.218*
Project duration scale level	2.39 (1.10)	2.88 (0.78)	3.15 (0.95)	3.40 (0.96)	3,123	6.12***	.318***
Average labor employed	142 (382)	45 (90)	38 (36)	80 (126)	3,123	1.99	−.142
Percentage of academic degrees	20.2 (29.9)	55.1 (27.2)	59.3 (25.5)	66.6 (17)	3,123	15.2***	.452***

*p < .05 **p < .01 ***p < .001

for four levels of technological uncertainty. The scale value associated with budget was from 1 (less than $100,000) to 6 (more than $1 billion). The project's duration scale value was from 1 (less than six months) to 6 (more than eight years). The other two variables were the average number of employees during execution and the percentage of people holding academic degrees. The table also contains the results of ANOVA (Analysis of Variance) tests for each variable, and Pearson correlation coefficients between these variables and technological uncertainty.

The data in table 2 clearly show that higher uncertainty requires increased budgets and longer projects; yet the average number of workers employed on the project is not related to technological uncertainty. The increase in budget and time of higher-tech projects can be attributed to the project's complexity and not to the need to employ more people. However, higher-tech projects employ more academic workers than do lower-tech projects.

A major distinction between projects is demonstrated by ascending levels of engineering activities with the increase in technological uncertainty (see table 3). The first variable—the number of activities included in the project's planning network—varies from 1 (fewer than 100) to 4 (more than 10,000). The second and third variables describe the number of design cycles performed before the design was frozen and the quarter in which the design freeze took place (zero means that the design was frozen before the project's initiation). Design reviews and planning indicate the level of effort invested in performing the engineering tasks in the project. Planning includes three variables: the level of use of computerized planning methods, detailed milestones, and integrative planning of budget and schedule (all on a Likert scale of 1 to 7). As one can see, these variables are positively associated with technological uncertainty, indicating the need for better planning and control in high- and super-high-tech projects.

The remainder of table 3 describes several combined variables of the project engineering process (on Likert scales of 1 to 7). For example, the risk management measure represents variables for issues such as initial identification of project risks, probabilistic assessment of risks, and inclusion of a detailed plan for risk mitigation. The systems engineering measure includes four variables, such as the use of structured systems engineering procedures, use of configuration management, and use of various types of software. Quality management represents three variables measuring the extent to which a total quality plan was prepared, quality goals were selected, and statistical control was performed in the project.

All engineering variables increase with technological uncertainty when we move from low-tech projects to high-tech projects. For some

TABLE 3

Descriptive statistics and ANOVA results for various levels of technological uncertainty: Engineering- and design-related variables

| | TECHNOLOGICAL UNCERTAINTY | | | | ANOVA | | |
Variables	LT Mean (S.D.)	MT Mean (S.D.)	HT Mean (S.D.)	SHT Mean (S.D.)	df	F	Correlation
Activities scale level	1.50 (.83)	1.66 (.72)	1.93 (.69)	2.30) (.48	3,121	12.16***	.301***
Number of design cycles	1.03 (.33)	2.07 (.60)	2.60 (.95)	2.70 (1.2)	3,121	28.7***	.608***
Design freeze quarter	.25 (.52)	1.95 (1.0)	2.3 (.83)	2.6 (.96)	3,121	37.65***	.581***
Design reviews	3.13 (2.3)	5.29 (1.9)	5.97 (1.3)	5.6 (1.8)	3,117	12.66***	.416***
Planning	3.92 (1.9)	4.83 (1.4)	5.20 (1.4)	6.06 (1.1)	3,120	5.95***	.351***
Risk management	1.87 (1.7)	2.38 (1.5)	2.8 (1.4)	3.25 (.94)	3,89	2.07	.255*
Systems engineering	2.74 (2.2)	3.95 (1.8)	4.99 (1.5)	4.58 (1.8)	3,92	6.31**	.364***
Quality management	3.59 (2.3)	3.87 (1.8)	4.72 (1.7)	4.85 (1.5)	3,96	2.35	.247*

*$p < .05$ **$p < .01$ ***$p < .001$

variables (design reviews and systems engineering), there is no further increase for super-high-tech projects. In conclusion, higher-technology projects require more design cycles, later design freeze, and increased attention to design considerations, risk management, systems engineering, and quality management.[27]

APPENDIX 5B

PROJECT TECHNOLOGY
AND TRADITIONAL
PROJECT MANAGEMENT

A S WE HAVE SEEN, moving along the uncertainty dimension is associated mainly with the way technical problems are resolved. It affects the number of design cycles, the time committed to design changes, the need to build prototypes, the extent of testing, and the frequency and complexity of trade-off decisions. Each of these concerns may have an impact on traditional project management, as shown in table 4.

TABLE 4

Technological uncertainty and the PMBoK knowledge areas

PMBoK knowledge area	LEVEL OF TECHNOLOGICAL UNCERTAINTY			
	Low-Tech	Medium-Tech	High-Tech	Super-High-Tech
Integration	Simple integration based on previous experience; quick transfer to operations and sales	Focus on integration of elements new to the company; involve customers in new areas to ensure meeting their requirements	Extensive cross-functional and customer involvement; extensive testing during integration; integrate organizational functions to create market awareness	Integration focused on core functions to prove system concept validity; extensive effort in integration of newly developed technologies; integrate users' feedback based on fast prototyping
Scope	Tight scope control from project initiation; allow only changes requested and approved by customer	Allow changes only before design freeze; tight scope control after design freeze	Define top-down work from scratch; allow more time for design cycles; tight scope control after design freeze to ensure product integrity	Flexible scope management to enable changes based on technological feasibility and prototype testing
Time	Tight schedule control from the start; plan for early start of most activities; small reserve for external risks	Keep management reserve to allow some time for new parts; tight schedule control after elimination of initial risks; time to market is important for competitiveness	Plan enough time for integration and testing to eliminate all product faults	Allow for enough product versions before final product is defined; be flexible about incorporation of new technologies and ideas; make contingency plans for possible difficulties
Cost	Budget based on detailed design and previous experience; tight budget control	Design to cost and tight budget control; small reserve for unforeseen technological difficulties	Detailed cost control based on careful planning; allocate budget for thorough testing; beware of potential overruns due to unnecessary additions	Flexible cost control before final product definition; allocate resources for prototypes and testing; relatively large reserve for contingency plans
Quality	Strict adherence to contractual specifications; use of well-known and reliable components	Focus on technological areas new to the firm; design for reliability, manufacturability, and maintainability	Extensive quality planning and quality assurance; continuous debugging throughout the project; design for reliability, manufacturability, and maintainability	Emphasis on product performance; other aspects of quality less important due to product innovativeness; some quality planning in later stages of project

(continued)

TABLE 4 *(continued)*

Technological uncertainty and the PMBoK knowledge areas

PMBoK knowledge area	LEVEL OF TECHNOLOGICAL UNCERTAINTY			
	Low-Tech	*Medium-Tech*	*High-Tech*	*Super-High-Tech*
Human Resources	Efficiency-conscious people; rigid management style	Well-organized, cross-functional team members; creative and innovative people in development functions; semirigid management style	Leaders with high technical skills; creative and innovative people in development functions; flexible management style in first phases; rigid management style after design freeze	Leaders with exceptional technical skills and capability to assess potential value in not-yet-developed technologies; creative and innovative people in various functions; allow freedom to express and test new ideas; highly flexible management style
Communications	Short and quick, less intense communication channels; most channels are formal	Formal communication and documentation, complemented by some informal interaction	Numerous formal and informal communication channels for interaction among team members; formal documentation of final decisions	Extensive and frequent informal communication; if possible, consider co-location; formal documentation of final decisions
Risk	Almost no internal or technological risk; risk management is focused on external sources	Identify possible risk areas and focus on them to avoid delays and budget overruns	Extensive risk management plan; create contingency plans and redundancies to protect from failures	Look for trouble; high risk due to many unknowns; different design approaches coupled with contingency plans
Procurement	Use only off-the-shelf items; secure supply sources before project start	Use off-the-shelf items when possible; involve suppliers in definition and design of special-purpose components and subsystems	Involve suppliers in definition and design of major components and subsystems; use multiple sources to guarantee lower cost and avoid delays in market introduction	Use any available source, including trial versions, to guarantee technological feasibility in first prototypes; secure supply sources for final version

EMPIRICAL RESULTS FOR PROJECT COMPLEXITY

A S MENTIONED IN appendix 5A, the quantitative portion of our studies strengthens the validity of the qualitative findings. Here, we look at complexity.[28] Table 5 contains information about the resources consumed by various project types. It includes the descriptive statistics for various levels of complexity. The scale values in budget terms are from 1 (less than $100,000) to 6 (more than $1 billion). The project's duration scale values are from 1 (less than six months) to 6 (more than eight years). The other two variables are the average number of employees during execution and the percentage of people holding academic degrees. Table 5 also contains the results of ANOVA (Analysis of Variance) tests for each variable, and Pearson correlation coefficients between these variables and project complexity, represented by a scale of 1 (assembly) to 3 (array).

As we found, there seems to be an association between complexity and size. Both budget and duration significantly increased with scope. In contrast, we found that the percentage of workers having academic degrees tends to decrease with complexity, probably because building high-complexity projects requires a large number of builders and craft workers and a smaller portion of academic personnel, who are usually engaged in design, planning, analysis, and testing.

We also observed a major distinction between projects based on managerial variables. Table 6 includes the descriptive statistics, ANOVA, and correlation coefficients obtained for such variables. The first two variables

TABLE 5

Project resources for various levels of project complexity

	PROJECT COMPLEXITY			ANOVA		
Variable	*Assembly* Mean (S.D.)	*System* Mean (S.D.)	*Array* Mean (S.D.)	df	F	Correlation
Project budget scale level	2.47 (0.99)	3.47 (0.81)	4.55 (0.88)	2,124	31.45***	.548***
Project duration scale level	2.50 (0.96)	3.00 (0.90)	3.66 (1.11)	2,124	8.12**	.308***
Average labor employed	11 (17)	54 (79)	393 (623)	2,124	18.26***	.359***
Percentage of workers with academic degrees	57.2 (28.0)	49.6 (31.3)	23.3 (23.1)	2,124	4.52*	−.229**

*p < .05 **p < .01 ***p < .001

are on a scale of 1 to 5 and represent a combination of a few subvariables. For example, the systems engineering measure includes four subvariables, such as use of structured systems engineering procedures, use of configuration management, and use of various types of software. As you can see, the use of systems engineering and quality management practices increases significantly in system and array projects compared with assembly projects, but systems engineering is more common in system projects than in array projects. Finally, the number of project activities and the extent of planning, control, and documentation all seem to increase significantly with project complexity.

The number of activities included in the project's planning network is coded into four levels: 1 (fewer than 100); 2 (between 100 and 1,000); 3 (between 1,000 and 10,000); and 4 (more than 10,000). The other variables in table 6 are seven-point scale combined measures representing the extent to which formal methods were used in each of these groups of variables.

Table 6 clearly indicates the need to resort to more formal procedures when project complexity increases. All managerial variables in the table are significantly associated with complexity. An interesting exception is project planning. The highest level of planning is found in system projects rather than in array projects.

TABLE 6

Descriptive statistics and ANOVA results for various levels of project complexity

	PROJECT COMPLEXITY			ANOVA		
Variable	Assembly Mean (S.D.)	System Mean (S.D.)	Array Mean (S.D.)	df	F	Correlation
Systems engineering	3.20 (1.9)	4.84 (1.6)	3.81 (2.5)	2,93	8.55***	.264***
Quality management	3.52 (1.9)	4.63 (1.8)	4.28 (1.6)	2,97	3.71*	.214*
Activities	1.18 (.47)	1.89 (.68)	2.66 (.86)	2,122	46.2***	.524***
Work breakdown structure	3.75 (2.2)	5.09 (1.6)	5.91 (.91)	2,105	7.07**	.340***
Planning	3.99 (1.7)	5.26 (1.4)	4.66 (1.5)	2,121	7.95**	.247**
Control	3.90 (1.5)	4.82 (1.3)	5.14 (1.2)	2,124	5.88**	.282**
Documentation	4.75 (1.6)	5.45 (1.1)	5.91 (.96)	2,123	4.49*	.168

$*p < .05$ $**p < .01$ $***p < .001$

PROJECT COMPLEXITY AND TRADITIONAL PROJECT MANAGEMENT

TABLE 7 SHOWS how different levels of complexity may affect project management processes according to the major PMBoK knowledge areas.

TABLE 7

Project complexity and PMBoK knowledge areas

PMBoK knowledge area	LEVEL OF PROJECT COMPLEXITY		
	Assembly	*System*	*Array*
Integration	Simple integration; quick transfer to operations and sales	Extensive integration period to make sure the entire system is functioning as planned; cross-functional and customer involvement; gradual integration of subsystems; extensive testing during system integration	Integration of subsystems by subcontractors; rare cases of full-scale integration by main contractor
Scope	Allow only changes that may improve cost effectiveness; scope may change due to special requirements of OEM manufacturers	Allow more time for design cycles; tight scope control after design freeze to ensure product integrity	Tight scope control; early design freeze of array architecture to allow work of systems-level contractors
Time	Tight schedule control from the start; small reserve for external risks	Plan enough time for subsystem testing, system integration, and testing to eliminate all product faults	Keep management reserve to allow for delays by contractors; plan enough time for total array coordination of functions
Cost	Budget based on detailed design and previous experience; design to cost; tight budget control	Detailed cost control based on careful planning; allocate budget for thorough testing; beware of potential overruns due to unnecessary additions	Overall budget managed by main contractor; flexibility in allocation of budget to contractors; keep management reserve to allow for prolonged on-site coordination
Quality	Strict adherence to contractual specifications; use of well-known and reliable components; design for reliability and manufacturability	Extensive quality planning and quality assurance; continuous debugging throughout the project	Emphasis on interface between systems; incorporation of central and/or remote test and fault analysis

(continued)

TABLE 7 (continued)

Project complexity and PMBoK knowledge areas

PMBoK knowledge area	LEVEL OF PROJECT COMPLEXITY		
	Assembly	System	Array
Human resources	Main focus on technical skills and design for efficiency, cost, and time	Leaders with high system skills as well as technical skills; well-organized, cross-functional team members; flexible management style in first phases, rigid management style after design freeze	Leaders with exceptional managerial skills, extensive prior experience, and human relations skills; prefer a program manager with good diplomatic skills and ability to deal with local and governmental authorities; highly flexible management style
Communications	Short and quick, mostly informal channels; formal documentation of final decisions	If possible, consider co-location; numerous formal and informal communication channels for interaction among team members; formal documentation of final decisions	Mostly formal communication and documentation with major contractors; formal documentation of all decisions having contractual implications
Risk	Minimal risk management focused on incorporation of technologies and external sources that might cause delays and overruns	Extensive risk management plan; contingency plans and redundancies to protect from failures	Risk associated mainly with systems working together; risk management of each system conducted as a stand-alone by its contractor
Procurement	Use off-the-shelf items when possible; secure supply sources before project start	Involve suppliers in definition and design of major components and subsystems; use multiple sources to guarantee lower cost and avoid delays inmarket introduction	Use contractors with prior expertise in development of required subsystems; prefer contractors sharing a similar culture

PROJECT PACE AND TRADITIONAL PROJECT MANAGEMENT

TABLE 8 DESCRIBES how various levels of project pace affect project management according to the major PMBoK knowledge areas. As you can see, with increased pace, management attention is increasingly focused on reducing the risk of project delays.

TABLE 8

Project pace and the PMBoK knowledge areas

PMBoK knowledge area	LEVEL OF PROJECT PACE			
	Regular	*Fast/Competitive*	*Time-Critical*	*Blitz*
Integration	Gradual integration until final system is completed and tested	Intensive integration and testing to ensure timely entry to the market	Carefully planned periods of integration to ensure product preparedness on time	No time for integration in blitz projects
Scope	Use of regular scope management techniques	Flexible scope management to enable changes based on market feedback and competitors' actions	Tight scope control to avoid unnecessary changes that might delay the project	No scope control
Time	Time is not critical; take the necessary time to ensure product integrity	Time to market is important for competitiveness; use fast tracking and early freeze of requirements and design to ensure quick delivery to market; top management monitors time by major milestones completion	Time is extremely critical; use all available resources to meet time goals; make contingency plans for possible difficulties; plan enough time to eliminate all product faults; top management is closely involved and monitors time performance frequently	Time is extremely critical; use all available resources to solve crisis situation; prepare contingency plans for possible situations; ongoing involvement of top management to guarantee timely resolution of crisis
Cost	Detailed cost control based on careful planning	Allocate resources for fast prototypes and market testing; time takes precedence over cost	Allocate budget for alternative solutions and thorough testing to guarantee prompt time completion	Cost is not an issue
Quality	Focus on continuous incremental improvement in product quality	Extensive quality planning and quality assurance to guarantee time to market	Extensive quality planning and assurance to prevent any delay	No specific emphasis on quality

Human resources	No particular focus on project team selection; flexible management style	Cross-functional teams; semirigid management style	No-nonsense people who can see the criticality of time constraint; rigid management style	Task force trained in advance and released from other duties; use outside personnel to solve critical problems
Communications	Most communication focused on professional issues	Extensive and multiple communication channels across all functional areas; formal documentation complemented by some informal interaction	Short and frequent communication channels; co-locate team members in same facility, if possible	Extensive informal and ongoing communication throughout the crisis
Risk	No specific focus on risk of delays	Extensive risk management plan; identify potential risk areas early; different design approaches to reduce risk of delays	Identify potential risk areas early; create contingency plans and redundancies to protect from failing to meet the deadline	Special importance of contingency plans prepared in advance for various scenarios
Procurement	Use various supply sources, as required; secure supply sources for final version of product	Involve suppliers in definition and design of major components and subsystems; use multiple sources to guarantee lower cost and avoid delays in market introduction	Use off-the-shelf items, when possible; rely on known suppliers; create umbrella contracts for fast acquisition of components and materials without the need to renew contracts	Use any available source, including trial versions; prepare emergency procurement procedures and channels in advance

NOTES

Chapter 1

1. Why GM's Plan Won't Work," *BusinessWeek*, May 9, 2005.

2. Robert Kanigel, *The One Best Way: Frederick Winslow Taylor and the Enigma of Efficiency* (New York: Penguin Books, 1997).

3. In fact, Michael Porter wrote in 1996 that "operational efficiency is not a competitive advantage." Michael E. Porter, "What Is Strategy?" *Harvard Business Review* (Nov–Dec 1996): 61–78.

4. Notice that the Project Management Institute defines a project as "a temporary endeavor undertaken to create a unique product or service," and project management as "the application of knowledge, skills, tools, and techniques to project activities in order to meet project requirements." *A Guide to the Project Management Body of Knowledge* (Newtown Square, PA: Project Management Institute, 2004).

5. The Standish Group, *Extreme Chaos* (West Yarmouth, MA: The Standish Group International Inc., 2001).

6. Gerrit Klaschke, *What the CHAOS Chronicles 2003 Reveal* (San Diego, CA: Cost Xpert Group, 2003).

7. Robert G. Cooper, *Winning at New Products* (Reading, MA: Addison-Wesley Publishing Company, 1993); Robert G. Cooper, *Winning at New Products: Accelerating the Process from Idea to Launch,* 3rd ed. (Reading, MA: Perseus Books, 2001).

8. *The Bull Survey* (London: Spikes Cavell Research Company, 1998).

9. Aaron J. Shenhar and Dov Dvir, *Managing R&D Defense Projects* (Tel-Aviv: Institute for Business Research, Tel-Aviv University and Ministry of Defense, 1993).

10. Lynda M. Applegate, Ramiro Montealegre, James H. Nelson, and Carin-Isabel Knoop, "Implementing the Denver International Airport Baggage-Handling System (A)," Case 9-396-311 (Boston: Harvard Business School, November 6, 1996); Paul Stephen Dempsey, Andrew R. Goetz, and Joseph S. Szyliowicz, *Denver International Airport: Lessons Learned* (New York: McGraw Hill, 1997).

11. Steve Kemper, *Code Name Ginger: The Story Behind Segway and Dean Kamen's Quest to Invent a New World* (Boston: Harvard Business School Press, 2003).

12. Brian Sauser, Aaron J. Shenhar, and Richard Reilly, "Why Projects Fail: How Contingency Theory Can Provide New Insights," working paper, Stevens Institute of Technology, Hoboken, NJ, 2005.

13. Peter W. Morris, *The Management of Projects* (London: Thomas Telford, 1997).

14. *A Guide to the Project Management Body of Knowledge,* 2004.

15. Ibid.

16. *Organizational Project Management Maturity Model (OPM3)* (Newtown Square, PA: Project Management Institute, 2003).

17. Terry Williams, "Assessing and Moving on from the Dominant Project Management Discourse in the Light of Project Overruns," *IEEE Transactions of Engineering Management* 52, no. 4 (2005): 497–508.

18. *A Guide to the Project Management Body of Knowledge,* 2004.

19. This statement was offered by Jeff K. Pinto and Jeff G. Covin in "Critical Factors in Project Implementation: A Comparison of Construction and R&D Projects," *Technovation* 9 (1989): 49–62.

20. Several exceptions were offered by various studies, as we report later, but none has affected the profession at large. The PMI's PMBoK does not make a distinction among project types.

21. Alex Laufer, in his book *Simultaneous Management* (New York: AMACOM, 1998), explored the concepts of dealing with uncertainty and accuracy of planning. His conclusion is simple: to deal with a project's uncertainty, you need to plan, act, and then keep planning or replanning.

22. You can see this model as a "Balanced Scorecard" for projects. The concept of the Balanced Scorecard was developed by Harvard's Robert S. Kaplan and David P. Norton to build a success dimension framework for planning the success of corporations. Their framework includes four dimensions: customer, internal, innovation and learning, and financial. *The Strategy-Focused Organization: How Balanced Scorecard Companies Thrive in the New Business Environment* (Boston: Harvard Business School Press, 2000).

Chapter 2

1. A short review of the Sydney Opera House construction project can be found at http://www.aviewoncities.com/sydney/operahouse.htm. The full story can be found in Peter Murray, *The Saga of Sydney Opera House: The Dramatic Story of the Design and Construction of the Icon of Modern Australia* (London: Spon Press, 2003).

2. For example, as Jeffery K. Pinto and Dennis R. Slevin note, "There are few topics in the field of project management that are so frequently discussed and yet so rarely agreed upon as that of the notion of project success" ("Project Success: Definitions and Measurement Techniques," *Project Management Journal* 19, no. 1 (1988): 67).

3. A summary of the development of the Ford Taurus can be found at http://media.ford.com/article_display.cfm?article_id=15702. Lewis C. Veraldi, the father of the Taurus, retired from Ford Motor Company three years after the launch of the Taurus (Jon Lowell, "Ford's 'Clean-up' Hitter: Lewis C. Veraldi Retires," *Ward's Auto World,* December 1989).

4. Pascal G. Zachary, *Showstopper! The Breakneck Pace to Create Windows NT and the Next Generation at Microsoft* (New York: The Free Press, 1994).

5. Fred Guterl, "Design Case History: Apple's Macintosh," *IEEE Spectrum* (December 1984): 34–43.

6. David Baccarini, "The Logical Framework Method for Defining Project Success," *Project Management Journal* 30, no. 4 (1999): 25–32.

7. Aaron J. Shenhar, Dov Dvir, Ofer Levy, and Alan Maltz, "Project Success: A Multidimensional Strategic Concept," *Long-Range Planning* 34 (2001): 699–725; and Aaron J. Shenhar, Dov Dvir, and Ofer Levy, "Mapping the Dimensions of Project Success," *Project Management Journal* 28, no. 2 (1997): 5–13.

8. Robert S. Kaplan and David P. Norton, *The Balanced Scorecard* (Boston: Harvard Business School Press, 1996); and Robert S. Kaplan and David P. Norton, *The Strategy-Focused Organization: How Balanced Scorecard Companies Thrive in the New Business Environment* (Boston: Harvard Business School Press, 2000).

9. Shenhar et al., "Project Success: A Multidimensional Strategic Concept"; and Alan C. Maltz, Aaron J. Shenhar, and Richard R. Reilly, "Beyond the Balanced Scorecard: Refining the Search for Organizational Success Measures," *Long Range*

Planning 36 (2003): 187–204. See also Aaron J. Shenhar and Dov Dvir, "Long Term Success Dimensions in Technology-based Organizations," in *Handbook of Technology Management,* ed. Gerard H. Gaynor (New York: McGraw Hill, 1996), 32.1–32.15.

10. Mark Freeman and Peter Beale, "Measuring Project Success," *Project Management Journal* 1 (1992): 8–17.

11. Edward McSpendon, "Los Angeles Metro Rail: A World-Class Rail System," *PmNetwork* (January 1994): 17–23.

12. In Shenhar et al. ("Project Success: A Multidimensional Strategic Concept"), we used only four dimensions. Our later research has expanded our model to include the fifth dimension, impact on the team. See Maltz et al., "Beyond the Balanced Scorecard: Refining the Search for Organizational Success Measures."

13. A study performed by Stan Lipovetskey, Asher Tishler, Dov Dvir, and Aaron Shenhar has shown that of the four dimensions of project success, the respondents rated impact on the customer as the most important, and project efficiency as second in importance. The other two dimensions were usually rated much lower in importance. Nevertheless, for special types of projects other dimensions may gain in importance. For example, for a feasibility study, building the future is the main purpose. For more details, see Stan Lipovetskey, Asher Tishler, Dov Dvir, and Aaron Shenhar, "The Relative Importance of Project Success Dimensions," *R&D Management* 27, no. 2 (1997): 97–106.

Chapter 3

1. Aaron J. Shenhar, Dov Dvir, and Shlomo Alkaher, "From a Single Discipline Product to a Multidisciplinary System: Adapting the Right Style to the Right Project," *System Engineering* 6, no. 3 (2003): 123–134.

2. The Project Management Institute has initiated a study to find out whether and what classification systems are used by organizations. See Lynn Crawford, Brian Hobbs, and Rodney J. Turner, *Project Categorization Research Report* (Newtown Square, PA: Project Management Institute, Research Department, 2004).

3. Aaron J. Shenhar and Dov Dvir, "Toward a Typological Theory of Project Management," *Research Policy* 25 (1996): 607–632; Aaron J. Shenhar, "One Size Does Not Fit All Projects: Exploring Classical Contingency Domains," *Management Science* 47, no. 3 (2001): 394–414; and Aaron J. Shenhar and Dov Dvir, "How Projects Differ and What to Do About It," in *Handbook of Managing Projects,* eds. Jeffrey Pinto and Peter W. G. Morris (New York: Wiley, 2004).

4. The story was originally written by Takahashi Hidemine, http://web-japan.org/nipponia/nipponia16/start.html.

5. http://pocketcalculatorshow.com/walkman/history.html.

6. Michael Maccoby, "Is There a Best Way to Build a Car?" *Harvard Business Review* 75, no. 6 (1997): 161–170; and Fred Kern, "Launching the BMW Z3: The 007 James Bond Edition," 2003, http://users.belgacom.net/bmw_z3/bmw_z3_history.htm.

7. John McQuaid, "Katrina Trapped City in Double Disasters," *New Orleans Times-Picayune,* September 7, 2005.

8. Shenhar and Dvir, "Toward a Typological Theory of Project Management"; Aaron J. Shenhar, "From Theory to Practice: Toward a Typology of Project Management Styles," *IEEE Transactions on Engineering Management* 41, no.1 (1998): 33–48; Shenhar, "One Size Does Not Fit All Projects"; and Shenhar and Dvir, "How Projects Differ and What to Do About It."

9. These categories were used by Steve Wheelwright and Kim Clark in their book *Revolutionizing Product Development* to indicate a company's aggregate of R&D projects (New York: The Free Press, 1992).

10. Shenhar and Dvir, "Toward a Typological Theory of Project Management"; Dov Dvir, Stan Lipovetsky, Aaron J. Shenhar, and Asher Tishler, "In Search of Project Classification: A Non-Universal Approach to Project Success Factors," *Research Policy* 27 (1998): 915–935; Shenhar, "From Theory to Practice: Toward a Typology of Project Management Styles"; and Shenhar, "One Size Does Not Fit All Projects."

11. Shenhar and Dvir, "How Projects Differ and What to Do About It."

12. A survey of classification systems used by companies can be found in Crawford et al., *Project Categorization Research Report.*

13. Eric Darton, *Divided We Stand: A Biography of New York's World Trade Center* (New York: Basic Books, 1999).

14. Angus K. Gillespie, *Twin Towers: The Life of New York City's World Trade Center* (New Brunswick, NJ: Rutgers University Press, 1999).

Chapter 4

1. Steven Wheelwright and Kim Clark have used these three terms to describe development projects. They also added a fourth type: R&D projects (which can also be categorized by technology level, as discussed later in chapter 5). Managers are advised to use these types to create an aggregate project portfolio to help an organization allocate its efforts in proportion to the need for and benefits from projects of each type. Steven C. Wheelwright and Kim B. Clark, *Revolutionizing Product Development* (New York: The Free Press, 1992).

2. For more details, see Burr Snider, "The *Toy Story* Story," *Wired*, December 1995, http://www.wired.com/wired/archive/3.12/toy.story.html.

3. William J. Abernathy and James M. Utterback, "Patterns of Industrial Innovation," *MIT Technology Review* 80, no. 7 (1978): 40–47.

4. William J. Abernathy and Kim B. Clark, "Innovation: Mapping the Winds of Creative Destruction," *Research Policy* 14 (1985): 2–22; and Rebecca M. Henderson and Kim B. Clark, "Architectural Innovation: The Reconfiguration of Existing Product Technologies and the Failure of Established Firms," *Administrative Science Quarterly* 35 (1990): 9–30.

5. Clayton M. Christensen wrote in his book *The Innovator's Dilemma*, "Markets that do not exist cannot be analyzed." *The Innovator's Dilemma: When New Technologies Cause Great Firms to Fail* (Boston: Harvard Business School Press, 1997).

6. Geoffrey A. Moore, *Crossing the Chasm* (New York: HarperCollins Publishers, 1991).

7. Christopher M. McDermott and Gina Colarelli O'Connor, "Managing Radical Innovation: An Overview of Emergent Strategy Issues," *Journal of Product Innovation Management* 19, no. 6 (2002): 424–438.

8. Charles O'Reilly and Michael Tushman introduced the term the *ambidextrous organization,* in which emerging businesses are managed separately from existing business with different cultures and processes, but under the same organizational umbrella. Charles O'Reilly and Michael L. Tushman, "The Ambidextrous Organization," *Harvard Business Review*, vol. 82 (April 2004): 74–81.

9. Christensen, *The Innovator's Dilemma*; Clayton M. Christensen and Michael E. Raynor, *The Innovator's Solution.* (Boston: Harvard Business School Press, 2003)

10. In his book *Mastering the Dynamics of Innovation* (Boston: Harvard Business School Press, 1994), James Utterback describes how the nature of organizations changes as an innovation's dominant design is adopted. He distinguishes between the organic and the mechanistic organization. As a product becomes standardized and is produced in a systematic process, interdependence among organizational sub-

units gradually increases, making it difficult and costly to incorporate radical innovation. It is seen as necessary to provide rigid coordination that establishes consistent routines and rules to minimize inefficiency and costs in operations. This type of structure is known as mechanistic.

11. Charles W. L. Hill, "Establishing a Standard: Competitive Strategy and Technological Standards in Winner-take-all Industries," *Academy of Management Executive* 11, no. 2 (1997): 7–25.

12. Steve Kemper, *Code Name Ginger: The Story Behind Segway and Dean Kamen's Quest to Invent a New World* (Boston: Harvard Business School Press, 2003). See also Jeffrey S. Pinegar and Gregory Cohen, "Book review on *Code Name Ginger: The Story Behind Segway and Dean Kamen's Quest to Invent a New World*," *Journal of Product Innovation Management* 21, no. 2 (2004): 221–224.

13. Steve Kemper (*Code Name Ginger*) lived in Kamen's house for many months. Kemper often talked with Kamen late in the evening and was able to examine Kamen's role in the process of the Segway development. The book illustrates in detail how Kamen's presence affected the project. In particular, three facets of Kamen's personality stand out: he was afraid that other manufacturers would discover and steal the project; he always had final authority over the direction of the product and refused to relinquish control; and he was the ultimate cheerleader and salesperson.

14. Kemper, *Code Name Ginger*, 195. This passage reveals perhaps the greatest lessons in the book and explains why Kamen was not concerned with the lack of market research. Market research that attempts to ask respondents for solutions always fails to generate innovative solutions, and evidently this was the only kind of market research Kamen had witnessed. However, customers are the best and only reliable source for identifying market needs, something Kamen perhaps did not realize.

15. Cliff Havener and Margaret Thorpe, "Customers Can't Tell You What They Want (Mythology of Product Development and Marketing Strategy)," *Management Review* 83, no. 12 (1994): 42–45.

16. Kemper, *Code Name Ginger*, 227.

Chapter 5

1. Lynda M. Applegate, Ramiro Montealegre, and Carin-Isabel Knoop, "BAE Automated Systems (B): Implementing the Denver International Airport Baggage-Handling System," Case 9-396-311 (Boston: Harvard Business School, 1996).

2. Aaron J. Shenhar, Rias vanWyk, Joca Stefanovic, and Gerard Gaynor, "Toward a Fundamental Entity of Technology" (paper presented at the International Association for Management of Technology conference, Washington, DC, 2004).

3. Aaron J. Shenhar, "From Low to High-tech Project Management," *R&D Management* 23, no. 3 (1993): 199–214; Aaron J. Shenhar and Dov Dvir, "Toward a Typological Theory of Project Management," *Research Policy* 25 (1996): 607–632; and Aaron J. Shenhar, "One Size Does Not Fit All Projects: Exploring Classical Contingency Domains," *Management Science* 47, no. 3 (2001): 394–414.

4. Such an association is based on previous studies, equating "high-tech" with extensive use of new technologies, and technological maturity with low uncertainty. See William L. Shanklin and John K. Ryans Jr., *Marketing High Technology* (New York: Lexington Books, 1984); Philip A. Roussel, Kamal N. Saad, and Tamara J. Erickson, *Third Generation R&D* (Boston: Harvard Business School Press, 1991); and Kathleen M. Eisenhardt and Behnam N. Tabrizi, "Accelerating Adaptive Processes: Product Innovation in the Global Computer Industry," *Administrative Science Quarterly* 40 (1995): 84–110.

5. Arthur D. Little, "The Strategic Management of Technology" (paper presented at the European Management Forum, Davos, Switzerland, 1981); Roussel et al., *Third Generation R&D*.

6. Little, "The Strategic Management of Technology."

7. Ibid.; Roussel et al., *Third Generation R&D*; and Eisenhardt and Tabrizi, "Accelerating Adaptive Processes."

8. L. J. Bourgeois III and Kathleen M. Eisenhardt, "Strategic Decision Processes in High Velocity Environments: Four Cases in the Microcomputer Industry," *Management Science* 34, no. 7 (1988): 816–835.

9. Little, "The Strategic Management of Technology."

10. See Charles R. Pellegrino and Joshua Stoff, *Chariots for Apollo* (New York: Athenaeum, 1985); and Ray Villard, "From Idea to Observation: The Space Telescope at Work," *Astronomy* (June 1989): 38–44.

11. Past research suggests that the new-product development process and outcomes depend on the level of perceived uncertainty regarding the external environment (e.g., Tom Burns and George M. Stalker, *The Management of Innovation* (London: Oxford University Press, 1994); Noel Capon, John U. Farley, Donald Lehmann, and James M. Hulbert, "Profiles of Product Innovators among Large U.S. Manufacturers," *Management Science* 38, no. 2 (1992): 157–169; and Billie Jo Zirger and Modesto A. Maidique, "A Model of New Product Development," *Management Science* 36, no. 7 (1990): 867–883). However, the research does not precisely explain how organizations adapt the development process when the external environment is perceived to be highly uncertain. There are various sources of perceived uncertainty about the environment: technological uncertainty, consumer uncertainty, competitive uncertainty, and resource uncertainty (Kim B. Clark, "The Interaction of Design Hierarchies and Market Concepts in Technological Evolution," *Research Policy* 14 (1985): 235–251; Robert B. Duncan, "Characteristics of Organizational Environments and Perceived Environmental Uncertainty," *Administrative Science Quarterly* 17 (1972): 313–327; Lawrence R. Jauch and Kenneth L. Kraft, "Strategic Management of Uncertainty," *Academy of Management Review* 11, no. 4 (1986): 777–790; and Frances J. Milliken, "Three Types of Perceived Uncertainty about the Environment: State, Effect, and Response Uncertainty," *Academy of Management Review* 12, no. 1 (1987): 133–143). Perceived technological uncertainty refers to an individual's perceived inability to accurately predict or completely understand some aspect of the technological environment (Kirk H. Downey, Don H. Hellriegel, and John W. Slocum Jr., "Environmental Uncertainty: The Construct and Its Application," *Academy of Management Journal* 18, no. 3 (1975): 562–577; and Milliken, "Three Types of Perceived Uncertainty about the Environment"). Song and Montoya-Weiss found that cross-functional integration, marketing and technical project synergy, and proficiency in the marketing and technical development activities differentially contribute to project performance in high versus low perceived technological uncertainty. Michael X. Song and Mitzi M. Montoya-Weiss, "The Effects of Perceived Technological Uncertainty on Japanese New Product Development," *Academy of Management Journal* 44, no. 1 (2001): 61–80.

12. A discussion of prototypes was provided by Steven C. Wheelwright and Kim B. Clark in their book, *Revolutionizing Product Development* (New York: The Free Press, 1992). Regarding product novelty, they recommend the use of a design cycle with prototyping as a managerial tool for improving product quality and shortening time to market. They suggest using prototypes in the development process of new products according their novelty level and hence freezing the design at different phases of the project.

13. National Research Council, *Improving Engineering Design: Designing for Competitive Advantage* (Washington, DC: National Academy Press, 1991).

14. Karl E. Weick, *The Social Psychology of Organizing,* 2nd ed. (Reading, MA: Addison-Wesley Publishing, 1979).

15. Aaron J. Shenhar, Dov Dvir, and Shlomo Alakaher, "From a Single Discipline Product to a Multidisciplinary System: Adapting the Right Style to the Right Project," *System Engineering* 6, 3 (2003): 123–134.

16. The objective is to keep the process flexible to adapt to emerging environmental changes (Ken Kamoche and Miguel Pina e Cunha, "Minimal Structures: From Jazz Improvisation to Product Innovation," *Organization Studies* 22, no. 5 (2001): 733–764). However, there are risks in being flexible for too long, such as freezing the wrong concept or delaying the completion date of the project.

17. Paul F. Crickmore, *Lockheed SR-71: The Secret Missions Exposed,* 3rd ed. (Oxford: Osprey Publishing, 2000); Richard H. Graham, *SR-71 Revealed: The Inside Story* (Osceola, WI: MBI Publishing, 1996); http://www.sr-71.org; and http://www.nasm .si.edu/research/aero/aircraft/lockheed_sr71.htm.

18. The skunk works story is told by Johnson in his biographical book. According to Wikipedia, "The term *skunk works* came from the Al Capp comic strip *Li'l Abner,* which was popular in the 1940s. In the comic, the 'Skonk Works' was a backwoods still operated by Big Barnsmell, known as the 'inside man at the Skonk Works.' In his secret facility, he made 'kickapoo joy juice' by grinding dead skunks and worn shoes into a smoldering vat" (http://en.wikipedia.org/wiki/Skunk_works). Kelly Johnson and Maggie Smith, *Kelly: More Than My Share of It All* (Washington, DC: Smithsonian Books, 1990).

19. In the mid-1980s, Barry Boehm, then a chief scientist at TRW Inc., devised spiral development as a way to reduce risk on large software projects. Boehm stressed a cyclical approach in which customers evaluated early results and in-house engineers identified potential trouble spots at an early stage. Although Boehm formulated spiral development for software engineering, the Department of Defense has adapted the technique as part of its evolutionary acquisition strategy to get newer technologies into large platforms, such as assault vehicles and computer systems, much more quickly.

20. Charles R. Pellegrino and Joshua Stoff, *Chariots for Apollo: The Making of the Lunar Module* (New York: Atheneum, 1985).

21. Marianne W. Lewis, M. Ann Welsh, Gordon E. Dehler, and Stephen G. Green, "Product Development Tensions: Exploring Contrasting Styles in Project Management," *Academy of Management Journal* 45, no. 3 (2002): 546–564.

22. Aaron J. Shenhar, "Project Management Style and the Space Shuttle Program: A Retrospective Look," *Project Management Journal* 23 (1992): 32–37.

23. Richard S. Lewis, *The Voyage of Columbia, the First True Space Ship* (New York: Columbia University Press, 1984).

24. Marianne Lewis et al., "Product Development Tensions."

25. *Report of Columbia Accident Investigation Board,* vol. 1. (Washington, DC: National Aeronautics and Space Administration, 2003), 6.

26. "Even as the design grew in technical complexity, the Office of Management and Budget forced NASA to keep—or at least promise to keep—the Shuttle's development and operating costs low. In May 1971, NASA was told that it could count on a maximum of $5 billion spread over five years for any new development program. This budget ceiling forced NASA to give up its hope of building a fully reusable two-stage vehicle and kicked off an intense six-month search for an alternate design . . . NASA made bold claims about the expected savings to be derived from revolutionary technologies not yet developed . . . During 1970, NASA's leaders hoped to secure

White House approval for developing a fully reusable vehicle to provide routine and low cost manned access to space. However, the staff of the White House Office of Management and Budget, charged by Nixon with reducing NASA's budget, was skeptical of the value of manned space flight, especially given its high costs. To overcome these objections, NASA turned to justifying the Space Shuttle on economic grounds. If the same vehicle, NASA argued, launched all government and private sector payloads and if that vehicle were reusable, then the total costs of launching and maintaining satellites could be dramatically reduced. Such an economic argument, however, hinged on the willingness of the Department of Defense to use the Shuttle to place national security payloads in orbit. When combined, commercial, scientific, and national security payloads would require 50 Space Shuttle missions per year. This was enough to justify—at least on paper—investing in the Shuttle." *Report of Columbia Accident Investigation Board,* vol. 1, 22.

27. Joseph J. Trento, *Prescription for Disaster* (New York: Crown Publishers, 1987).

28. Shenhar, "Project Management Style and the Space Shuttle Program."

29. Technology readiness level (TRL) is a metric/measurement of the maturity of a particular technology and the consistent comparison of maturity between different types of technology. It includes the following levels: Level 1: Basic principles observed and supported. Level 2: Technology concept and/or application formulated. Level 3: Analytical and experimental critical function and/or characteristic proof-of-concept. Level 4: Component and/or breadboard validation in laboratory environment. Level 5: Component and/or breadboard validation in relevant environment. Level 6: System/subsystem model or prototype demonstration in a relevant environment. Level 7: System prototype demonstration in a space environment. Level 8: Actual system completed and "flight qualified." Level 9: Actual system "flight proven" through successful mission operation. *See* Aaron Shenhar, Dov Dvir, Dragan Milosevic, et al. "Toward a NASA-specific Project Management Framework," *Engineering Management Journal* 17, no. 4 (2005): 8–16.

Chapter 6

1. Kenneth Boulding was perhaps the first one to conceptualize the idea of systems and subsystems. In his famous 1956 article, "General System Theory: The Skeleton of Science," he wrote that everything in our universe is made of systems and subsystems, and he identified nine levels. Kenneth E. Boulding, "General System Theory: The Skeleton of Science," *Management Science* 2 (1956): 197–208. See also David L. Marples, "The Decisions of Engineering Design," *IEEE Transactions on Engineering Management* EM-8 (1961): 55–71; and Christopher Alexander, *Notes on the Synthesis of Form* (Cambridge, MA: Harvard University Press, 1964).

2. Kim B. Clark, "The Interaction of Design Hierarchies and Market Concepts in Technological Evolution," *Research Policy* 14 (1985): 235–251.

3. Eberhardt Rechtin, *Systems Architecting* (Englewood Cliffs, NJ: Prentice Hall, 1991).

4. See, for example, Johannes M. Pennings, "Structural Contingency Theory: A Reappraisal," *Research in Organizational Behavior* 14 (1992): 267–309; and Harold D. Doty and William H. Glick, "Typologies as a Unique Form of Theory Building: Toward Improved Understanding and Modeling," *Academy of Management Review* 19, no. 2 (1994): 230–251.

5. Dov Dvir, Stan Lipovetskey, Aaron J. Shenhar, and Asher Tishler, "In Search of Project Classification: A Non-uniform Mapping of Project Success Factors," *Research Policy* 27 (1998): 915–935.

6. For a detailed description of the development of the Blackbird, see Clarence L. "Kelly" Johnson and Maggie Smith, *Kelly: More Than My Share of It All* (Washington, DC: Smithsonian, 1985).

7. S. J. Manne and L. Collins, "Reconstructuring an Aging Infrastructure," *Project Management Journal* (April 1990): 9–24.

8. Jack K. Lemley, "The Channel Tunnel: Creating a Modern Wonder of the World," *PmNetwork* 6 (1992): 14–22.

9. Wayne F. Cascio, *The Guide to Responsible Restructuring* (Darby, PA: DIANE Publishing Co., 1995).

10. Ford Motor Co., *Ford Facts* (Dearborn, MI, 1994); David Sedgwick, "Fixing Ford," *Detroit News,* September 18, 1994, 1–5; "Corporate Scoreboard," *BusinessWeek*, March 6, 1995, 101; Ford Motor Co., "Ford to Realign Worldwide Automotive Processes and Organization to Manage Them," Public Affairs Office News Release, April 21, 1994.

11. Oscar Suris, "Retooling Itself, Ford Stresses Speed, Candor," *Wall Street Journal*, October 27, 1994, B1–B10.

12. Greg Gardner, "Report Card Time: Ford Shows Big Gains in Annual 'Productivity' Gauge," *Ward's AutoWorld*, August 1, 1998.

13. Harold Kerzner, *Project Management: A Systems Approach to Planning, Scheduling, and Controlling*, 8th ed. (New York: John Wiley & Sons, 2003); Jack R. Meredith and Samuel J. Mantel Jr., *Project Management: A Managerial Approach,* 5th ed. (New York: Wiley, 2003); Dennis Lock, *Project Management*, 8th ed. (Aldershot, Hampshire, UK: Gower Publishing Company, 2003).

14. For an explanation of how to build the WBS of a project, see, for example, G. D. Lavold, "Developing and Using the Work Breakdown Structure," in *Project Management Handbook,* eds. David I. Cleland and William R. King (New York: Van Nostrand Reinhold, 1988), 302–323.

15. Aaron Shenhar, Asher Tishler, Dov Dvir, Stan Lipovetskey, and Thomas Lechler, "Refining the Search for Project Success Factors: A Multivariate Typological Approach," *R&D Management* 32, no. 2 (2002): 111–126.

16. Lemley, "The Channel Tunnel."

17. The International Space Station is the largest and most complex international scientific project in history, and it represents a move of unprecedented scale off the home planet. Led by the United States, the International Space Station draws upon the scientific and technological resources of sixteen nations: Canada, Japan, Russia, eleven nations of the European Space Agency, and Brazil. More than four times as large as the Russian Mir space station, the completed International Space Station will have a mass of about 1,040,000 pounds. It measures 356 feet across and 290 feet long, with almost an acre of solar panels to provide electrical power to six state-of-the-art laboratories (http://www.shuttlepresskit.com/ISS_OVR/). See also the entry "Strategic Defense Initiative," *Columbia Encyclopedia,* 6th ed. (New York: Columbia University Press, 2004); http://www.bartleby.com/65/st/StratDI.html); and Janet A. McDonnell, *After Desert Storm: The U.S. Army and the Reconstruction of Kuwait* (Honolulu, HI: University Press of the Pacific, 2002).

18. Mike Hobday, Howard Rush, and Joe Tidd, "Innovation in Complex Products and Systems," *Research Policy* 29, no. 7–8 (2000): 793–804; Paul Nightingale, "The Product-Process-Organization Relationship in Complex Development Projects," *Research Policy* 29 (2000): 913–930; and Aaron J. Shenhar, "From Theory to Practice: Toward a Typology of Project-Management Styles," *IEEE Transactions on Engineering Management* 45, no. 1 (1998): 33–47.

19. Andrew P. Sage and William R. Rouse, "An Introduction to Systems Engineering and Systems Management," in *Handbook of Systems Engineering and Man-*

agement, eds. Andrew P. Sage and William R. Rouse (New York: Wiley Press, 1999); and Lee K. Hansen and H. Rush, "Hotspots in Complex Product Systems: Emerging Issues in Innovation Management," *Technovation* 18, no. 8/9 (1998): 555–561.

20. The needs and the seeds concept is used by Sharp Corporation to identify and decide whether to pursue business opportunities. It matches the identified needs of customers with the company's capabilities. "Sharp Corporation's Technology Strategy," Case 9-793-064 (Boston: Harvard Business School, revised April 1995).

21. Kevin Forsberg, Hal Mooz, and Howard Cotterman, *Visualizing Project Management,* 2nd ed. (New York: Wiley, 1997).

22. Eberhardt Rechtin and Mark W. Maier, *The Art of System Architecting* (New York: CRC Press, 1997).

Chapter 7

1. Kathleen M. Eisenhardt and Shona L. Brown, *Competing on the Edge: Strategy as Structured Chaos* (Boston: Harvard Business School Press, 1998); Kathleen M. Eisenhardt and Shona L. Brown, "Time Pacing: Competing in Markets That Won't Stand Still," *Harvard Business Review* 3, no. 4 (1998): 59–69; and Shona L. Brown and Kathleen M. Eisenhardt, "The Art of Continuous Change: Linking Complexity Theory and Time-paced Evolution in Relentlessly Shifting Organizations," *Administrative Science Quarterly* 42 (1997): 1–34.

2. Marco Iansiti and Alan MacCormack discuss the way projects should be managed in uncertain and dynamic environments that present fundamental challenges to managers. Between successive product generations, significant evolutions can occur in both the customer needs a product must address and the technologies it employs to satisfy these needs. Furthermore, even within a single development project, firms must respond to new information or risk developing a product that is obsolete the day it is launched. *Developing Products on Internet Time* (Boston: Harvard Business School Press, 1999).

3. *Mars Climate Orbiter Mishap Investigation Board Phase I Report* (Washington, DC: National Aeronautics and Space Administration, 1999).

4. Thomas A. Young, "Confusing Lines of Responsibility and Accountability Created," *Mars Program Independent Assessment* (Washington, DC: National Aeronautics and Space Administration, 2000), slide 46.

5. Noel Hinners, personal interview, February 4, 2004.

6. Aaron J. Shenhar, Dov Dvir, Thomas Lechler, and Michael Poli, "One Size Does Not Fit All: True for Projects, True for Frameworks" (paper presented at the First PMI Research Conference, Seattle, July 2002).

7. Eliyahu M. Goldratt, *Critical Chain* (Great Barrington, MA: North River Press, 1997).

Chapter 8

1. Steve Jobs, interviewed in "How Big Can Apple Get?" *Fortune,* February 21, 2005, 66–76.

2. For more details on project portfolio management, see Gerald I. Kendall and Steven C. Rollins, *Advanced Project Portfolio Management and the PMO: Multiplying ROI at Warp Speed* (Fort Lauderdale, FL: J. Ross Publishing, 2003); Harvey A. Levine, *Project Portfolio Management: A Practical Guide to Selecting Projects, Managing Portfolios, and Maximizing Benefits* (San Francisco, CA: Jossey-Bass, 2005); and Stephen S. Bonham, *IT Project Portfolio Management* (Norwood, MA: Artech House Books, 2005).

3. Many authors have studied project portfolio management. Bob Cooper is perhaps the most influential. Robert G. Cooper, Scott J. Edgett, and Elko J. Kleinschmidt, *Portfolio Management for New Products*, 2nd ed. (Cambridge, MA: Perseus Books, 2001) contend that a portfolio must be strategically aligned. This means that all projects are "on strategy" and that the breakdown of spending across projects, areas, markets, and so on must mirror the strategic priorities. Several portfolio methods are designed to achieve strategic alignment. One of them is the concept of *strategic buckets*. The process starts at the top with developing the business strategy and continues with formulating the product innovation strategy, outlining the business goals, and agreeing on where and how to focus the new product efforts. Next, you decide how to split up your resources: "Given the strategy, where should you spend your money?" You can make these splits by project types, product lines, markets or industry sectors, and so on. Thus, strategic buckets, or envelopes of resources, are established. Then, within each bucket or envelope, you rank all projects—active, on hold, and new—until all resources in that bucket are allocated. The result is multiple portfolios, one portfolio per bucket.

4. Aaron J. Shenhar, Dov Dvir, Thomas Lechler, and Michael Poli, "One Size Does Not Fit All: True for Projects, True for Frameworks" (paper presented at the PMI Research Conference, Seattle, July 2002).

5. Clayton M. Christensen, Michael E. Raynor, and Scott D. Anthony, "Six Keys to Building New Markets by Unleashing Disruptive Innovation, Management Gurus: The Importance of Disruptive Ideas & Innovation Chaos," http://hbswk.hbs.edu/item/3374.html.

6. Tom Burns and George M. Stalker, *The Management of Innovation* (London: Tavistock, 1961).

7. In contrast to the exploratory nature of many project management studies, the innovation literature has been richer in its theoretical development. A central notion in this development was the distinction between incremental and radical innovation (Burns and Stalker, *The Management of Innovation;* Edwin Mansfield, *Industrial Research and Technical Innovation* (New York: Norton, 1968); Gerald Zaltman, Robert Duncan, and Jonny Holbek, *Innovations and Organizations* (New York: Wiley, 1973); Michael Moch and E. V. Morse, "Size, Centralization and Organizational Adaptation of Innovations," *American Sociological Review* 42 (1977): 716–725; Stewart P. Blake, *Managing for Responsive Research and Development* (San Francisco: Freeman and Co., 1978); William J. Abernathy and James M. Utterback, "Patterns of Industrial Innovation," *Technology Review* (June–July 1978): 40–47; Chris Freeman, *The Economics of Industrial Innovation*, 2nd ed. (Cambridge, MA: MIT Press, 1982); John E. Ettlie, W. P. Bridges, and R. D. O'Keffe, "Organizational Strategy and Structural Differences for Radical vs. Incremental Innovation," *Management Science* 30 (1984): 682–695; and Robert D. Dewar and Jane E. Dutton, "The Adoption of Radical and Incremental Innovations: An Empirical Analysis," *Management Science* 32 (1986): 1422–1433). A new category called "system innovation" was mentioned by Donald G. Marquis ("The Anatomy of Successful Innovations," *Innovation* 7 (1969): 28–37), who perhaps was the first to introduce a conceptual model for the innovation process. According to this model, innovation is characterized by continuous interactions between technology and markets until the final realization of the product.

The study of innovation types has taken new directions during the past thirty years, characterizing innovations in newer, more refined, and sometimes ambiguous ways (Hubert Gatignon, Michael L. Tushman, Wendy Smith, and Philip Anderson, "A Structural Approach to Assessing Innovation: Construct Development of Innovation Locus, Type, and Characteristics," *Management Science* 48, no. 9 (2002): 1103–1122).

For example, Rebecca M. Henderson and Kim B. Clark ("Architectural Innovation: The Reconfiguration of Existing Product Technologies and the Failure of Established Firms," *Administrative Science Quarterly* 35 (1990): 9–30) linked different types of technological change to product class. According to this view, products are composed of core technology components and their linkages (architecture), yielding four types of technological change: incremental, radical, modular, and architectural. Architectural innovation involves changes in linking mechanisms between subsystems, and modular innovation involves changes in subsystems. Michael L. Tushman and Philip Anderson ("Technological Discontinuities and Organizational Environments," *Administrative Science Quarterly* 31 (1986): 439–465) distinguish between types of innovations that build on existing competencies and those that destroy existing competencies. A different direction by Clayton M. Christensen (*The Innovator's Dilemma* (Cambridge, MA: Harvard Business School Press, 1997); "Disruptive Technologies: Catching the Wave," Teaching Note 5-699-125, Boston: Harvard Business School Publishing, 1998) suggested a distinction between sustaining and disruptive innovation, based on whether the innovation can be built upon or is destroying existing capabilities. In a recent attempt to put some order into these inconsistencies, Gatignon et al. ("A Structural Approach to Assessing Innovation") developed a comprehensive set of measures to assess an innovation's locus, type, and characteristics.

8. Charles Perrow, "A Framework for the Comparative Analysis of Organizations," *American Sociological Review* 32 (1967): 194–208; James D. Thompson, *Organizations in Action* (New York: McGraw-Hill, 1967); Mansfield, *Industrial Research and Technical Innovation;* Zaltman et al., *Innovations and Organizations*; Moch and Morse, "Size, Centralization and Organizational Adaptation of Innovations"; Blake, *Managing for Responsive Research and Development*; Abernathy and Utterback, "Patterns of Industrial Innovation"; Chris Freeman, *The Economics of Industrial Innovation*, 2nd ed. (Cambridge, MA: MIT Press, 1982); Jay R. Galbraith, "Designing the Innovating Organization," *Organizational Dynamics* (Winter 1982): 5–25; Robert A. Burgelman, "A Process Model of Internal Corporate Venturing in the Diversified Major Firm," *Administrative Science Quarterly* 28 (1983): 223–244; Ettlie, Bridges, and O'Keffe, "Organizational Strategy and Structural Differences for Radical vs. Incremental Innovation"; Robert Drazin and Andrew H. Van de Ven, "Alternative Forms of Fit in Contingency Theory," *Administrative Science Quarterly* 30 (1985): 514–539; Dewar and Dutton, "The Adoption of Radical and Incremental Innovations: An Empirical Analysis"; and Johannes M. Pennings, "Structural Contingency Theory: A Reappraisal," *Research in Organizational Behavior* 14 (1992): 267–309.

9. Abernathy and Utterback, "Patterns of Industrial Innovation."

10. Henderson and Clark, "Architectural Innovation."

11. Ibid.

12. Christensen, *The Innovator's Dilemma*; Clayton M. Christensen and Michael E. Raynor, *The Innovator's Solution* (Boston: Harvard Business School Press, 2003); Clayton M. Christensen, *Seeing What's Next* (Boston: Harvard Business School Press, 2004).

13. "Gartner Group's Dataquest Says Nokia Became No. 1 Mobile Phone Vendor in 1998," Gartner Group Press Release, 1999. http://www.gartner.com/5_about/press_room/pr19990208a.html.

14. This case is based on an article by Benjamin Fulford, "Another Dimension," *Forbes,* July 2, 2002.

15. Geoffrey A. Moore, *Crossing the Chasm: Marketing and Selling High-Tech Products to Mainstream Customers,* 2nd ed. (New York: HarperCollins, 1999).

16. Everett M. Rogers, *Diffusion of Innovations,* 4th ed. (New York: The Free Press, 1995).

17. Bill Yenne and Morton Grosser, eds., *100 Inventions That Shaped World History* (San Mateo, CA: Bluewood Books, 1983).

18. Raytheon Company, "Technology Leadership: Magnetron Tubes," http://www .raytheon.com/about/history/leadership/index.html.

Chapter 9

1. *A Guide to the Project Management Body of Knowledge,* 3rd ed. (Newtown Square, PA: Project Management Institute, 2004).

2. Lynn Crawford, Brian Hobbs, and Rodney Turner (*Project Categorization Systems* (Newton Square, PA: Project Management Institute, 2004) have studied categorization systems used by companies. According to their findings, many organizations don't use any explicit framework for categorization. They divided the reasons organizations may categorize projects into two groups: strategic alignment and capability specialization. Strategic alignment is focused on ensuring that the organization is doing the right set of projects and that the projects undertaken are aligned with the organizational strategy and with the organization's capacity to undertake and complete projects. Capability specialization is focused on doing projects right.

3. Alex Laufer, *Simultaneous Management* (New York: AMACOMM, 1996).

4. Josh Weston, presentation to Stevens Institute of Technology Executive Leadership students (Hoboken, NJ, July 29, 2006).

5. Eli Goldratt, in his book *Critical Chain* (Great Barrington, MA: North River Press, 1997), introduced the concept of "project buffers" to indicate the slack that projects need to leave at the discretion of the project manager. Rather than have each activity retain its own slack, projects are better off if they plan their scheduled activities without slack and use a total project slack for those activities that turn out to be late.

6. For example, Christoph H. Loch, Arnoud DeMeyer, and Michael T. Pich have developed a framework for project risk management based on unforeseeable uncertainties and project complexities (*Managing the Unknown: A New Approach to Managing High Uncertainty and Risk in Projects,* Hoboken, NJ: John Wiley & Sons, Inc., 2006). They introduced the concepts of *selectionism* and *learning* to deal with various types of uncertainty and complexity.

7. *A Guide to the Project Management Body of Knowledge,* Chapter 11.

8. Loch et al., *Managing the Unknown.*

9. Our research was not specifically focused on calculating project risks. We therefore offer these initial ideas as a possible direction for further research.

10. Alex Laufer, *Simultaneous Management.*

11. We are grateful to Max Wideman, who helped us develop the work package framework. See Max R. Wideman and Aaron J. Shenhar, "Professional and Personal Development Management," in *Project Management for the Business Professional: A Comprehensive Guide,* ed. Joan Knutson (New York: John Wiley, 2001).

12. Karen A. Brown, Thomas G. Schmitt, Richard J. Schonberger, and Stephen Dennis, "Quadrant Homes Applies Lean Concepts in a Project Environment," *Interfaces* 34, no. 6 (2004): 442–450.

13. James P. Womack and Daniel T. Jones, *Lean Thinking* (New York: Simon and Schuster, 1996).

14. *BusinessWeek,* March 21, 2005.

Chapter 10

1. Numerous books and articles have been written about the development process of consumer products. Here is a partial list: Bruce T. Barkley and James H. Saylor, *Customer-Driven Project Management: Building Quality in to Project Success* (New York: McGraw-Hill Professional, 2001); Robert G. Cooper, *Winning at New Products*, 3rd ed. (Reading, MA: Perseus Books Group, 2001); Milton D. Rosenau, Abbie Griffin, George A. Castellion, and Ned F. Anschuetz, eds., *The PDMA Handbook of New Product Development* (New York: Wiley, 1996); Robert J. Thomas, *New Product Development: Managing and Forecasting for Strategic Success* (New York: John Wiley and Sons, 1993).

2. A more detailed description of the management process of industrial and business projects is given in the following books: Michael A. Cusumano and Kentaro Nobeoka, *Thinking Beyond Lean: How Multi-Project Management Is Transforming Product Development at Toyota and Other Companies* (New York: Free Press, 1998); Jeffery K. Pinto and Pelka Rouhiainen, *Building Customer Based Project Organization* (New York: Wiley, 2001); Joint Development Board, *Industrial Engineering Projects* (Oxford, UK: Routledge, 1997).

3. An excellent description of a huge public transportation project constructed in Boston can be found in Dan McNichol and Andy Ryan, *The Big Dig* (New York: Silver Lining Books, 2000). See also Peter Vanderwarker, *The Big Dig: Reshaping an American City* (Boston: Little Brown and Company, 2001).

4. PMI has published a special extension to the PMBoK for government projects, elaborating on the methodology and techniques that are especially important for such projects. *Government Extension to a Guide to the Project Management Body of Knowledge* (Newtown Square, PA: PMI, 2002).

5. Jennifer Bean and Lascelles Hussey, *Project Management for Non Profit Organizations: Ensuring Projects Deliver Their Objectives in Time and on Budget* (London: HB Publications, 2005).

6. The stories of several major space projects can be found in Alex Laufer and Edward J. Hoffman, *Project Management Success Stories: Lessons of Project Leadership* (New York: Wiley, 2000).

7. There are some specific project management books, most of them on construction and software development. There are also some books on automobile or pharmaceutical projects, but very few on other types of projects.

Chapter 11

1. See for example, Aaron J. Shenhar, "Strategic Project Leadership: Toward a Strategic Approach to Project Management," *R&D Management* 34, no. 5 (2004): 569–578.

Appendixes

1. Paul R. Lawrence and Jay William Lorch, *Organization and Environment: Managing Differentiation and Integration* (Boston: Harvard University, 1967); Robert Drazin and Andrew H. Van de Ven, "Alternative Forms of Fit in Contingency Theory," *Administrative Science Quarterly* 30 (1985): 514–539; Johannes M. Pennings, "Structural Contingency Theory: A Reappraisal," *Research in Organizational Behavior* 14 (1992): 267–309.

2. Aaron J. Shenhar, "One Size Does Not Fit All Projects: Exploring Classical Contingency Domains," *Management Science* 47, no. 3 (2001): 394–414.

3. For example, Stewart P. Blake (*Managing for Responsive Research and Development*, San Francisco: Freeman & Co., 1978) has suggested a normative distinction between minor change (alpha) projects and major change (beta) projects; and Steven C. Wheelwright and Kim B. Clark (*Revolutionizing Product Development*, New York: The Free Press, 1992) have mapped in-house product development projects according to the degree of change they make in the product portfolio. Some have adapted the radical versus incremental distinction (e.g., Chee Meng Yap and William E. Souder, "Factors Influencing New Product Success and Failure in Small Entrepreneurial High-technology Electronics Firms," *Journal of Product Innovation Management* 11 (1994): 418–432; Shona L. Brown and Kathleen M. Eisenhardt, "The Art of Continuous Change: Linking Complexity Theory and Time-paced Evolution in Relentlessly Shifting Organizations," *Administrative Science Quarterly* 42 (1997): 1–34; and William E. Souder and Michael X. Song, "Contingent Product Design and Marketing Strategies Influencing New Product Success and Failure in U.S. and Japanese Electronics Firms," *Journal of Product Innovation Management* 14 (1997): 21–34), and others have suggested more refined frameworks (e.g., Lowell W. Steele, *Innovation in Big Business* (New York: Elsevier Publishing Company, 1975); Niv Ahituv, Michael Hadass, and Seev Neumann, "A Flexible Approach to Information System Development," *MIS Quarterly* (June 1984): 69–78; James I. Cash Jr., Warren F. McFarlan, and James L. McKenney, *Corporate Information Systems Management* (Homewood, IL: Irwin, 1988); and Alan W. Pearson, "Innovation Strategy," *Technovation* 10, no. 3 (1990): 185–192).

4. Dov Dvir, Stan Lipovetsky, Aaron J. Shenhar, and Asher Tishler, "In Search of Project Classification: A Non-Universal Approach to Project Success Factors," *Research Policy* 27 (1998): 915–935.

5. In search of such a framework, one could look back at 1967, when three influential works were published independently. They have had a significant impact on contingency theory. Paul Lawrence and Jay Lorch (*Organization and Environment: Managing Differentiation and Integration*) focused on how different rates of change in technology, science, and markets affect an organization's ability to cope with these changes. Using one integrated score of uncertainty, they concluded that in a more diverse and dynamic field, effective organizations must be highly differentiated and integrated, whereas in a more stable and less diverse environment, effective organizations can be less differentiated, but they must still achieve a high degree of integration. James D. Thompson (*Organizations in Action*, New York: McGraw-Hill, 1967) suggested that coping with uncertainty is the central problem for complex organizations and that technology and environments are major sources of uncertainty. And Charles C. Perrow ("A Framework for the Comparative Analysis of Organizations," *American Sociological Review* 32 (1967): 194–208) used an integrated viewpoint on technology and complex organizations, at the same time treating technology as the independent variable and structure as the dependent variable. Using technology to distinguish between analyzable and unanalyzable problems, he identified four types of industries: craft, routine, nonroutine, and engineering.

6. To deal with complexity, the hierarchical nature of systems and their subsystems has long been the cornerstone of general systems theory (Kenneth Boulding, "General Systems Theory: The Skeleton of Science," *Management Science* (April 1956): 197–208; John P. Van Gigch, *Applied General Systems Theory,* 2nd ed. (New York: Harper and Row, 1974); and Aaron J. Shenhar, "On System Properties and System-

hood," *International Journal of General Systems* 18, no. 2 (1991): 167–174). Boulding, for example, suggested a hierarchical classification of systems that includes nine levels, starting with the lowest type of static structures and going up to transcendental systems. Obviously, because products are composed of components, and systems of subsystems, hierarchies in products are almost always addressed in practitioners' books and monographs that deal with engineering design problems (e.g., Gehard Pahl and Wolfgang Beitz, *Engineering Design* (New York: Springer-Verlag, 1984); William Lewis, and Andrew Samuel, *Fundamentals of Engineering Design* (New York: Prentice Hall, 1989); and Eberhardt Rechtin, *Systems Architecting,* Englewood Cliffs, NJ: Prentice Hall, 1991).

7. Several important studies have further characterized the nature of innovation as competence enhancing or destroying (Philip W. Anderson and Michael L. Tushman, "Technological Discontinuities and Dominant Design: A Cyclical Model of Technological Change," *Administrative Science Quarterly* 35, no. 4 (1990): 604–633; and Clayton M. Christensen, *The Innovator's Dilemma,* Boston: Harvard Business School Press, 1998), as core or peripheral (Carliss Y. Baldwin and Kim B. Clark, *Design Rules: The Power of Modularity,* Cambridge, MA: MIT Press, 2000), and as architectural or generational (Rebecca M. Henderson and Kim B. Clark, "Architectural Innovation: The Reconfiguration of Existing Product Technologies and the Failure of Established Firms," *Administrative Science Quarterly* 35 (1990): 9–30; and Hubert Gatignon, Michael L. Tushman, Wendy Smith, and Philip W. Anderson, "A Structural Approach to Assessing Innovation: Construct Development of Innovation Locus, Type, and Characteristics," *Management Science* 48, no. 90 (2002): 1103–1122).

8. Although classic theory was focused on sustaining organizations, two compelling phenomena in the modern organization must be addressed: first, any framework for project distinction must reflect the temporary nature of projects and the common time limitation that exists to finish a task. Second, the high velocities with which decisions are made and the shortened life cycles of products and markets also make time an inseparable factor in any modern look at the organization. Kathleen M. Eisenhardt and Behna N. Tabrizi, "Accelerating Adaptive Processes: Product Innovation in the Global Computer Industry," *Administrative Science Quarterly* 40 (1995): 84–110; and Shona L. Brown and Kathleen M. Eisenhardt, "The Art of Continuous Change: Linking Complexity Theory and Time-paced Evolution in Relentlessly Shifting Organizations," *Administrative Science Quarterly* 42 (1997): 1–34.

9. Aaron J. Shenhar and Dov Dvir, "Toward a Typological Theory of Project Management," *Research Policy* 25 (1996): 607–632; and Aaron J. Shenhar and Dov Dvir, "How Projects Differ and What to Do about It," in *Handbook of Managing Projects,* Jeffrey Pinto and Peter Morris, eds. (New York: Wiley 2004).

10. Geoffrey C. Bowker and Susan Leigh Star, *Sorting Things Out: Classification and Its Consequences* (Cambridge, MA: MIT Press, 1999).

11. Barbara H. Kwasnik, "The Role of Classification Structures in Reflecting and Building Theory," *Proceedings of the 3rd ASIS SIG/CR Classification Research Workshop: Advances in Classification Research* 3 (1992): 63; quotation from Georges Rey, "Concepts and Stereotypes," *Cognition* 15 (1983): 237–262.

12. Kwasnik, "The Role of Classification Structures," 63.

13. Elin K. Jacob, "Classification and Categorization: Drawing the Line," *Proceedings of the 2nd ASIS SIG/CR Classification Research Workshop: Advances in Classification Research*, Washington, DC (1991): vol. 2, 67–83.

14. Ibid.; and Howard Gardner, *The Mind's New Science: A History of the Cognitive Revolution* (New York: Basic Books, 1987).

15. Jacob, "Classification and Categorization," 78.

16. Ibid., 67.

17. Facet analysis involves "analyzing a phenomenon in terms of fundamental aspects and then re-synthesizing it into a useful expression" (Kwasnik, "The Role of Classification Structures," 72). This approach is attributed to Ranganathan (in Kwasnik, "The Role of Classification Structures," and in S. L. Star, "Grounded Classification: Grounded Theory and Faceted Classification," in *Proceedings of Information Systems and Quality Research Conference, IFIPS WG 8.2,* Philadelphia, 1997).

18. Bowker and Star, *Sorting Things Out,* 231.

19. Ibid., 232.

20. Kwasnik, "The Role of Classification Structures," 72.

21. Lynn Crawford, Brian Hobbs, and Rodney Turner, *Project Categorization Systems* (Newtown Square, PA: Project Management Institute, 2004).

22. Michel Foucault, *The Order of Things* (New York: Random House, 1970), 147; quotation from Jeffrey Parsons and Yair Wand, "Choosing Classes in Conceptual Modeling," *Communications of the ACM* 40, no. 6 (1997): 7.

23. Bowker and Star, *Sorting Things Out,* 230.

24. Ibid., 267.

25. John H. Payne and Rodney J. Turner, "Company-wide Project Management: The Planning and Control of Programmes of Projects of Different Types," *International Journal of Project Management* 17, no. 1 (1999): 55–60 ; and Rodney J. Turner, *The Handbook of Project-based Management,* 2nd ed. (London: McGraw-Hill, 1999).

26. Shenhar, "One Size Does Not Fit All Projects." See also Dvir et al., "In Search of Project Classification"; and Aaron J. Shenhar, Dov Dvir, and Shlomo Alakaher, "From a Single Discipline Product to a Multidisciplinary System: Adapting the Right Style to the Right Project," *System Engineering* 6, no. 3 (2003): 123–134.

27. Eisenhardt and Tabrizi, "Accelerating Adaptive Processes."

28. Shenhar, "One Size Does Not Fit All Projects." See also Dvir et al., "In Search of Project Classification."

INDEX

actual management style, 51
adaptive diamond model, 49–50
  illustrated, 50
adaptive project management
  as extension of traditional project
    management, 12
  features of, 11–12
  implementation of, 208
  importance of, 206–207
adoption cycle, 152
agile development model, 94
Air Force, missile projects of, 8
Amana, 157
Apollo project, 83
  compared with space shuttle program,
    98–99
  diamond model of, 95
  history of, 94–95
  success of, 95–96
Apollo 13 project, 129, 223
Apple iPod, 139
Apple Lisa, 23, 28
Apple Macintosh, 23, 72, 105
architectural innovation, 148–149
architecture, system, 117
array complexity, 103
  and traditional project management,
    242–244
array projects, 48–49, 103, 104
  characteristics of, 114
  described, 105
  descriptive statistics for, 239–241
  management of, 108, 109
  formality and bureaucracy in, 109
  nonreliance on industry standards, 110
  planning of, 178
assembly complexity, 103
  and traditional project management,
    242–244
assembly projects, 48, 103, 104
  characteristics of, 114
  described, 104
  descriptive statistics for, 239–241
    informality of, 109
    planning of, 178
AT&T, switching software project at,
  202

BAE Automated Systems, 80
base technologies, 82
Bell, Alexander Graham, 149
blitz projects, 49, 127, 129–131
  characteristics of, 132
  as response to crisis, 129
  distinguished from time-critical projects,
    129
  evolution of, 129–130
  management of, 129–130
  planning of, 178
  team autonomy in, 133–134
  top management and, 134
BMW Z3, 43–44
Bowker, Geoffrey, 228
Brasilia, 199
breakthrough products, 47, 153
  adoption of, 152–153
  development of, 153–154
breakthrough projects, 64
  distinguished from platform projects, 151
  examples of, 67–68
  project management of, 71, 232
  risks and opportunities of, 70–75
Brown, Shona, 123
budget goals, 21, 22
build-to-print projects, 82
Burns, Tom, 147
business and direct success, 30
  and project, 28

categorization. *See* classification, project
cellphone industry, 149
Challenger accident, 96, 97
Chernobyl, 202
Christensen, Clayton, 71–72, 149

Chunnel project, 105, 199
  complexity of, 111
  diamond model of, 112
  history of, 110–111
Clark, Kim, 63, 148
classification, project
  attributes and labels in, 229–230
  designing, 229
  functions of, 227
  principles of, 227–228
  purposes of, 227
  questionnaire for, 224–225
  system characteristics, 228–229
Columbia accident, 97
comparability, 228
complexity, product, 101–102
  related to project complexity, 102–104
complexity, project, 41, 101–102, 207
  in diamond approach, 13, 14
  effect on project management, 53–54,
    107–113
  and formality, 108–110
  illustration of, 43–44
  levels of, 48–49
  and planning, 178
  product complexity and, 102–104
  risks and benefits of increased, 53
  and traditional project management,
    242–244
  types of, 54–55
  in UCP model, 223
configuration items, 117
construction industry, 198
  diamond model of projects in, 201
  project characteristics in, 200
  project management in, 199
consumer (B2C) projects, 190
  characteristics of, 191, 192
  diamond model of, 190
  focus of, 192
contingency approach to project
    management, 221–223
contingency reserves, 88
  importance of, 170
contingency theory, 41
contractors, 108
contracts, types of, 93–94
control, 228
Cooper, Robert, 5, 132
cost-benefit analysis, 144
cost-plus contracts, 93, 94
craft work, 182
  defined, 181
crashing, of projects, 93
crisis, and blitz projects, 129

Critical Chain, 128
critical path method (CPM), 8
Crossing the Chasm, 152, 153, 166
customers
  in adoption cycle, 152–153, 154
  impact of project on, 27, 30
  and project goals, 142
  and project management, 189–197
  types of, 190

delays, coping with, 88
Dell Computer, 192
Denver International Airport, 6
  baggage-handling system of, 80
  diamond model of, 15, 81
  history of, 79–80
derivative products, 46
derivative projects, 64
  project management of, 71, 232
design
  initiating, 167–168
  outsourcing of, 184–186
  phased, 94
  uncertainty, 167
design cycles, 86
  determining, 168–169
design freeze, 86, 168, 169
detailed work plan, 178
diamond approach, 207
  adaptive, 49–53
  bases of, 13, 14
  described, 46–49
  examples of, 15, 41–49
Digital Equipment Corp., 149
disruptive innovation, 149, 150
dominant design, 72
DuPont, 8

early adopters, in adoption cycle, 152, 154
early majority, in adoption cycle, 152, 154
  capturing, 153–154
earned value report, 109
efficiency, project, 27, 30
  adaptive approach to, 179–180
Eisenhardt, Kathleen, 123
emerging technologies, 83
engineering, systems, 116–117
engineering work, 182
  defined, 181
environment, of project, 40
equipment/device industry, 198
  diamond model of projects in, 201
  project characteristics in, 200

project management in, 199
Eurotunnel, 111
evolutionary innovation, 147
execution, project phase, 163
executive review board, 93
expectations, adaptation of, 32–33
external projects, 141

failure, of projects, 34–35
  cases of, 6
  criteria for, 164, 206
  early identification of, 209
  reasons for 7
  technological risk and, 84, 85
fast/competitive projects, 49, 127, 128,
    245–247
  characteristics of, 132
  planning of, 178
FCS project, 37–39
  complexity of, 112
  diamond model of, 51
  lessons to be learned from, 39
FEMA (Federal Emergency Management
    Agency), 45
financial middleware software
  case study of, 75–76
  diamond model of, 76–77
fixed-price contracts, 93, 94
flash memory case, 151–152
Ford 2000 project, 105–107
  diamond model of, 107
Ford Taurus, 22
future
  preparation for, 28
  of project management, 213

Gemini program, 95
General Motors, products of, 3
globalization, 3
goals, project, 40
  customers and, 142
Goldratt, Eli, 128
government/public (B2G) projects, 190
  characteristics of, 191, 197
  competitive bidding system and, 196
  customer-producer relations in, 196–197
  diamond model of, 190
  focus of, 196, 197
Guggenheim Museum (Bilbao), 199

handbook, for project management, 210
Hanks, Tom, 129

Harmony project
  background for, 118
  complexity issues in, 119
  diamond model of, 120
  goals of, 118
Henderson, Rebecca, 148
high-tech projects, 48
  characteristics of, 89
  descriptive statistics for, 233, 235
  management style in, 87, 92, 93
  traditional project management view of,
    236–238
  uncertainty of, 82, 83
Hinners, Noel, 126
Howard, Ron, 129
Hubble space telescope, 83

Iansiti, Marco, 123
IBM PC, 72
Ibuka, Masaru, 41
incremental innovation, 67, 147
industrial (B2B) projects, 190, 192
  characteristics of, 191, 193
  diamond model of, 190
  focus of, 193
  goals of, 192
  scope of, 193
industries
  differences in project management
    based on, 198, 199, 202–203
  types of, 198
industry standards, creating, 72–73
innovation
  business built on, 139–140
  and customer adoption cycle, 152–153,
    154
  incremental vs. radical, 67
  portfolio management for, 140–144
  project management approaches to,
    145–146
  resource allocation for, 140, 142
  types of, 147–151, 208
innovator's dilemma, 149, 150
innovators, in adoption cycle, 152, 154
intangible outcomes, 182
  defined, 180
integration, system, 117
Intel, and flash memory, 151
internal projects, 141–142
International Space Station, 113
Internet browser, as breakthrough, 67
inventive work, 182
  defined, 181
iPod (Apple), 139

iron triangle, 10
ISO Insurance, Market Watch project of,
    145–147

Jobs, Steve, 65
Johnson, Clarence L. "Kelly," 90
JVC VHS standard, 72

Kamen, Dean, 73
Kaplan, Robert, 24
Katrina (Hurricane), 44–46
Kennedy, John F., 94
key technologies, 83
Kuwait reconstruction, 113
Kwasnik, Barbara, 227

laggards, in adoption cycle, 152, 154
late majority, in adoption cycle, 152, 154
Laufer, Alex, 166, 176, 177
level of effort document, 109
linear phased design, 94
Lisa (Apple), 23, 28
Lockheed Martin, 90
Los Angeles Metro, 25–26
low-tech projects, 48
    characteristics of, 89
    descriptive statistics for, 233, 235
    management style in, 87, 92, 93
    traditional project management view of,
        236–238
    uncertainty of, 82
Lucas, George, 65

Macintosh (Apple), 23, 72, 105
management style, required vs. actual,
    50–51
Manhattan Project, 8
market change, 148
Market Watch project
    diamond model of, 146–147
    goals of, 145–146
    risks of, 146
    success of, 147
markets
    and project management, 189–197
    See also customers
Mars Climate Orbiter (MCO), 6
    breakthrough nature of, 124–125
    causes of failure of, 124, 125
    diamond model of, 126
    management of, 125–126

pace of, 128
Mars Polar Lander (MPL), 124
master plan, 177
Masuoka, Fujio, 151
material complexity, 103
media corporation case
    cost-benefit analysis of, 144
    diamond model of, 142–143
    project selection in, 140–141
    resource allocation in, 142
medium-tech projects, 48
    characteristics of, 89
    descriptive statistics for, 233, 235
    management style in, 87, 92, 93
    traditional project management view of,
        236–238
    uncertainty of, 82–83
Microsoft Windows, 22
microwave oven case, 154–159
    diamond analyses of, 156–158
    history of, 155–156, 158
middle-level plan, 177
modular innovation, 148–149
Moore, Geoffrey, 68, 152, 153
Morita, Akio, 42
Motorola, cell phone technology of, 149

NASA
    Apollo program of, 83, 94–96
    breakthrough projects of, 83
    Gemini program of, 95
    Mars Climate Orbiter of, 6, 124–126,
        128
    Mars Polar Lander of, 124
    space shuttle program of, 96–99
Navy, Polaris project of, 8
New Orleans, LA, Hurricane Katrina and,
    44–45
new-to-the-world products. See
    breakthrough products
New York City Transit Authority,
    modernization project of, 105
novelty, product, 46–47
    and project novelty, 231–232
novelty, project, 207
    classification of, 63
    in diamond approach, 13
    distinguishing projects based on, 66–68
    effect on project management, 53
    effect on projects, 63–66
    engines of, 63
    levels of, 64
    misclassification of, 75–77
    and planning, 179

product novelty and, 231–232
risks and benefits of, 52, 173
NTCP model
    illustrated, 47
    impact on project management, 53–55
    See also diamond approach

operational projects, 141, 142
    diamond model of, 143–144
operations, 3, 4
O'Reilly, Charles, 71
organizational breakdown structure
    (OBS), 9
organizational efficiency, 4
organizational project management
    maturity model (OPM3), 9
organizational structure, 108
original design manufacturers (ODMs),
    184–185
outsourcing, 184
    diamond model of, 185
    caveats regarding, 186
    of routine activities, 185–186

pace, 41, 207
    in diamond approach, 13, 14
    effect on organization, 133
    effect on project management, 54,
        132–134
    illustration of, 44–46
    levels of, 49, 127
    and planning style, 178
    risks and benefits of increased, 53
    and team autonomy, 133–134
    in UCP model, 223
pacing technologies, 83
peer reviews, 87
personal computer, as breakthrough, 67
pharmaceutical/health care industry, 198
    diamond model of projects in, 201
    project characteristics in, 200
    project management in, 199, 202
phased design, 94
pilot projects, 170, 208
Pixar Animation Studios, 65
planning
    adaptive approach to, 175–179
    importance of early, 209
    levels of, 9, 208
    project phase, 163
    project type and, 178–190
    rolling wave of, 176–177
    success dimensions and, 33, 206

traditional approach to, 175
platform complexity, 103
platform products, 46
platform projects, 64, 66–67
    distinguished from breakthrough
        projects, 151
    project management of, 71, 232
portfolio management, 140
    project selection, 141–142
    resource allocation in, 142
portfolio selection, 140–141
    criteria for, 51–53, 207–208
    policy for, 210–211
Post-it notes (3M), 64
process industry, 198, 209
    diamond model of projects in, 201
    project characteristics in, 200
    project management in, 202
products
    complexity of, 102–104
    innovative level of, 46–47
    novelty of, 46–47
    success of, 23
program evaluation and review techniques
    (PERT), 8
program management office, 108
programs. *See* array projects
project management
    adaptive, 11–12. *See also* adaptive
        project management
    as asset, 209
    of blitz projects, 129
    bureaucracy levels in, 108–110
    characteristics of, 206
    complexity and, 107–113
    contingency approach to, 221–223
    creativity in, 39–40
    defined, 5
    education for, 212–213
    evolution of, 8
    future of, 213
    goals of, 206
    handbook for, 210
    importance of, 209
    industry context of, 198–203
    of innovation, 145–146
    market requirements and, 189–197
    need for new policies in, 209
    need for redefinition of, 7–8
    novelty level and, 71
    NTCP dimensions and, 53–55, 164, 166
    pace and, 132–134
    personnel for, 209, 211–212
    and project success, 24–25
    organizational framework for, 210

project management (*continued*)
  project phase, 163
  project type and, 165
  responsibilities of, 33–34
  role of scholars in, 213
  skills in, 88
  style of, 87
  of system projects, 115–118
  technological uncertainty and, 84–99
  tools of, 109–110
  traditional, 9. *See also* traditional
    project management
  traditional drivers of, 10
  traditional failures of, 9–10
  training for, 211
  of uncertainty, 170–175, 206
project team
  for blitz projects, 133–134
  communication in, 87
  impact of project on, 28, 30
  procedures of, 7, 8
  skills needed in, 88
Project Management Body of Knowledge
  (PMBoK), 9
Project Management Institute (PMI), 8–9
projects, 3
  business and direct success of, 28
  categorization of, 141–142
  classification of, 224–230
  commonalities and differences among,
    39–40
  complexity of, 48–49
  cost-benefit analysis of, 144
  defined, 5
  diamond model of, 13–15, 142–144
  distinguishing among, 40–41
  as drivers of innovation, 3
  efficiency of, 27, 179–184, 208–209
  environment of, 40
  failure of, 6–7
  goals of, 40
  impact on customer of, 27
  impact on future of, 28
  impact on team of, 28
  importance of, 4–5
  increasing share of, 4
  investment in, 209
  learning from, 212
  linear model of, 161–162
  novelty of, 66–72
  organizational structure of, 108
  phases of, 163
  pilot, 170, 208
  planning of. *See* planning
  premature shortening of, 93

  problems of, 7–8
  resource allocation for, 142
  review of, 93
  risk of. *See* risk, project
  selection of, 140–141, 207–208, 210–211
  selection criteria for, 51–53
  success assessment questionnaire for,
    219–220
  success/failure criteria for, 12, 21–23,
    164, 206
  success rate of, 5–6
  tasks of, 40
  technological level of, 47–48, 84–99
  type identification of, 162, 164, 165
  uncertainty reduction in, 166–167,
    169–170
prototyping, 85
  importance of, 169–170, 209

Quadrant homes, 183–184
qualitative risk analysis, 172
quantitative risk analysis, 172

radical innovation, 67, 147
Rail Construction Corporation, 26
Raytheon, 155, 156
regular paced projects, 127
  characteristics of, 132
regular projects, 49
  pace and, 245–247
required management style, 51
requirements, product, 167–168
  and design uncertainty, 167
  determining, 168
  initial vs. final, 168
  reassessing, 169
research and development (R&D)
  cutting costs of, 184
  keeping in-house, 186
  outsourcing of, 184, 185
resource allocation, 142
revolutionary innovation, 147
risk, project, 171
  defined, 172
  diamond model of, 171–172, 173–175
  identification of, 172
  monitoring and control of, 172
  response planning, 172
  traditional analysis of, 172–173
risk management, 172
  diamond analysis in, 173–175
  traditional approach to, 172–173
Rogers, Everett, 152

Samsung, 151
Sears, 149
Segway, 6
    as breakthrough, 67
    diamond model of, 73–74
    history of, 73
    lessons to be learned from, 75
Simultaneous Management, 176
Skunk works, 91, 133
Snow White and the Seven Dwarfs, 65
software industry, 198
    diamond model of projects in, 201
    project characteristics in, 200
    project management in, 202
Sony Betamax, 72
Sony Walkman, 41–42, 64
space shuttle program
    diamond model of, 98
    difficulties of, 97
    history of, 96
    NASA conception of, 96
Spencer, Percy, 155, 156
spiral phased design, 94
SR-71 Blackbird, 105
    described, 90
    development of, 91
    diamond model of, 91
    success of, 91–92
stage-gate, 132
Stalker, George, 147
Standish Group, 5
Star, Susan, 228
strategic projects, 141, 142
    diamond model of, 143–144
Strategic Defense Initiative (SDI, "Star
    Wars"), 83, 113
subcontractors, 108
subsystem complexity, 103
success, project
    criteria for, 12, 21–23, 164, 206
    dimensions of, 26–29, 31–32
    as dynamic concept, 29–32
    leading to product success, 23
    maximizing chances of, 32–35
    multidimensionality of, 23–26
    questionnaire for assessing, 219–220
    rate of, 5–6
    responsibility for, 24
    technological uncertainty and, 84–85
    time and, 29–30
    and types of projects, 31–32
super-high-tech projects, 48, 88
    characteristics of, 89
    descriptive statistics for, 233, 235
    management style in, 90, 92, 93

traditional project management view of,
    236–238
    uncertainty of, 82, 83
sustaining innovation, 149
Sydney Opera House, 21
    pace of, 127, 223
system architecture, 117
system complexity, 103
    and traditional project management,
        242–244
system integration, 117
system projects, 48, 103, 104
    business viability of, 116
    characteristics of, 114
    configuration issues in, 117
    cooperation in, 116, 117–118
    customer interests in, 116
    described, 104–105
    descriptive statistics for, 239–242
    environments of, 113
    failure factors of, 115
    formality and bureaucracy in, 109
    management of, 115–118
    operation of, 115
    optimization of, 116
    planning of, 178
    skills for, 115
    subsystems in, 113
    typical difficulties of, 113, 115
    user involvement in, 117
system scope, 48–49
systems engineering, 116–117

tangible outcomes, 182
    defined, 180
Tappan Industries, 157
task, of project, 40
technological uncertainty, 47–48
    and contract type, 93–94
    and delays, 88
    effects of, 81–85
    and implementation risks, 173
    and management style, 87, 92–94
    and peer reviews, 87
    and project communication, 87
    and project planning, 179
    and traditional project management,
        236–238
technology, 207
    defined, 81
    in diamond approach, 13–14
    effect on project management, 53
    innovation in, 148
    risks and benefits of, 52

technology (*continued*)
  uncertainty of, 47–48, 81–85
technology readiness level (TRL), 99
termination price report, 109
termination, project phase, 163
3M Post-it notes, 64
time, 21, 22
  causes of constraints based on, 123
  competition based on, 123
  impact on success, 29–30
  See also pace
time-critical projects, 49, 127, 128–129
  characteristics of, 132
  distinguished from blitz projects, 129
  pace and, 245–247
  planning of, 178
time-paced strategies, 123
Tobin, Austin, 55
Toshiba, flash memory and, 151
Toy Story
  complexity of, 112
  diamond model of, 69–70
  making of, 65
Tozzoli, Guy, 55
traditional project management, 9
  complexity and, 242–244
  features of, 11
  pace and, 245–247
  uncertainty and, 236–238
Transmanche Link, 111
triple constraint, 10
Tushman, Michael, 71

UCP model, 222–223
  illustrated, 222
uncertainty, project, 41
  of design, 167, 169
  effect on project management, 84–92,
    206
  illustration of, 41–42
  impact of, 171
  managing, 164–171, 206, 208
  and project success, 84–85

technology and, 47–48. *See also*
    technological uncertainty
  types of, 54
  reducing, 166
  types of, 166–167
  in UCP model, 222–223
  See also risk, project
United Airlines, 80

visibility, 228

Walkman project (Sony), 41–42
Walt Disney Company, 65
Western Union, 149
Weston, Josh, 170
Weyerhaeuser Company, 183
Wheelwright, Steven, 63
wire coating project, 193–194
  diamond model of, 195
work breakdown structure (WBS), 9,
    107–108
work package management, 180
  improving efficiency through, 181–183,
    208–209
  operational, 4
  organizational, 4
  work outcomes in, 180
  work package classification, 181
  work types in, 181
work packages, 9
World Trade Center project, 55–56
  diamond model of, 56–57
  success of, 58

Y2K compliance projects, 128, 130–131
Yamasaki, Minoru, 55

Z3 project (BMW), 43–44

ABOUT THE AUTHORS

Aaron J. Shenhar is the Institute Professor of Management and the founder of the Project Management Program at Stevens Institute of Technology, the Howe School of Technology Management. He has also been a visiting professor at the University of Minnesota and Tel-Aviv University. He is the first winner of the Project Management Institute Research Achievement Award and was named Engineering Manager of the Year by the Engineering Management Society of the IEEE. He is a fellow and member of the science council for the Center for Program/Project Management Research at NASA's University Space Research Association.

Prior to joining academia, he was involved in managing projects, innovation, R&D, and high-tech businesses for almost twenty years. Working for the defense industry, he served as an executive at Rafael, the Armament Development Authority of Israel, where he was appointed Corporate Vice President, Human Resources, and later, President of the Electronic Systems Division.

In his second career, Shenhar's research and teaching center on project management, technology and innovation management, product development, and the leadership of professionals in technology-based organizations. His writings—over one hundred fifty publications, including more than sixty research articles—have influenced and shaped project management research and education throughout the world. He is also serving as a consultant to the aerospace industry and to major global corporations such as 3M, NASA, Honeywell, Trane, the U.S. Army, BMG Entertainment, Lockheed Martin, Dow Jones & Co., and Israel Aircraft Industry.

Shenhar holds five academic degrees, including a BSc and MSc in engineering from the Technion in Israel, MSc's in statistics and engineering economic systems, and a PhD in engineering from Stanford University. Professor Shenhar is the founder of the Technological Leadership Institute, a management consulting company that focuses on aligning business and technology.

Dov Dvir's career combines years of practical and academic experience. He is the head of the management department at Ben Gurion University School of Management in Israel. He is also a visiting professor at Stevens Institute of Technology. Dvir was the founder and head of the technology management department at the Holon Center for Technological Education.

Prior to his academic career, he worked for the Israel military and defense industry, where he participated in all phases of engineering and management, from project manager up through executive posts. He served as the commander of a large technological center in the Israeli Defense Forces at the rank of colonel.

Dvir accumulated more than eighty publications, including more than thirty research articles. His work focuses on research, teaching, and consulting in project management, technology and innovation management, and entrepreneurship.

Dvir holds a BSc in engineering from the Technion in Israel, an MBA and MSc in operations research, and a PhD in management from Tel-Aviv University.